FLOWERS

MALCOLM HILLIER

PHOTOGRAPHY BY STEPHEN HAYWARD

A Dorling Kindersley Book

 Dorling Kindersley

LONDON, NEW YORK, SYDNEY, DELHI, PARIS,
MUNICH, and JOHANNESBURG

US Editor • *Mary Sutherland*

US Editorial Director • *LaVonne Carlson*

US Publisher • *Sean Moore*

Project Editors • *Irene Lyford, Lesley Malkin*

Project Art Editor • *Wendy Bartlet*

DTP Designers • *Louise Paddick, Louise Waller*

Senior Managing Editor • *Mary-Clare Jerram*

Senior Managing Art Editor • *Lee Griffiths*

Production Controllers • *Sarah Coltman, Mandy Inness*

First American Edition, 2000
2 4 6 8 10 9 7 5 3 1

Published in the United States by
DK Publishing, Inc.
95 Madison Avenue
New York, New York 10016

DK Publishing offers special discounts for bulk purchases for sales promotions
or premiums. Specific, large-quantity needs can be met with special editions,
including personalized covers, excerpts of existing guides,
and corporate imprints. For more information, contact:
Special Markets Department, DK Publishing, Inc.,
95 Madison Avenue, New York, NY 10016 Fax: 800-600-9098.

Library of Congress Cataloging-in-Publication-Data

Hillier, Malcolm.
    Flowers / Malcolm Hillier.- 1st American ed.
    p.cm.
    ISBN 0-7894-5954-X
    1.Flower arrangement. 2. Flowers. 1. Title

SB449.H487 2000
745.92'2-dc21   00-029485

Reproduced in Italy by GRB Editrice Srl
Printed and bound in Spain by Artes Graficas Toledo
D.L. TO: 1182-2000

See our complete catalog at
www.dk.com

CONTENTS

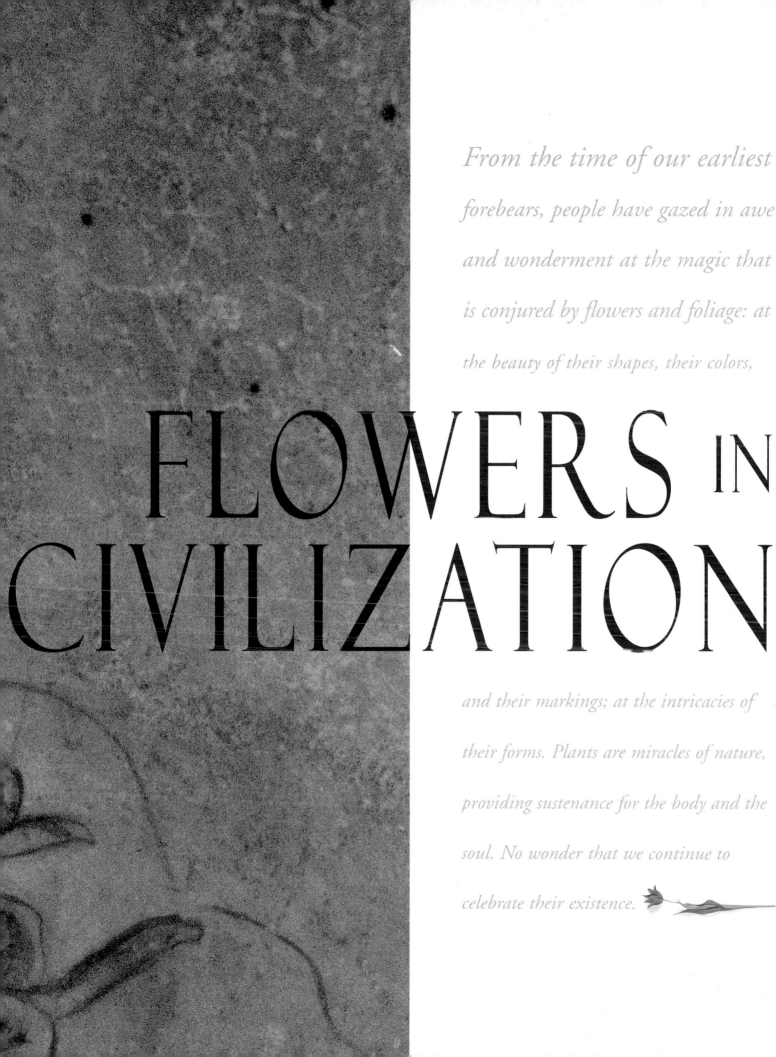

From the time of our earliest forebears, people have gazed in awe and wonderment at the magic that is conjured by flowers and foliage: at the beauty of their shapes, their colors,

FLOWERS IN CIVILIZATION

and their markings; at the intricacies of their forms. Plants are miracles of nature, providing sustenance for the body and the soul. No wonder that we continue to celebrate their existence.

FLOWERS IN CIVILIZATION

SOME OF THE earliest surviving images, artifacts, and buildings are those of ancient Egyptian dynasties, which date back earlier than 2500 BC. Theirs was a society in which symbols, rituals, and the beauty of the human form played a large and significant role. Two plants recur constantly in Egyptian symbolism – the waterlily and the papyrus. Both plants were used decoratively in buildings, and were offered as tributes to gods and dignitaries and incorporated into garlands for the dead.

SYMBOLS OF LIFE

It is easy to see why, in a dry country that is so profoundly dependent on its river for survival, these plants, which need constantly to have their feet in water, came to be seen as both symbols of life and miracles of nature, and why the strong, dramatic shapes of their leaves and flowers captured the artistic imagination of these cultured people. Hapi, the Egyptian god of the waters, who was believed to seasonally raise the level of the Nile enough to flood the waterways and irrigation canals of its valley, is always depicted in carvings

OFFERING TO THE SUN GOD
This carved stone frieze shows King Akhenaten offering up bunches of lotus flowers on long stems to the sun god Aten, who is depicted with hands at the end of the sun rays. The King would have worn a linen tunic and used cosmetics made from plants.

and paintings surrounded by water plants such as these.

FLORAL MOTIFS

Many state buildings in Egypt were raised on thick stone columns with carved bases and capitals that frequently depicted the waterlily, the papyrus, and the fronds of the date palm *Phoenix dactylifera*. The walls of such grand ceremonial buildings, as well as those of tombs, were decorated with carved and painted scenes depicting both everyday life and state occasions. Flowers are often shown as offerings in these scenes, sometimes in bunches, sometimes as arrangements, as well as being used to adorn the human figure, in the form of garlands for the hair and threaded together as necklaces or collars. Many stone, gold, and silver vases, in which the flowers were arranged and floated, were made in the shape of waterlilies. It is now known that the flowers once thought of as the lotus are not in fact the sacred lotus, *Nelumbo nucifera*. They are a species of white, often night-flowered, waterlily, *Nymphaea lotus* (the Egyptian lotus), which has fragrant blooms that can be up to 12in (30cm) in diameter. Poppy, iris, olive, cornflower, rosemary, lupine, and narcissus have all been found in Egyptian funerary headdresses and necklaces, some dating back as far as 2500 BC, but it was not until two thousand years later that the rose was introduced into Egypt from China via Greece.

ENHANCING HUMAN BEAUTY

The beauty of the human form was of paramount importance in Egyptian culture, and plants were used to make a range of cosmetics and perfumes, in what amounted to a major industry. From the evidence of tomb paintings, it is surprising how contemporary the faces of the ancient Egyptians appear to us today: rich gold and enameled jewelry embellished with flower motifs bedeck slender necks and

wrists; cheek bones are accentuated by makeup, while liners and shadow highlight the eyes. Perfumed bunches of flowers, or just a single bloom, were carried to ceremonies by both men and women, and original recipes for perfumes have recently been discovered. At banquets, the guests would be dressed in fine linen, the women adorned with beautifully crafted necklaces, bangles, rings, and headdresses. The banquet tables would be laid out with delicacies and decorated with bowls of flowers and garlands, and the air would be filled with their delicious perfumes.

SYMBOLIC PLANTS IN TOMB PAINTING
Funnel vases, in the shape of lotus flowers and leaves, stand beside two mummies in this frescoed tomb painting of Nebamun and Ipuky, dating from 1380 BC. On the right is a stylized papyrus standard – a plant from which the ancient Egyptians made paper. Egyptian mummies were wrapped in linen and frequently anointed with floral perfume.

CEREMONIAL GARLANDS ▶

This frescoed roundel shows the Greek god Dionysus (or Bacchus) and a maenad (a female participant in the rites of Dionysus) adorned with ceremonial garlands of roses, ivy, and jasmine. The rose was sacred to the Roman goddess Venus, the goddess of beauty, while ivy was sacred to Dionysus, the Greek god of wine and originally a vegetation god. In classical times, ivy also symbolized immortality.

INSPIRATION THROUGH THE AGES ▼

In this wall painting from Stabia, which survived the eruption of Mount Vesuvius in 79 AD, Flora, the Roman goddess of spring, gathers the flowers of the asphodel – a plant mentioned by the Greek poet Homer in his *Odyssey*. Following the excavations of classical ruins in the eighteenth century, floral motifs such as this influenced painters and designers, including the British architect Robert Adam (1728–92).

ANCIENT GREECE AND ROME

Both learning and physical beauty were of great importance to the ancient Greeks and Romans, in whose cultures the "body beautiful" attained cult status. Just as we now go to health clubs to tone ourselves up, so too did both the Greeks and Romans, and we have evidence of the success of their efforts in many of the surviving pieces of sculpture of the period. To celebrate their physical perfection, whether in the sports arena or at ceremonial events, both the Greeks and Romans employed flowers and leaves, often in the form of headdresses and garlands.

The Greek terracotta vases with their illustrations of everyday and ceremonial life, which were produced in such abundance, were created simply as decorative pieces and were never intended to hold flowers. They would have been superb for displaying cut flowers both for decoration and for their perfume, but there is no evidence of such use in the first century of the first millennium.

AROMATIC HERBS AND PETALS

At the beginning of the first millennium AD, Pliny the Elder, the author of the vast *Natural History* encyclopedia, wore a headdress of rosemary, as this highly aromatic herb was believed to sharpen the workings of the mind. In classical times, the fragrant leaves of the herb bay laurel were used to make the garlands for victorious athletes, heads of state, and elders. When a recently discovered tomb of a young Roman woman was opened, she was found to be lying on a bed of bay laurel leaves. Flower petals also played a significant role in classical life. For very special occasions,

ROMAN MOSAIC
This mosaic from the Roman emperor Hadrian's villa, dating from the second century AD, is now located in the Vatican in Rome. There is some doubt about its complete authenticity: Tulips, here intertwining with roses, lily, chicory, anemones, morning glory, and carnations, were probably not growing in Italy when the mosaic was created.

the floors of Roman villas were strewn with flower petals and leaves (usually roses and bay leaves), while the guests wore sweet perfumes and carried scented flowers. The Romans also prepared sorbets flavored with orange blossom and rose oils, using ice that was transported from the Alps and kept in underground stores.

It is not until the thirteenth and fourteenth centuries, however, that we find evidence of flowers being cut and arranged in Islamic culture. Frescoes, tiles, and tomb decorations of this period reveal richly decorated ceramic vases with rather formal arrangements of flowers fountaining out of them. Later, in the sixteenth century, onyx water basins filled with floating, perfumed rose petals were suspended in the canals beside the main thoroughfares of the Persian city of Isfahan. Carpets with flower and vase emblems were designed to represent the paradise gardens. In Turkey, a favorite present was a small, narrow, specimen vase carrying a single tulip; these vase offerings were also depicted on tiles.

HOME OF THE DAMASK ROSE

Syria, whose capital, Damascus, is reputedly the oldest in the world, is believed to be the home of the damask rose – in particular *Rosa × damascena* var. *bifera*, the "autumn damask," which is still used to make the highly perfumed oil attar of roses. The origins of this hybrid rose are unknown but it was certainly grown in Syria in the eleventh century and probably much earlier, for it is thought to be the "Rose of Paestum" described by both the Roman poet Virgil (70–19 BC) and Pliny the Elder (23–79 AD), a Roman scholar. The rose was carried by the Arabs to North Africa, from there to Spain, and then to South America, hence its many names: Alexandrian Rose, Rose of Castile, and Mission Rose. Its heady perfume is without a doubt the most sumptuous of any rose.

SYMBOLS OF PARADISE

The moguls – the Muslim dynasty that ruled India from the sixteenth to the end of the eighteenth century – enjoyed a rich cultural life in which the arts flourished and flowers were

MAIDEN WITH LOTUS
This evocative, fifth-century fresco from Sri Lanka shows a young Sigiriya maiden holding two lotus buds in one hand and a sweetly scented frangipani blossom (known as "temple tree") in the other.

THE GARDENS OF ISLAM

By the first millennium AD, gardens were being cultivated as tranquil havens in the rugged, often desert, landscape of the Middle East, particularly in Syria and Iran (which was formerly known as Persia). These gardens were usually walled and four-square, and included water features. The word "paradise" actually derives from the Persian word for enclosed garden, "*pairidaeza.*"

regarded as symbols of earthly as well as heavenly paradise. Perfumed flowers, in particular, played a significant part in religious ceremonies as well as in everyday life. Favorite flowers included jasmine, iris, narcissus, hyacinth, oleander (*Nerium oleander*), the highly prized tulip, and, of course, the rose – the flower that, according to Islamic legend, sprang from Allah's sweat.

Such was the Mogul delight in floral beauty that much of the art of this period – frescoes, drawings, and paintings – contains visual references to flowers. These are often arranged in a vase or in a group of vases, or sometimes singly, as delicate, individual specimens.

TILES IN ISLAMIC ART ▲

For religious reasons, most Islamic art concentrates on natural forms and designs rather than on living creatures. Dating from the twelfth century, these Iranian tiles, depicting plant and flower arabesques, are typical of this art form. Blooms such as the rose, the lotus (both in its Egyptian and its Chinese form), the chrysanthemum, and the palmetto are all included and, as with most Islamic art, the entire surface of the tiles is covered with ornamentation to create a sense of tranquillity.

◄ TWO PRINCES CONVERSING

In this delicately detailed eighteenth-century gouache painting on paper, two Indian princes sit on a flower-embossed rug under a canopy in the moonlight. The small specimen vases placed around them contain perfumed narcissus, roses, and poppies. In the pool behind, waterlilies float serenely – the epitome of paradise.

CHINESE FLOWER-ARRANGING TRADITIONS

From the earliest times, China has enjoyed a flourishing tradition of flower arranging. Arrangements usually consisted of one or two types of flowers displayed in an exquisite ceramic, metal, or basketware container – often one that had been designed specifically for the purpose. Chinese arrangements had seasonal themes, each creation being thought of as a painting with a unique structure, textures, light, and shade. One cardinal rule applied:

flowers and leaves never covered the rim of the vase.

For centuries, the favorite plants in China have been the chrysanthemum, the tree peony, the sacred lotus, peach and apricot blossoms (symbols of purity), the narcissus (named the sacred lily or "water fairy"), orchids, the pine, which represented longevity, and the bamboo, a symbol of courage. Combined with their elegant and refined vessels, these plants have inspired the exquisite flower arranging imagery in Chinese painting, screen prints, and fabrics.

◄ NEW YEAR FESTIVAL
In this nineteenth-century picture, a family watches as the father sets off fireworks in honor of the Chinese kitchen god during their New Year festival. Nearby, on a garden bench, are containers of blossoms, narcissus, and tree peonies. The rocks in the foreground represent sacred miniatures of a mountainous landscape.

WICKER BASKET ►
Vibrantly colored lotus, tulip, iris, and other stylized flowers are informally displayed in the spherical bowl of this vase, which has an open-work band displaying camellias. This type of arrangement was a symbol of good wishes on special occasions. The Chinese were the first to design wicker baskets specifically for flowers; this one could be displayed either standing or hanging.

TEA CEREMONY ▶
Flowers form an integral
part of the Japanese tea
ceremony, a ritual that
represents the inner core of
Japanese aesthetic. In this
depiction by the artist
Toshikata, which dates from
the late-nineteenth to early-
twentieth century, flowers
are being prepared prior to a
tea ceremony, when they
will be placed in the alcove
as an offering to Buddha.

◀ NAGEIRE-STYLE DISPLAY
In this eighteenth-century
wood block print by Suzuki
Haronobu, a Wakashu looks
at a painting of Mount Fuji
– the highest mountain in
Japan, famous for its
symmetrical, snow-capped
cone – while he stands beside
a nageire-style ikebana
arrangement of blossoms in
a bamboo container.

JAPANESE IKEBANA ▶
Dating from the second half
of the nineteenth century,
this silk and gilt thread
embroidery on satin depicts
a wicker basket as the base
for a branch of blossoms,
chrysanthemum flowers,
and bamboo leaves, all of
which are symbolically
significant. The symmetry
of the arrangement is based
upon the curving branch
of blossoms, with the
chrysanthemum blooms
balanced toward its base.

THE ART OF IKEBANA

The Japanese took inspiration from the early Chinese flower arranging style of the sixth century AD. This they developed over the centuries into the prescribed art of ikebana. Translated as "living plant material," ikebana is an art that combines Buddhism and the Japanese belief in the sacred nature of plants; each form of arrangement represents an outlook on the universe. Strict rules called "tatebana" were formulated to govern the arranging of flowers designated for special religious occasions and, later, arrangements for everyday domestic display and for the tea ceremony, known as "nageire." In both of these forms, flowers, leaves, and stems are arranged in a way that maximizes their natural beauty. The proportions of the container and its arrangement are strictly defined by the rules; so, too, is the overall shape of the flower arrangement and the disposition of the stems to give balance within the overall shape.

EVOLVING STYLE

There have been many schools of ikebana, but toward the end of the nineteenth century, a new form of the art was introduced, in which flowers, branches, leaves, and sometimes fruit and vegetables, were arranged in a low, flat bowl to resemble a landscape. By this time many new flower varieties had been introduced from the West, which in turn became aware for the first time of the art form. In this way ikebana began to evolve, gradually becoming looser until the art reached its present-day state. The basic premise is retained, perhaps in an even stronger way, that plant ingredients should be arranged to take advantage of their natural beauty and that the whole arrangement should be an abstraction of the sacred nature of plants.

MONASTIC TRADITIONS

In the West, in the first millennium AD and the early part of the second millennium, the monasteries kept the arts alive, and most references to flowers are to be found in highly decorative and gilded manuscripts. One of these was the famous book of private devotion, *Très Riches Heures*, which was executed for the Duc de Berry by the Limburg brothers in 1413. This illuminated manuscript contains many representations of landscape with flowers. The medieval gothic tradition culminated in 1561 with an amazing and highly inspirational volume, *Mira Calligraphiae Monumenta*, containing a wealth of illustrated manuscript and still lifes, in which elaborate calligraphy is adorned with flowers, fruits, vegetables, insects, reptiles and shells, as well as several flower arrangements.

THE RENAISSANCE

Early in the fourteenth century, beginning in Italy, a wave of new thought, learning, and artistic endeavor spread out across Europe in what we now call the Renaissance. The Church was the foremost patron of this movement, and this was reflected in many of the paintings that set out to illustrate biblical events. Giotto, Mantegna, Botticelli, Leonardo da Vinci, and Michelangelo – some of the greatest names in the history of painting – all produced works that included flowers and arrangements of flowers such as iris,

A VICTORIOUS SAINT GEORGE
This triumphant, armor-clad knight, painted by Andrea Mantegna in 1466, was the patron saint of both Venice and England. In an allusion to the victory of the Christian faith, he tramples a slain dragon underfoot. Above him is suspended a victor's garland made from fruits and herbs. The garland was probably bound onto a rope, though grapevine and fig stems were sometimes used for this purpose.

VIRGINAL PURITY
The background of this work by Botticelli (1446–1510) depicts three arrangements of pink and white roses on stands. Both are symbols of purity that were traditionally associated with the Virgin Mary.

LA PRIMAVERA
A highly imaginative artist, Arcimboldo (1527–93) painted symbolic figures using flowers, fruits, and vegetables. These were considered to be in poor taste until they inspired the surrealists in the twentieth century.

cornflower, narcissus, columbines, and roses. The Madonna lily, *Lilium candidum*, which, in biblical times, was the lily of the field, appears in many paintings of the Annunciation where the purity of the Virgin is accentuated by this most pure and white of all flowers. The presence of flowers conveyed a common symbolism for the viewer, the better to render the story or event. Thus the red *Rosa gallica* becomes a symbol of love while the white rose, *Rosa alba*, is associated with the Virgin Mary, who is seen as "a rose without thorns." The columbine, *Aquilegia vulgaris*, with its flowers that look like flying doves, is employed as a symbol for the Holy Ghost. The violet, *Viola odorata*, with its diminutive head, becomes a symbol of humility that is associated with the infant Christ.

During the Renaissance, the public learned to expect a fidelity to nature in painting and sculpture: the ultimate goal for artists was perfect form, harking back to ancient Greek and Roman classical art. A single blossom could inspire a truth of nature, as could a sweeping landscape. Previously the art of painting had been relegated to mere symbolism – an imitation of nature that neglected this truth. The first true Renaissance painter, Giotto, rose to prominence declaring, "I am the man through whom the extinct air of painting lived once more."

Eventually Renaissance aesthetics preached the concept of the picture frame as a "window" through which the spectator looked into the re-created natural world of the artist. Plants and flowers played a prominent role in this process, as best seen in the paintings, sketches, and drawings of the period's supreme master, Leonardo da Vinci. His landscapes reflect the new mood of naturalism in which we continue to find inspiration, comfort, and joy today.

DUTCH AND FLEMISH FLOWER PAINTINGS

By the fifteenth century in northern Europe, flowers had assumed a major role in art. The flower still lifes of the fifteenth to eighteenth centuries were commissioned by private patrons rather than by the Church, and the Netherlands, with its developing plant and flower industry, emerged as a natural source for such paintings.

These still lifes of flowers afforded a means of capturing for perpetuity the ephemeral beauty of flowers and of showing flowers as a symbol of the fleeting nature of life. Many symbolic objects, or "vanitas," were used in these paintings: nests of eggs and the luscious pomegranate represent birth; the skull, skeleton, and toad represent death; jewelry shows vanity, while the salamander nourishes good and banishes evil. A timepiece ticks away the minutes, while bubbles – the most transitory of all beautiful things – vanish in a moment. In these sumptuous paintings, leaves and petals are devoured by pests, a glorious rose falls, the locust feasts: all symbols of life's transience.

THE INFLUENCE OF THE TULIP

The tulip, at this time the most precious of all flowers, plays a leading role. These are the wonderful striped and splashed, frilled and twisted blooms in cream, green, and scarlet, in plum and mauve, rust and white, twisting flowers like exotic birds in flight. Irises parade their dappled falls, great peonies burst their seams, and you can almost smell the perfume of voluptuous roses. Diminutive narcissus and violets peep from behind the skirts of green leaves, while grapes, peaches, and nectarines glisten with their seductive sweetness. Executed in quantity, these wondrous paintings have inspired floral artists all over the world.

BOY WITH FRUIT BASKET ▲
Caravaggio (1571–1610) created a naturalistic style using observation and sharp contrasts of light and dark to depict the lushness of fruits and leaves. This style became a distinctive trademark of his work.

OMNIA VANITAS ▶
The skull in this eighteenth-century Dutch painting by an unknown artist reminds us symbolically of the transitory nature of life, as do a bursting bubble, fallen rose, expired candle, and half-read book.

STILL LIFE OF TAZZA WITH FLOWERS ▼
In this seventeenth-century oil painting by Jan Brueghel the Younger, a tazza is circled with a delicate garland of flowers. A timepiece and a scattering of jewels depict the passage of time and vanity.

NINETEENTH-CENTURY EUROPE AND AMERICA

During the first two-thirds of the nineteenth century, European interest in flower arranging blossomed and – as depicted in flower paintings of the time – became much less inhibited. Symbolism and mystery were abandoned, however: these paintings simply reveled in the beauty of the flowers and their purely decorative qualities.

As interest in arranging flowers developed in the United States and Europe, no dinner party was complete without flower arrangements for the house and the table, and women began to carry posies of flowers to parties. Flowers had become a middle-class fashion item, to be given as gifts and represented in prints, books, and couture. It is no coincidence that the "language of flowers" set codes of etiquette during this period.

As plants were increasingly collected from all over the world, more and more species became available to the flower arranger. Flowers were still arranged in the informal manner of the Dutch and Flemish paintings, but often appeared very simply in jugs and glass vases. These vases, epergnes, and tazzas, as well as traditionally shaped urns, were made in large quantities, and the quality of the

VICTORIAN LIFE STYLE ▲
The rise of color printing in the second half of the nineteenth century brought a proliferation of style manuals and texts that every middle-class hostess consulted for advice and inspiration. In this Victorian drawing-room collage, dating from 1880–1890, elaborate floral displays are depicted among the main elements of the room.

GENERAL GRANT AND FAMILY ▶
In this hand-colored lithograph by A.L. Weise and Company, dating from 1866, a typical nineteenth-century American interior centers around key elements of domesticity. The themes of music, literature, and family are punctuated by a diminutive flower arrangement near the center of the composition, echoed by the leaves outside in the garden.

materials from which they were constructed (china, glass, or metal) and their decoration were of the highest standard.

The greatest flower painter of this period was the Frenchman Henri Fantin-Latour (1836–1904), who worked from the middle of the nineteenth until the beginning of the twentieth century. In France, Fantin-Latour was admired for his portraiture, but it was his flower paintings and still lifes that captured the imagination in Britain, where the industrial revolution had brought wealth to a new section of the public, eager to spend their money on art.

Toward the end of the nineteenth century, the impressionists, a group of experimental artists who were inspired by light and nature, rose to prominence. Manet, Monet, Degas, Vuillard, Renoir, and Bonnard all painted arrangements of flowers – sometimes in intimate domestic interiors that were suffused with light.

Vincent Van Gogh (1853–90) was greatly influenced by the impressionist group when he went to Paris in 1886. His subsequent paintings of wheat fields, sunflowers, irises, and cherry blossoms are overwhelming in their power, not only in the depiction of the flowers and plants themselves, but in the sweeping application of the paint.

LILIES IN A VASE (1888) ▲
Fantin-Latour said that his aim in this and many of his other paintings was to capture the fleeting, fresh flowers that "are not petrified in the stage of perfection as they were by the flower painters of an earlier age."

TWENTIETH-CENTURY FLORAL ART

By the twentieth century, the floral tradition had become diverse and multifaceted, drawing upon all the influences of previous centuries, and formality and informality could now happily co-exist. This diversity is reflected in the work of a wide range of twentieth-century painters.

The work of Odilon Redon (1840–1916), who was a disciple of Henri Fantin-Latour, straddles the nineteenth- and twentieth-century traditions. A symbolist, his works have a dreamlike quality and strangeness that later placed him as a forerunner of the surrealists. His paintings and pastels, particularly of flowers, are truly amazing, the colors exquisite, the relationship between vase and flowers, flowers and figures, and, in particular, between flowers and the human head, is always fascinating.

FLOWERS THROUGH THE LENS

During the twentieth century, photography became another valuable artistic means of capturing natural images from life. In a photograph we are allowed to see the intricacy and beauty of nature in a way that had never been experienced before. At the turn of the century, the German photographer Karl Blossfeldt made a series of studies of plant material, which elevate each stem, each flower, and each seed to become works of sculptural quality.

In the 1980s, black and white photographs by Robert Mapplethorpe captured flowers in a new way. "Hard-edged and decadent," they have a strength of line and form that equal his striking imagery of the human face and figure. At the turn of the new millennium, the American photographer John Dugdale made a series of masterful cyanotype studies of flowers, which seem to express not only their radiant beauty but also their inner meaning – the very essence of the flower and of the life that it represents.

Thanks to photography, we can now look at the work of the great garden designer Gertrude Jekyll, who, in the early part of the century, created beautiful flower arrangements, especially of wild plants, which were to become the "English Country Style." These arrangements set aside the formality that had become a part of the late nineteenth century and have been an inspiration ever since.

WESTMINSTER ABBEY
For the wedding of HRH Prince Andrew and Miss Sarah Ferguson in 1986, 30,000 apricot, peach, pale pink, and cream flowers were arranged in Westminster Abbey, London by members of NAFAS.

OPHELIA AMONG THE FLOWERS (1905–08)
Toward the end of his life, Redon was captivated by the mythological and floral worlds. Here, with jasmine in her hair, Ophelia floats, almost becoming a dreamlike creation of flowers in turquoise, blue, and scarlet.

HOUSTON MAGNOLIA
In this miracle of light, the American photographer John Dugdale captured the essence of a fresh magnolia flower that was flown to his New York studio after he had marveled over its beauty and fragrance in Texas.

A CONTINUING TRADITION

In the 1930s, when Constance Spry opened her flower school, her creations were made in this same spirit. During the following decade, interest in arranging flowers continued unabated although World War II threw the cut flower industry into a perilous state.

In 1959, a group of flower arranging clubs joined together to form a British association, The National Association of Flower Arrangement Societies (NAFAS), which has now become an international organization. As well as keeping alive the art of flower arranging on a domestic scale, the Society has been involved with the arrangement of flowers for many major events, including the wedding of HRH Prince Andrew and Miss Sarah Ferguson in Westminster Abbey, London, in 1986.

From the single bloom on a café table to cascades of flowers in a banquet hall, from the jug of flowers on the kitchen window sill to floral floats in civic parades, the tradition of flower arranging continues, allowing us to ensure that nature's beauty is never far from our eyes.

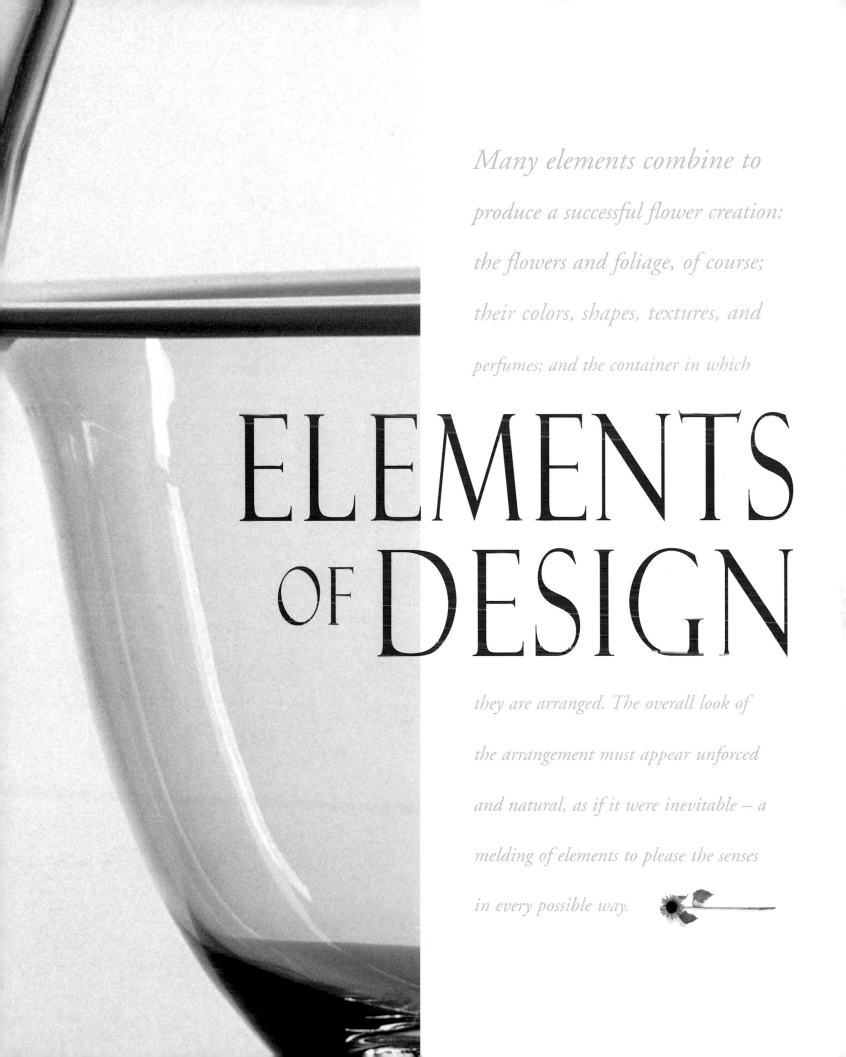

Many elements combine to produce a successful flower creation: the flowers and foliage, of course; their colors, shapes, textures, and perfumes; and the container in which

ELEMENTS OF DESIGN

they are arranged. The overall look of the arrangement must appear unforced and natural, as if it were inevitable — a melding of elements to please the senses in every possible way.

COLOR

OF ALL THE ATTRIBUTES we notice in flowers, color is perhaps the most immediate. It invariably creates the most powerful visual impact, while the choice of particular colors can generate a range of different emotional responses. To understand just how color produces such different effects and moods, we need to understand a little about color theory and how colors relate to one another. This relationship is commonly explained using a color wheel (*right*), which is composed of primary, secondary, and tertiary colors.

PRIMARY COLORS

Red, blue, and yellow are the three primary colors: they cannot be created by mixing other colors. All the colors in the spectrum, however, can be produced by combining the primaries and adding black or white. Secondary colors are created by mixing two of the primary colors. In the color wheel each secondary lies opposite the third unmixed primary.

Red

Yellow

Blue

tertiary

secondary

tertiary

primary

tertiary

secondary

SECONDARIES

Green, orange, and violet are the three secondary colors of the color wheel and are produced by mixing two primaries together: blue and yellow to make green, red and yellow for orange, and red and blue for violet. Colors that lie opposite each other on the color wheel – for example, primary yellow and secondary violet, or primary blue and secondary orange – are known as complementary colors and actually enhance one another when they are placed side by side.

These combinations can create stunning visual effects.

primary

tertiary

secondary

tertiary

primary

tertiary

Orange

Green

Violet

TERTIARIES

Turquoise, indigo, purple, scarlet, gold, and lime green are tertiary colors and are made by mixing various combinations of primaries and secondaries that lie adjacent to one another on the color wheel. Blue and green make turquoise, violet and blue make indigo, red and yellow together make gold, and green and yellow combined make lime-green. On the right-hand side of the color wheel are the warmer colors; on the left, the cooler hues. By adding white, which creates lighter hues, or black, which deepens a color, a variety of paler or darker versions of all these colors can be produced.

Turquoise

Indigo

Purple

Scarlet

Gold

Lime-green

PROPERTIES OF COLOR

Understanding the particular characteristics of any color ensures that the most appropriate flowers can be used in an arrangement to harmonize the piece and create the right style and mood. Whether saturated or pale, intense or tinted, certain colors can be used effectively to create either an elegant or a rustic effect, or a vibrant or demure look.

Passionate red

The hottest and most concentrated of colors in the spectrum, red is extremely vibrant and instantly eye-catching. Red evokes powerful emotions, symbolizing love and passion but also confusion and danger. It can be a warm and positive color, yet also provocative and angry.

Mellow yellow

The closest of colors to white, yellow is therefore also the brightest. Clean and fresh, it induces feelings of happiness and security. It is also a warm color, evocative of spring and summer. Its clarity and radiance make it seem to leap out at the eye. It is the easiest of colors to use and mixes well in arrangements.

Tranquil blue

Pure blue is a cool color that is a fairly uncommon hue in a flower; most blue flowers lean toward the red or green end of the spectrum. Blue evokes tranquillity and creates a feeling of space and height, but it can also look muted and drab when mixed with intense colors such as red.

Fiery orange

Orange is a warm color, the color of autumn and the dying embers of a fire. The brightest of oranges are sunny and welcoming; the deeper hues have a wistful quality that does not bring out the best in other colors, especially purple and violet.

Serene green

Green is the most serene of colors. It is cooling and calming, gentle and refreshing, and the natural opposite of red on the color wheel. It is the most constant color in flower arranging and fortunately complements all other hues.

Demure violet

Violet lies at the dark, moody end of the spectrum. It is an enigmatic color, demure and withdrawn yet carrying an intense, secretive beauty. It harmonizes well with adjacent colors, but really only shines and radiates when paired with yellow.

COMPLEMENTARY COLORS

Mixing colors is always an exciting process. For sheer vibrancy that almost takes the breath away, those colors that lie opposite one another on the spectrum are the ones that create the most stunning effects. Contrasting opposites occur between a primary and a secondary color such as red and green, or two tertiaries, such as lime-green and purple. Such bold contrasts in color will enliven a look even more. This is particularly true when a small amount of one color is mixed with a large quantity of its complementary opposite. The small selection of color seems to becomes even more intense, thus creating a greater impact.

Blue and orange

Perhaps the most vibrant color opposites of all are primary blue and secondary orange. Although true blue hues are rarely found in flowers, with many so-called blue flowers actually betraying hints of lilac and mauve, it is the cooler notes of blue, when contrasted with the sunny sharpness of orange, which cause a blue flower to become so intense and lively. Likewise, the startling brightness of orange becomes even more luscious if set against a mass of blue flowers.

Yellow and violet

Primary yellow is the most joyous color of the spectrum, and it marks the start of the warm half of the color wheel; by contrast, violet is a more somber, subtle color. When mixed together, however, the extraordinarily luminous concentration of yellow flowers becomes even brighter than before, while the interludes of deep violet shades seem to almost vibrate in intensity. Lime-green foliage and blooms will also create a visually stunning impact when set against deep pinks, violets, and purples.

Red and green

The fiery heat of red shades set against the cool, refreshingly restful hues of green make this an immensely exciting pair of complementary colors. It is a combination that occurs naturally in the garden, where the green foliage of the plants immediately offsets any flush of red blooms.

Contrasting opposites: red & green

Contrasting opposites: blue & orange

Contrasting opposites: violet & yellow

HARMONIES AND GENTLE CONTRASTS

A harmonious relationship between colors is usually determined by the order and proportion of colors used. The most successful combinations of harmonious colors are those that lie close to one another on the color spectrum and which combine to create an effect that is pleasing and easy on the eye. As the color pairings move farther apart on the color wheel, so the contrasts become greater. The range of mixes can also be complicated by the ubiquitous presence of green, and/or the degree of lightness or darkness of a particular hue.

Adjacent harmonies

Those hues that lie adjacent to one another on the color wheel are comparatively easy to harmonize and unify. For instance, the tertiary scarlet, combined with either red or orange, which lie on either side of scarlet, will produce a richly satisfying blend of saturated, harmonized color. Although these hues appear to be uniformly intense, they combine together with an assured ease that is visually satisfying, and likewise with such combinations as orange and yellow, yellow and green, turquoise and blue, and so on.

Primary contrasts: red & blue

Gentle contrasts: lime-green & peach

Close contrasts: scarlet & purple

Gentle contrasts

Those colors that lie close, though not adjacent, to each other on the color wheel will generate a series of gentle contrasts. When combined, they create a heightened visual effect while still harmonizing. This is particularly true if these gentle contrasts cross the border between the hotter and cooler ends of the spectrum, either side of warm lime-green and cool purple. The correct proportion and mix of colors will heighten the concentration of each flower with subtle vibrancy.

Moderate contrasts

Creating a look that enhances the visual impact of a flower arrangement without producing a startling result can be achieved by combining colors that lie up to three or four positions apart on the color wheel. This mix of colors will usually include any two of the three primary colors. Such a combination of yellow with blue, red with blue, or red with yellow, can create strong effects. Include paler or darker secondaries and tertiaries, such as pale pink and peach, if you want to tone down the impact.

Close harmonies: orange & yellow

Medium contrasts: purple & green

Close harmonies: orange, cream, & yellow

CHANGING BACKGROUNDS

There are no hard and fast rules for choosing which colors will best complement each other, but there are general guidelines for achieving the most interesting and dynamic effects. To illustrate the way in which different colors interact to produce different effects, this harmonious arrangement of yellow, cream, and green poppies, eustoma, and goldenrod in a simple glass vase has been pictured against five differently colored backgrounds, and demonstrates dramatically the power and influence of color.

BLUE, a primary color, shows up yellow (another primary) surprisingly well. The flowers stand out bright and fresh against this background; the green foliage, which is closer to blue, becomes muted.

GREEN is considered a harmonizing color. A deeper green would have made the flowers stand out and the foliage almost disappear; here the richer golden yellow flowers still create impact against this lighter shade.

YELLOW is a strong color that can detract from more muted hues. While easy on the eye, the effect of this yellow background on the flowers is such that they lose all definition and almost vanish.

NEUTRAL, with its off-white hue, is close to yellow in tone, but since it is so pale it harmonizes well with the flowers while still showing them off. The pale green leaves begin to merge gently with the neutral wall.

RED, with its rich, dark hues, makes both the flowers and foliage of this arrangement stand out dramatically. Here are complementary green and red at their most effective, while the yellow blooms glow luminously.

JUXTAPOSING COLORS

Any two colors placed together will have an immediate effect on each other, and any harmonization or contrast between the two will immediately be accentuated. Here, the same arrangement of rich purple and violet anemones, burgundy ranunculus, and purple liatris in a glass container have been set against the same five colored backgrounds as on the previous pages. The effects created by this display, however, are dramatically different from those of the previous yellow, cream, and green arrangement.

BLUE is relatively close to purple and violet on the color wheel. As a result the flowers in the vase harmonize with the blue background, so losing their individual strength and clarity.

GREEN lies far enough from purple on the color wheel to provide an effective contrast to these flowers. This makes the blooms seem more saturated, while the foliage of the anemones appears to recede.

RED is closely associated with many of the purples and violets in this arrangement. The anemones in particular almost disappear into the background, while the green foliage leaps out of the picture.

NEUTRAL shades are perfect for showing off these rich colors as they create an effective contrast to both flowers and foliage. The lightness of the background makes the flowers look larger and brighter.

YELLOW is the direct opposite of violet on the color wheel and so provides the most effective contrast for these flowers. This wall of yellow makes the arrangement appear at its strongest and richest.

CONTAINER SHAPES

THE SHAPE OF a container is a crucial factor in any flower arrangement. Having a selection of vessels to choose from makes an enormous difference to the quantity, size, and type of flowers and foliage that you will be able to select and buy. Bear in mind that the style and diameter of the neck of the container will have a marked influence on the overall shape of the final arrangement. Aside from the question of shape, the color and any decorative qualities on the exterior of a container are also worth considering.

fluted trumpet vase

large rectangular vase

rounded "goldfish" bowl

urn-shaped pedestal

small round vase

SELECTION OF SHAPES

There is now an enormous range of different container shapes available on the market – from a low, shallow bowl to a tall cylinder, from a classical urn shape to a tazza, from a goldfish bowl to a trumpet vase – all of them produced in an increasingly inventive and interesting array of materials. It is certainly true that some container shapes are much better for arranging flowers than others: any container that holds stems in place satisfactorily will make the task of placing flowers in an attractive and pleasing way much easier. Trumpet and cylindrical shapes are among the most effective containers in which to arrange flowers and foliage; both the rims and the edges at the bottom of these vases will hold the ingredients securely in place, like pencils in a mug.

The rounded shape of a goldfish-bowl-shaped container is more difficult to work with, particularly when the flower heads are heavy. When this is the case, the stems will tend to rise up to the widest part of the bowl and can easily lift up out of their water as a result. Narrow-topped vases, on the other hand, automatically

tall cylindrical vase

narrow-necked vase

large tazza

small square vase

narrow-waisted vase

restrict the amount of stems and foliage that can be placed in them, but this factor can also be beneficial if you do not wish to buy too much material for your arrangement.

Low, shallow bowls that curve outward, wide cylindrical or rectangular vases, and tazzas are not easy containers to arrange flowers and foliage in, unless you simply float flower heads on the surface of the water. If you do decide to use such containers for arranging flowers, the first stems at least will usually need to have some form of support. Foam, pinholder, marbles, or wire mesh

are all possibilities. If the bowl or vase is made of clear glass and you use foam as a support, you will have to devise a means of hiding it – for example, by putting a layer of green moss against the inner edges, which can then be held in place by the foam.

If you wish to select just four basic vases for everyday flower arrangements at home, I suggest that you choose a cylindrical vase 9in (23cm) tall, a narrow rectangular vase measuring 8 × 8 × 3in (20 × 20 × 8cm), a trumpet-shaped vase approximately 7in (18cm) tall, and a round bowl in which to float flower heads.

DISPLAY SHAPES

THERE ARE NO HARD AND FAST RULES concerning the shape of an arrangement, and so long as the display doesn't look top-heavy or precariously balanced, any shape that looks comfortable in its setting should be fine. There are, however, several factors to consider when planning the eventual look. The scale of the arrangement should be in keeping with the size of the setting and, in general, the flowers should not be more than twice the height of the vase. Consider whether the arrangement will suit a formal or casual setting, for instance, and be sure that it does not block anyone's path or restrict their view at a table.

THE THREE-DIMENSIONAL ASPECT

A flower arrangement should always look complete and balanced in its setting. While this doesn't mean that a display must always look as finished at the back as at the front (which would increase the cost and amount of plant materials), it does mean that the arrangement should look good at every angle from which it can be seen. It should also give the impression that the back of the arrangement would look as good as the front if it were on view.

Giving the display a three-dimensional effect usually achieves this, even if the display is going to sit flush against a wall. Arrange the flowers so that they don't just face to the front, but lean back, up, and out to the sides to achieve a rounded effect. Make sure that arrangements are positioned comfortably in a container to achieve the right balance – and do check that any foam, wires, chicken wire, or tube extensions are concealed.

Curved display

The most common shape in flower arranging is one that creates a rounded, fan-shaped effect rising from a container. Depending on the particular situation and setting, this can be a front-facing or all-around display, and its size can be as variable as the selection of flowers you choose. Aim for soft, broken curves and natural groupings of moderately contrasting flowers and colors.

Triangular display

Triangular-shaped arrangements can vary from a low, flattened, three-pointed display such as the one above (which would be particularly suitable as a round centerpiece for a dining table) to a tall, front-facing triangular arrangement that will also look effective when viewed from the side. This type of arrangement is more complicated to achieve successfully than a curved display.

Conical display

The diameter of the mouth of a vase is a determining factor in the final shape of an arrangement; a conical vase, which is a good container for easy arranging, creates a very attractive shape for flowers and foliage. To achieve a conical effect, give the display a good height by seeing that the flowers are at least twice as high as the vase. This shape is good for all-around and front-facing displays.

Asymmetrical display

A tilted, triangular shape can work well, particularly if the stems are also visible through the transparent sides of a rectangular glass vase. This type of display works best if it is one-dimensional, so be sure that the front-to-back depth of the vase is narrow enough to hold the display securely. This arrangement is just one flower deep, but it looks equally beautiful from the front and the back.

Low all-around display

An ideal arrangement for table centers and coffee tables, this display has as its base a ring of foam that ensures the flowers can be arranged into a compact, almost flat, low mound shape. Since these arrangements are mostly seen from above, they need to look good from every angle and should be evenly arranged. To maintain the impact of this display, keep the plant materials simple.

Rectangular display

The effect of this arrangement is similar to that of a windowbox of flowers, so it is best to use a long box-shaped container. The flowers are arranged so that they stand upright, imitating growing plants. This type of arrangement works best if it is created as a three-sided display with just the suggestion of a back, and then positioned against a wall, mirror, or on a shelf.

TEXTURE

TEXTURE IS A SENSUAL as well as a visual element of flower arranging. The appearance and feel of various plant materials, such as leaves and petals, bark and moss, stems and seedheads, combined with the textural surface of a container, become major elements in the makeup of a flower display. Being aware of the possibilities of combining textures can add an extra dimension to every arrangement.

TEXTURED CONTAINERS

Whether it is the uneven texture of roughly woven twigs or wicker, or the smooth, cool, silky surface quality of glass, the texture of a container will influence and accentuate the overall look of an arrangement. Wicker, bark, and rough terracotta containers work particularly well with seedheads, pinecones, and any dried plant materials. Yet such rough textures also work effectively when they are juxtaposed with the waxy smoothness of orchids, for example, or the velvety petals of peonies. Mixing and matching such a wide variety of textures guarantees that you will produce more sensual creations.

Brass and copper
Although brass and copper both have smooth surfaces, any interesting burnished and tarnished areas can easily be seen and felt. Such materials work well with autumn colors and dried flowers.

Galvanized steel
This material has a crystalline surface texture that improves with age. The flower-bucket shape of most galvanized steel containers is perfect for large and small fresh flower arrangements.

Glass
Sometimes silky smooth, sometimes like wax, glass also looks effective when it is roughly etched like chipped ice. This material makes for one of the best containers for fresh flower arrangements.

Terracotta
With its warm tones, rough texture, and pitted surface, terracotta is a popular choice. Although it is a porous material, terracotta will serve very well if the container is first lined with plastic.

Woven raffia
Raffia, which is made from the stalks of the palm *Raphia*, has a crinkly texture that is accentuated when it is woven. Use it as ties for bouquets or woven into baskets for a natural look and feel.

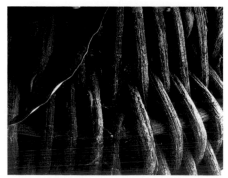

Woven twigs
Layering texture upon texture, each twig in a woven basket has a rough grain running through the surface of its woody stem. The shape of the basket often serves to accentuate these textures.

COMBINING TEXTURES

A flower arrangement will become more fascinating and exciting if unusual combinations of textures are incorporated to create a visually stimulating display. Try taking the textures of rough and smooth to extremes: combine delicate but brittle shells with creamy flower bouquets, velvety petals with the hard coldness of marble, or twigs and pinecones with patinated bronze. Every flower will also have its own textures, such as the seed capsules of sunflowers, the fragile throats of orchids, the rich, sumptuous softness of rose and peony petals, the rough quality of sage leaves, or the spiky notes of butcher's broom.

Similar textures

The ruff of silky textured deep-red feathers looks wonderful when mixed with rich, velvety crimson peonies in this wedding bouquet, making it sensuous to touch and beautiful to behold.

Contrasting textures

A polished satin-finished steel pot filled with a brush of chopped papyrus leaves creates a spiky crown effect across the immaculately smooth, domed ball. Little waxy berries add textural detail.

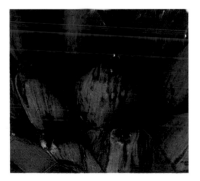

Complementary textures

This basket made from plaited palm leaves has a similar texture to the fleshy leaves of the artichoke flower. Both the poppy heads and the sea holly echo this tactile textural pattern.

We all need inspiration, and
the wealth of arrangements in these
pages will act as a catalyst to help
in your own creations. The chapter
is divided into four sections – Flowers for
the Home, Thanksgiving and Christmas,

INSPIRATIONS

Wedding and Church, and Flowers for

Giving. These four sections are preceded

by a visual index to help you access the

projects, each of which is described in

terms of its seasonal application, longevity,

and level of difficulty.

FLOWERS FOR THE TABLE

THE MOST IMPORTANT PLACE in a house tends to be the table where we eat, especially when it is part of the kitchen. As such, it deserves to have an offering of flowers, be it a jug with flowers from the garden, floating blossoms in a bowl, an opulent table center-piece, or a garland surrounding each plate for a party.

Arrangements that are low enough to

See pages 82–83

See pages 260–261

See pages 240–241

See pages 104–105

place on dining and reception tables

See pages 192–193

See pages 128–129

See pages 102–103

See pages 248–249

without obscuring diners' views

See pages 276–277

See pages 64–65

See pages 118–119

See pages 112–113

FLOOR-STANDING DISPLAYS

LARGER DISPLAYS CAN LOOK magnificent when they are placed on the floor. Whether an arrangement is displayed in front of a fireplace, in a hallway, corridor or landing, on a turn of the stairs, or against a wall, flowers add character and charm, while at the same time lending a homey touch to our rooms.

Ideal for special events, floral displays that

See pages 282–283

See pages 156–157

See pages 116–117

See pages 114–115

are best viewed from above or are large

See pages 164–165

See pages 258–259

See pages 152–153

See pages 266–267

enough to stand alone on the floor

See pages 92–93

See pages 242–243

See pages 256–257

See pages 274–275

POSIES AND BOUQUETS

A SIMPLE BUNCH of flowers can be as informal or as elegant as you choose. For brides or bridesmaids, I like posies more than any other sort of arrangement.

A beautifully wrapped bouquet tied with a stunning bow, however, makes a memorable gift that can be easily cut and arranged in a vase by the recipient.

Beautifully wrapped bouquets and posies

See pages 294–295

See pages 286–287

See pages 244–245

to feature as wedding flowers or as special

See pages 250–251

See pages 238–239

See pages 236–237

occasion gifts for family and friends

See pages 296–297

See pages 268–269

See pages 254–255

CANDLES AND TINY LIGHTS

NOT ONLY do we all look our best by the soft, golden glow of candlelight, but candles and flowers make an enchanted combination. We can dispense magic with light on a dining or side table, in the garden, or on a Christmas tree. Do bear in mind, however, that lighted candles should never be left unattended.

Create a magical atmosphere with

🌲 *See pages 186–187*

🌲 *See pages 206–207*

🏠 *See pages 104–105*

the golden glow of candlelight, or with the

🏠 *See pages 172–173*

🏠 *See pages 118–119*

🌲 *See pages 202–203*

🌲 *See pages 198–199*

inclusion of tiny, twinkling lights

🌲 *See pages 212–213*

🏛 *See pages 246–247*

🌲 *See pages 216–217*

FRAGRANT DISPLAYS

SMELL IS PROBABLY the most powerful of our senses. The evocative perfume of a particular flower can take us right back to an early childhood experience or to a memorable holiday. Always have a few scented flowers in the house – the scent of even a single rose bloom can provide the most intense pleasure.

Let the sweet scent of flowers waft through

🏠 See pages 88–89

🏠 See pages 68–69

🏠 See pages 106–107

🏠 See pages 74–75

your rooms or perfume a church or

🏠 See pages 126–127

🏠 See pages 162–163

🎀 See pages 290–291

🏠 See pages 112–113

marquee for a wedding or christening

⛪ See pages 264–265

🎀 See pages 288–289

🏠 See pages 60–61

🏠 See pages 76–77

QUICK CREATIONS

WE FREQUENTLY HAVE LITTLE TIME to put flowers and foliage together, but there are many easy ways of arranging flowers. Even when minimal effort is needed, a simple vase containing a few choice flowers or some flower heads floating in a bowl of water can generate intense and immediate pleasure.

Simple creations that are easy to prepare

See pages 188–189

See pages 170–171

See pages 234–235

See pages 112–113

can be just as beautiful as the more

See pages 108–109

See pages 110–111

See pages 160–161

See pages 154–155

complicated, time-consuming displays

See pages 78–79

See pages 122–123

See pages 72–73

See pages 150–151

STRUCTURED DISPLAYS

THE NATURE of these designs makes them more time-consuming to prepare than any other flower displays, but they are well worth the effort. Constructed of fresh and dried flowers and foliage, these set pieces can provide memorable visual treats for both everyday home situations or for more formal occasions.

Not all flower creations need a container:

See pages 210–211

See pages 226–227

See pages 148–149

See pages 272–273

these displays are constructed with flexible

See pages 218–219

See pages 208–209

See pages 270–271

See pages 190–191

rope or wire or on rigid, moss-filled bases

See pages 202–203

See pages 182–183

See pages 224–225

See pages 158–159

GRAND DESIGNS

SPECIAL OCCASIONS in the home, in church, or at a reception, require flowers that will stand out and proclaim their beauty. Creating the most appropriate large-scale display may take time and effort, but the result will add a dimension of visual excitement, drama, and impact to any memorable event.

Bold and dramatic, these displays have

See pages 132–133

See pages 232–233

See pages 90–91

See pages 142–143

maximum impact in form, color, and

See pages 124–125

See pages 234–235

See pages 156–157

See pages 210–211

texture, even when viewed from afar

See pages 214–215

See pages 100–101

See pages 252–253

See pages 168–169

DIMINUTIVE DISPLAYS

MOST OF OUR floral needs center around small-scale arrangements for the home, but small does not mean inferior – often a simple little creation has just as much impact as a much larger one. And, of course, just one or two flowers in specimen vases can look stunning beside each place setting at a dinner party.

Even the smallest creations have impact

See pages 128–129

See pages 276–277

See pages 112–113

See pages 70–71

when seen from close up: these are ideal

See pages 186–187

See pages 172–173

See pages 82–83

See pages 118–119

for dinner tables and small side tables

See pages 110–111

See pages 74–75

See pages 104–105

See pages 240–241

LASTING ARRANGEMENTS

LONG-STANDING DISPLAYS, created from preserved or dried plant material, are especially useful for standing in an unused hearth or on a staircase landing, where their colors are less likely to be faded by strong sunlight. For a selection of recommended, long-lasting fresh flowers and foliage, see pp.500–501.

Many long-lasting displays use dried or

See pages 164–165

See pages 190–191

See pages 176–177

See pages 148–119

preserved materials, whose color range is

See pages 184–185

See pages 296–297

See pages 200–201

See pages 210–211

more subdued than that of fresh plants

See pages 180–181

See pages 226–227

See pages 216–217

See pages 104–105

Find inspiration here among a wealth of floral ideas for the living room, hallway, bedroom, and kitchen, as well as special flowers for dinner parties or creations for alfresco entertaining in the garden.

FLOWERS FOR THE HOME

✳ availability of ingredients   ✳ longevity of display

✳✳ level of difficulty

CONE OF PINK AND GOLD

SPRING CERTAINLY PROVIDES us with a wealth of gold, but there is also plenty of pink, especially blossoms in soft, pale pink. Echoing the pink and gold coloration of this wonderful conical vase, I have put together pink flowering almond (*Prunus triloba*), *Bouvardia* 'Pink Luck', and the rich gold *Freesia* 'Springtime', complemented by pale green willow (*Salix*).

Ingredients

Bouvardia 'Pink Luck'

Prunus triloba

Freesia 'Springtime'

Salix babylonica

Alternative with *smyrnium*

In this denser version of the original display, new ingredients replace the golden freesias. The beautiful froth of bright, lime-green leaves and flowers is *Smyrnium perfoliatum*, which, rather like alchemilla (lady's mantle), provides a wonderful complement for any pink, yellow, red, or blue flowers. The display's highlight is now white, in the shape of white anemones with a faint pink tinge.

ARRANGING THE FLOWERS

• Select bouvardia stems that are well conditioned at the outset.

• Prolong the life of the bouvardia by adding flower food to the water in the vase. Encourage the conditioned water to rise in the bouvardia stems by adding a boost of hot water to the vase.

• Arrange the pink flowers of the display first, creating a spiky mop of flowering almond that curves above the vase. Then place the clear pink heads of the bouvardia so that they hover at the middle level.

• Place a gold band of the rich, burning, sweetly scented freesias at the lowest level. If their powerful color is intensified by gold on your vase, so much the better.

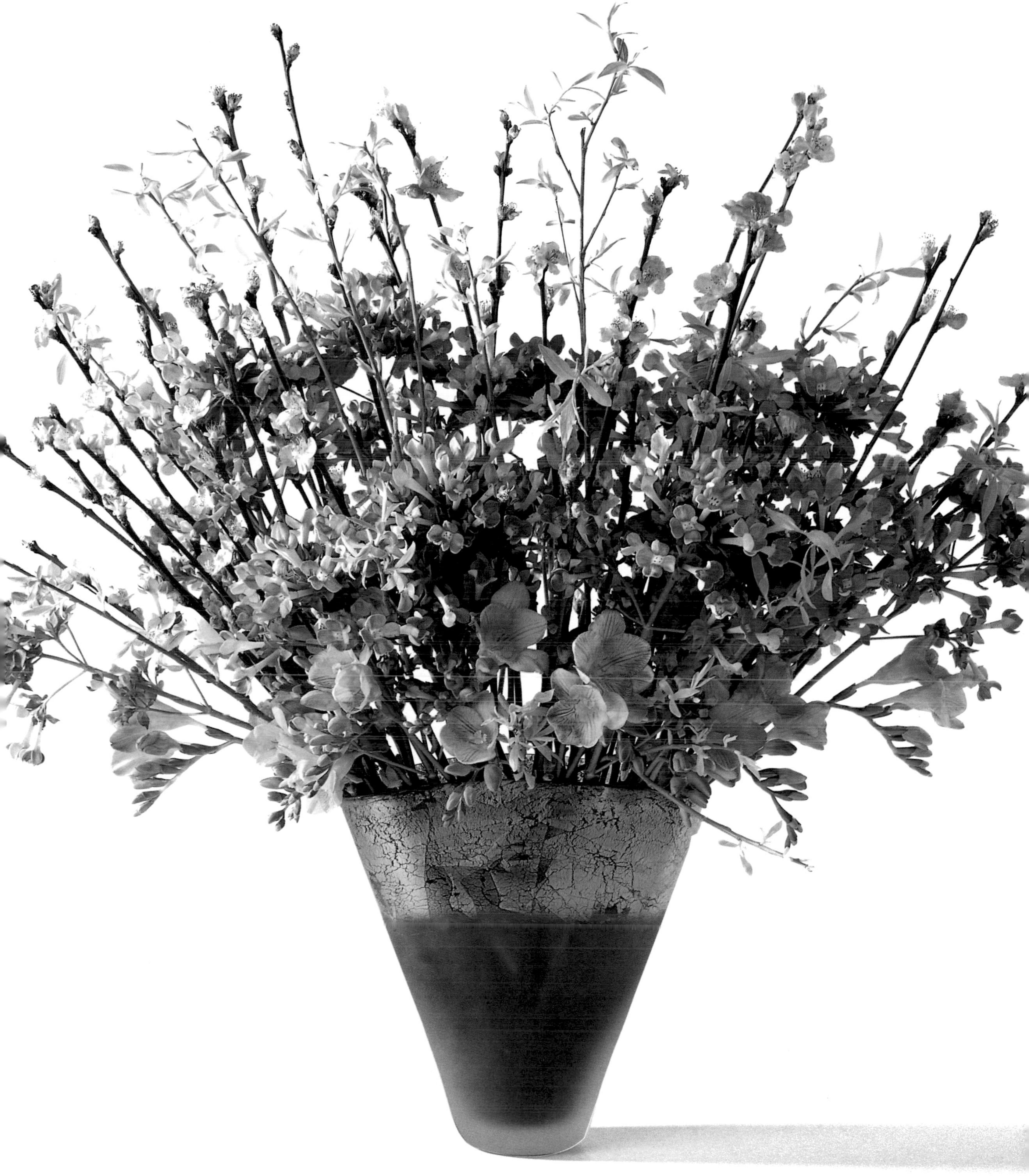

DRAMATIC SPRING FLOWERS

Ingredients

Camellia japonica 'Elegans'

Anemone coronaria De Caen Group

Tulipa 'Exotic Bird'

SPRING GIVES US not only soft pastels, but also much more intensely colored flowers. The cultivars of tulips (*Tulipa*), anemones, and camellias all have a plentiful supply of particularly rich colours. Here, scarlet tulips with a black blotch at the base of each petal combine with purple De Caen anemones and warm, bright pink camellias in a dramatic display to brighten a living room or garden table.

Alternative with *orange*

The red of the tulips, so lively when offset against the purple anemones in the main display, appears more mellow when they are combined with orange chincherinchees (*Ornithogalum dubium*) and fritillaries. This is because scarlet and orange are close to each other on the color wheel (*see pp.30–31*), lying on the warm side between yellow and red. The overall effect is still an invigorating mix, but it is much easier on the eye.

MAKE IT LAST
- Always buy anemones in bud, when they are just beginning to show color (*see p.310*); they will last well once they have been conditioned (*see pp.310–313*).
- All flowers have a longer vase life in cool places, but this is particularly the case with tulips. The arrangement would last longest if kept outdoors in a spot where it could be seen from the living room or kitchen. Cool winter weather should give the tulips a vase life of 21 days; however, a hard frost would destroy the flowers.
- Remove flowers from the stems of the camellia as they fade to encourage more buds to open.
- This glass-lined wire vase is an excellent shape in which to display flowers.

JELLY MOLDS

THE FLUTED SHAPES of these ceramic molds – once used for jellies and blancmanges – make them wonderful to use as vases; their creamy glaze is ideally suited to spring arrangements of scarlet-streaked, pale tulips (*Tulipa* 'Carnaval de Rio'), creamy hyacinths (*Hyacinthus orientalis*), and the fragile flowers of *Leucojum vernum*, the spring snowflake.

Ingredients

Hyacinthus orientalis 'City of Haarlem'

Tulipa 'Carnaval de Rio'

Leucojum vernum

FILL THE MOLDS

- Arranging flowers in wide-necked containers and bowls can be tricky; attach a few prongs to the base of each jelly mold with adhesive clay to help hold the first stems as they are placed.
- Tulips continue growing for several days and may lengthen considerably in the vase; cut them slightly shorter to begin with than the required eventual length.

- Tulips form very attractive shapes as they grow, but if they become too unruly, wrap them in a roll of newspaper and stand them in deep water overnight to straighten them (*see p.313*).
- Hyacinth stems bleed a glutinous sap that can encourage bacteria to grow, so be sure to add two or three drops of household bleach to the water.

FOIL VASE

THIS DELICATE, elegant glass vase is lined with small pieces of silver foil in patterns of green, black, orange, and bright pink. These colors are echoed in the flowers: the tulips (*Tulipa* 'Estella Rijnveld') have pink stripes and splashes; the berries of the two types of ivy (*Hedera*) are very pronounced and ordered, one green and the other ripening to black; and the silvery broom (*Cytisus*) echoes the silver foil. The flowers are arranged very simply, just springing up and out of the vase, and would be ideally suited to a glass or metal shelf.

Ingredients

Cytisus multiflorus

Tulipa 'Estella Rijnveld'

Hedera canariensis 'Gloire de Marengo'

Hedera helix f. *poetarum* 'Poetica Arborea'

Alternative with *fritillaries*

Nodding snakeskin fritillaries (*Fritillaria meleagris*) in plum and white match the foil vase perfectly. Although these incredible flowers look fragile, they should last up to six days if they are bought just as they are opening (*see p.310*).

PRACTICAL POINTS

• Vases with decoration on the inside, such as this, need a watertight lining or inner container to protect them (*see p.308*).
• The tulips will continue to grow in the vase and, although they may need to be cut back a little if they get too straggly, the sinuous curves into which their stems evolve are often most attractive.
• The vase life of many flowers can be shortened by the presence of tulips in the same arrangement, but this combination should last reasonably well.

SPRING YELLOWS

THIS EXOTIC APPROACH to spring color uses calla lilies (*Zantedeschia*) and dramatic crown imperials (*Fritillaria*), alongside stocks (*Matthiola*), day jessamine (*Cestrum*), and sandersonia, a delicate South African flower that blooms in summer but is available throughout the year from florists. The combination makes a modern arrangement that is ideal for a side table.

Alternative with *quince*

The addition of a few twigs of red-flowered ornamental quince (*Chaenomeles*), creates quite a different color emphasis. Although only a small amount of red is added, the whole arrangement seems much warmer. It is always worth experimenting with combinations – the results are often a pleasant surprise.

PREPARE THE MATERIAL

• Remove all the lower leaves of the crown imperials; they rot very quickly once they are submerged in water.

• If possible, change the water of this arrangement every day: the stems of both the stocks and the crown imperials rot easily. Always use a few drops of bleach or some flower food in the water to help keep harmful bacteria at bay.

• This arrangement is best placed some distance from any seating area, as the smell of the crown imperials is slightly unpleasant, but not enough to warrant excluding them from displays.

Ingredients

Fritillaria imperialis

Zantedeschia 'Aztec Gold'

Sandersonia aurantiaca

Cestrum diurnum

Matthiola incana

CHECKERED HEADS

A WONDROUS SIGHT, the snake's head fritillary (*Fritillaria meleagris*) has bell-shaped flowers patterned in checks, ranging in color around plum and maroon with incursions into pink, cream, and white. They look superb in this vase, which relates to their petals, along with another holding a few Christmas roses (*Helleborus niger*).

Ingredients

Fritillaria meleagris

Helleborus niger

Alternative with *tulips*

To the simple arrangement of snake's head fritillaries I have added some amazing tulips – a variety named 'Gavota' – turning out their petals to maximize their impact. Their flowers of plum, cream, and green are in the same color range as the fritillaries, and they seem to have strayed from a seventeenth-century painting. It is always exciting to chance upon such a fascinating color link between two flowers.

ARRANGING THE FLOWERS

• Find two containers that will happily complement each other in shape, color, and texture, looking also for colors that harmonize with the flowers.

• Cut the stems of the fritillaries. They appear to be extremely fragile, but actually last reasonably well once cut.

• Arrange the fritillaries quite densely with their leaves still on the stem, encouraging the robust leaves to spring up wildly.

• Take the hellebores (Christmas roses) and stick a pin through their stems several times just below the flower, then place them in warm water. The flowers will take in more water and therefore last longer.

• Arrange the heads of the hellebores so that they just skim the top of their vase.

VIBRANT ANEMONES

COLORS THAT LIE ADJACENT or close to each other on the color wheel (*see pp.30–31*) mostly harmonize, although bluish purple and orangish red can react quite vibrantly. Here, rich purple anemones (*Anemone coronaria* De Caen Group) and liatris (*Liatris spicata*), which is on the blue side of red, vie with orange-red ranunculus (*Ranunculus asiaticus*) (on the yellow side of red); these in turn sing out against the green anemone leaf bracts and stalks. Set against a rich Venetian red background, all this makes for an exciting display that revels in color, while the arrangement itself has been kept deliberately simple in form.

Alternative with *yellow*

Here the same rectangular glass vase and similarly shaped flowers are used to quite different effect. Harmonizing yellows, ranging from a rich egg-yolk yellow, through gold, to green-yellow and cream, give a bright, sunny arrangement. Again, just three types of flower are used: golden rod (*Solidago*), Iceland poppies (*Papaver nudicaule*), and eustoma.

Ingredients

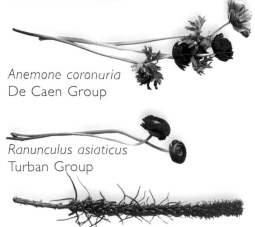

Anemone coronuria
De Caen Group

Ranunculus asiaticus
Turban Group

Liatris spicata

ARRANGE THE FLOWERS

• Although it looks simple, this kind of arrangement requires care to create.

• Start by propping some of the shorter flower stems almost vertically against the left side of the vase.

• Add more stems, allowing them to spray out gently; the first stems will help to hold them in place.

• The stems leaning out to the right of the vase should be the longest, so that the ends of their stems reach the bottom of the left side and hold them in place.

HANGING VASES

ADAPTING CONTAINERS can add great versatility to displays: this rich yellow jug with its matching small glasses hanging over the rim has a form you would never find in a vase. For both the jug and the glasses, I have used feathery, silvery leaved mimosa (*Acacia*) and ice-pink cherry blossoms (*Prunus mume*), and dill (*Anethum graveolens*). The mix of perfumes is delicious.

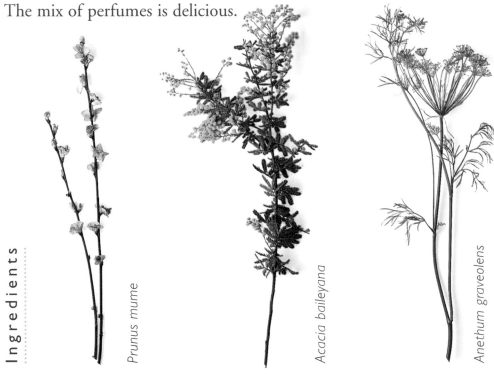

Ingredients

Prunus mume

Acacia baileyana

Anethum graveolens

PREPARE THE MATERIAL

- Care is needed to bring cut mimosa into flower and to maintain its fluffiness. Cut, scrape, and hammer the stems and then condition the flowers in lukewarm water, covering with a plastic bag to help them to open and stay fluffy.
- To prolong the life of this arrangement, add either flower food or a few drops of household bleach to the water: the stems of dill decay very rapidly and changing the water, particularly in the small containers, could be difficult.
- Even after the petals drop from the cherry blossoms, the stamens remain on the stems and continue to look attractive.

SUSPEND THE GLASSES

- It is best to arrange the flowers in the glasses before you hang them.
- Take a length of raffia and tie loops in the ends to hold two glasses. The raffia should be long enough to lay over the top of the jug, with the glasses hanging down the side, balancing each other. The flower stems will hold the raffia in place. Repeat with the other two glasses.
- Stagger the glasses down the height of the jug, tilting them whichever way looks best for the position you have chosen.
- Glasses that do not flare like these will need a raffia harness under as well as around them to make them secure.

VIOLETS AND BLUE

LYING IN THE SPECTRUM between clear blue and the warmer hues of plum and purple, violet is a powerful color that glows darkly but vividly – and all the more so when set off by a vibrant blue. Here, richly perfumed sweet violets (*Viola odorata*) are stunningly displayed in a tall, narrow, indigo and turquoise vase and a moon-shaped, translucent blue container, while a turquoise bowl offsets the luscious petals and intense black eyes of *Anemone coronaria* 'Mona Lisa Purple'.

Ingredients

Anemone coronaria 'Mona Lisa Purple'

Primula Polyanthus Group Crescendo Series

Viola odorata

Alternative with *primulas*

The sweet violets are retained in their intensely blue, translucent container. Next to them a turquoise bowl holds heads of deep violet polyanthus (*Primula* Polyanthus Group Crescendo Series), each flower with a bright gold center. The polyanthus will add its own fragrance to the delightful, old-fashioned perfume of the sweet violets.

DISPLAYING THE FLOWERS

• Seek out containers in colors that will resonate with the hues of the flowers you are arranging. The original function of the containers need not deter you – for example, the asymmetrical, bright blue container housing the violets is nothing more grand than a plastic wastebasket.

• Arrange the anemones in their container, making sure that they have adequate water.

• Set aside any long-stemmed leaves that have been supplied with the violets.

• Attach the short stems of the violets to wire supports, cutting the wires long enough to hold up the violets' heads just above the top of their container, with the stems trailing down inside.

• Wire short-stemmed polyanthus leaves in the same way, with their ends about 1½in (4cm) below the top of the container.

• Water the vases of violets to the brim, and fill them up frequently.

VIVID BLUES

INSPIRATION FOR THIS DISPLAY was provided by the intense colors of the matte glazes on this conical vase. The forget-me-nots (*Myosotis sylvatica*) are beautiful in the detail of their clear sky-blue flowers, while the blue of the willow gentian (*Gentiana asclepiadea*) is rich and warm. Such a simple arrangement would particularly suit a contemporary setting – maybe on a glass, stone, or metal side table. It would last well on a table outside but should be brought in if frost is forecast.

CHOOSING INGREDIENTS

• In many places, larch twigs (*Larix decidua*) are available during winter, when such fresh-looking greenery is scarce. The twigs can be kept in water in a cool place outside when other material in the arrangement has faded; they will last for several months and can be used again.

• The flowers of forget-me-nots are not long lasting once cut, but in a cool temperature, especially outside or in a porch where they can be admired as you go in and out of the house, they should look good for about five days. Their fleshy stems are not very long; it is important to keep the vase filled up so that the shorter stems stay well below the water.

• Gentians carry some of the bluest flowers of all and the willow gentian is no exception. Although summer-flowering, willow gentians are available all year from florists. For best results, remove most of their leaves as well as any fading flowers.

Alternative with *viburnum*

A much cooler and more serene arrangement can be created by replacing the vibrant blue willow gentians with the superb green-white flowers of snowball bush (*Viburnum macrocephalum*). Most of the leaves of the viburnum have been removed: this not only makes the flower heads last longer but gives a cleaner look to the display. Because of the delicate forget-me-nots, this design will also last best outside in cool temperatures.

Ingredients

Larix decidua

Gentiana asclepiadea

Myosotis sylvatica 'Music'

ORCHIDS AND REEDS

FLOWERS SEEM TO ARRANGE themselves in vases of this shape but, since even the smaller-flowered cymbidium orchids can be top-heavy, these are staked with reed bamboo, which also adds vertical interest to the arrangement. The beautiful, warm, golden-silver patina of the vase shows off any color, especially the green and gold seen here.

ARRANGING THE ORCHIDS

• Each stem of orchid is tied to a reed stake with two short lengths of raffia; no attempt has been made to hide the raffia, which adds a textural interest of its own.

• Remove the lower orchid flowers as they start to fade: this may encourage more buds to come out farther up the stem.

• Many orchids last well when cut, but it is still important to condition them (*see pp.310–313*). Even if you buy the orchids with their stems in tubes of water, recut the ends and recondition them.

Alternative with *red*

Here, a brilliant red anemone is set against the green, intensifying both colors, which lie opposite each other on the color wheel (*see pp.30–31*). Anemones have a superb color range, from pure white, through pinks, to deep purples and bright reds. The black centers and halo of white at the base of each petal intensify the red even more. They will not last as long as the orchids but can be either removed or replaced.

Ingredients

Cymbidium Kings Loch

Chamaedorea seifrizii

BREATH OF SPRING

LILY-OF-THE-VALLEY (*Convallaria majalis*) has one of the most evocative of all scents: for me it conjures up my childhood breath of pleasure as, each late spring, their tiny flowers exploded with fragrance beneath opening azaleas. This graceful curve of test tubes, each holding a few delicate stems, refreshes the flowers and leaves so that their short-lived beauty and piercingly delicious perfume can be enjoyed by all.

CREATING THE CONTAINER

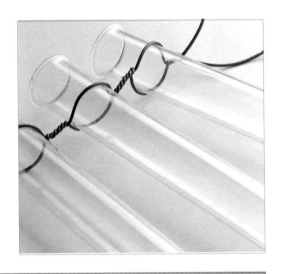

- For this display, you'll need 15 test tubes and a coil of plastic-coated garden wire.
- Cut two lengths of garden wire, each 5ft (1.5m) long. (If you want to wire together more or fewer test tubes, adjust the wire lengths accordingly.)
- Find the middle point of one wire by folding it in half, and bend it around one test tube, about ½in (1cm) below the rim.
- Twist the ends of the wire until the tube is held firmly in place by the wire loop.

- Twist the wire ends six or seven more times to create a ¾in (2cm) gap between the first tube and the next one.
- Take in the second test tube by twisting the wire ends around it, make another width of twisted wire, and continue until all the tubes are connected. Leave about ½in (1cm) of wire at the end, bent down the side of the final tube.
- Repeat with the second wire, starting 1in (2.5cm) up from the bottom of the test tubes and keeping the tubes parallel.

Alternative with *columbines*

Having wired up your row of test tubes, you can bend it into any shape, such as a triangle, square, or the circle shown here. Columbines (*Aquilegia*) are incredibly beautiful, underrated flowers that are available in late spring or early summer in an extraordinary range of mostly pastel colors. Another choice is strawberry-perfumed mock orange (*Philadelphus coronarius*). Arrange two or three stems of either type in each test tube.

Ingredients

Convallaria majalis

RADIANT SPIRES

AFRICAN CONTAINERS, one of hide and one of wood, set off tall, glowing spires of *Bulbinella hookeri*, a native of South Africa and New Zealand. In the hide pot (*left*), the feathery foliage and yellow heads of banksia (*Grevillea robusta*) mix with the orange spires; in a wooden pot, brilliant pot marigolds (*Calendula officinalis*) meld with the yellow spires.

Alternative with *asters*

While yellow and orange blooms harmonize easily, the addition of rich purple Michaelmas daisies (*Aster novi-belgii* 'Chequers') creates a violent contrast, making the marigolds appear even brighter and sunnier. This is because the two colors are opposite each other in the color wheel (*see pp.30–31*). Late summer is a good time for this display because bulbinellas, marigolds, and Michaelmas daisies are all in season then.

Ingredients

Grevillea robusta

Bulbinella hookeri

Bulbinella hookeri

Calendula officinalis

ARRANGING THE FLOWERS

- Check that rustic containers are watertight: in the case of the hide vase, I placed a cylindrical glass vase inside rather than using a plastic lining that could be pierced by the banksia.

- To improve the appearance of the marigolds and make them last longer, remove most of the leafy side-shoots and some of the larger leaves.

- Place the orange bulbinella spires and banksia at roughly the same height.

- Allow the yellow bulbinella spires to dominate the crown of the arrangement, with marigolds forming the lower tiers.

EARLY SUMMER SKIES

THE BRIDGE BETWEEN spring and summer is one of the most beautiful times of the floral year: plants are fresh and sparkling, their colors enhanced by the early summer skies. Among the beauties that flower at this time are Solomon's seal (*Polygonatum*) and snowball bush (*Viburnum macrocephalum*) – both white with green undertones – which I have added to some early, pale blue delphiniums in this etched glass vase. The blue backdrop intensifies the theme, but these flowers would look equally attractive against a green, yellow, or white background.

CHOOSING A VASE

• A conical vase always makes for simple, attractive arrangements: the bottom and rim hold the first few stems securely in place, making management of the rest of the arrangement easier, while the shape allows flowers and foliage to spring outward in a beautifully natural way.

• Be sure that the stems of the Solomon's seal (*Polygonatum*) curve outward, so that their demure little white and green flowers can be easily seen.

• To prolong the life of the flowers on the snowball bush, remove most of the lower leaves from the stems before arranging them in the vase. This will also help prevent the display from looking too leafy.

Ingredients

Viburnum macrocephalum

Delphinium 'Lord Butler'

Polygonatum x hybridum

SHADES OF PALE

A GENTLE DOME of white and blush flowers stands serenely beside a glass plate of papery garlic bulbs and ribbed mushrooms. Perfumed mock orange (*Philadelphus* 'Belle Etoile') and *Phlox paniculata* 'Fujiyama' jostle with *Eustoma grandiflorum* and *Scabiosa caucasica* 'Miss Willmott', while white spires of *Lysimachia clethroides* erupt in every direction.

ARRANGING THE FLOWERS

• Place a small disk of soaked wet foam on a florist's spike in the bottom of a pure white glass or china bowl. The foam will help hold the stems in place as you arrange them.

• Place the stems of mock orange, then the phlox and scabious, turning the bowl to see how they look from all round.

• Add the large, ice-pink eustoma flowers, aiming for an informal but balanced look; then add the lysimachia spires, allowing them to cascade out of the arrangement.

• Cut off dying mock orange and eustoma flowers to encourage new buds to appear.

Ingredients

Lysimachia clethroides

Phlox paniculata 'Fujiyama'

Eustoma grandiflorum Heidi Series

Philadelphus 'Belle Etoile'

Scabiosa caucasica 'Miss Willmott'

Allium sativum

ARRANGING THE GARLIC

• Find a plate that complements the vase you have chosen – the one I used here features swirls of clear and white glass.

• Lay out the garlic bulbs: the blush visible through their papery skin echoes the tinge of the mock orange flowers.

• Add the ribbed oyster mushrooms. If kept out for only a few hours, they may be refrigerated and eaten the following day.

MAJESTIC LILIES

ORIGINALLY FROM AFRICA, calla lilies (*Zantedeschia aethiopica*) are shade- and water-loving plants with magnificent spathes like crisp, white, furled napkins. Artists such as Georgia O'Keefe and Diego Rivera have featured these majestic flowers in their paintings – in some where the white spathes are echoed by the white skirts of women. Here, they are featured emerging from a metal windowbox set against a wall of garden greenery, but they would look equally magnificent indoors.

MAKING THE SCAFFOLD

- Bind five pieces of ⅜in (10mm) metal tubing, one 28in (70cm) long and four 24in (60cm) long, to form a scaffold above a 24in (60cm) long metal trough, with the longer rod at the top.
- Fill the trough with gravel and insert six tumblers level with the trough rim. Bind the support to the trough with wire.
- Place the callas in the tumblers, tying the stems to the support with raffia. Vary the number of stems in each tumbler.

Alternative with *birds of paradise*

Any tall flowers with large heads – such as these birds of paradise (*Strelitzia*) – can be arranged in this way. If the flowers are top-heavy, tie the stems to both sides of the top rail. Use the leaves as well, crossing the stems of some flowers and leaves to give an interesting shape to the top of the display. Lilies such as 'Casa Blanca', which can be top-heavy, could also be displayed like this, as could delphiniums, eremurus, agapanthus, heliconias, bamboo, or bunches of foliage.

Ingredients

Zantedeschia aethiopica 'Crowborough'

TALL TERRACOTTA POTS

TERRACOTTA POTS WEATHER over the years to give a wonderfully distressed finish. The simplicity and brilliant colors of gerberas seem well suited to these pots, the clusters of daisies just peeping above the rims to make very striking, yet easy to create, floor-standing arrangements for a special occasion. Forcers, placed over rhubarb to blanch it to perfection, make fascinating containers for these displays, but tall pots may be easier to find and can be substituted.

Ingredients

Gerbera jamesonii (red cultivar)

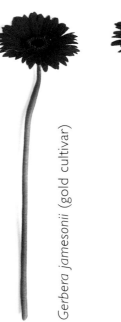

Gerbera jamesonii (gold cultivar)

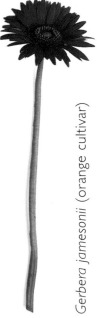

Gerbera jamesonii (orange cultivar)

Alternative with *pink*

Gerberas have a simple daisy shape that suits all seasons. They are available in flower shops throughout the year in a range of vibrant colors: in spring you could use yellows, cream, and white; in summer gaudy reds and pinks; and for autumn rusty oranges, dark reds, and maroons. Opposing colors can enliven each other (*see pp.30–31*): in the smaller arrangement here, a pleasantly clashing combination of pink and orange gives a bright look. Watch for gerberas with dark centers, since these always stand out beautifully in any arrangement.

USING TERRACOTTA

• Old forcers are open-ended (originally they would have had lids), so they need to have containers inside them to hold water.
• Place a brick at the base of each forcer, and stand a container on it with its rim about 2in (5cm) down from the top.
• Unglazed terracotta pots are porous and should be lined (*see pp.308–309*).
• The gerberas are cut so that their stems sit on the base of the water container and their heads are held just above rim level.
• Forcers can be used either way up, as long as they can be made stable.

SPRING COLOR IN SUMMER

YELLOW AND BLUE are colors that epitomize spring: golden daffodils and blue skies with scudding white clouds. Summer is full of warmer colors, but it is possible to recapture the fresh feeling that comes at the beginning of the growing season by putting together these spring colors with summer flowers. A strongly textured gray ceramic container makes a simple foil to the clear yellow flowers of spurge (*Euphorbia palustris*) mixed with double blue scabious (*Scabiosa lucida*), love-in-a-mist (*Nigella damascena* Persian Jewel Series), and the intense blue of hound's tongue (*Cynoglossum nervosum*), which all flower at the same time.

FRESH PALETTE

• Flower creations are dictated by what is available; when buying flowers, always keep an open mind, perhaps thinking of the color palette. The resulting display is often all the more interesting for a touch of improvisation.

• Brilliant blue cornflowers, which are available for most of the year at flower shops, could be substituted for any of the blues used here, and the result would still look fresh and springlike.

USE THE SETTING

- A narrow trough such as this is ideal for a side table in a hall where there is little space for a more rounded arrangement.
- Consider not only the container but also where it will be displayed. The placing of taller stems toward the ends of this arrangement echoes the upturned ends of the Chinese whatnot below.

- Do not overload your container; this very narrow ceramic trough holds just a single line of flowers.
- It is important to keep small containers filled up with fresh water, particularly if some of the flower stems do not extend to the bottom of the trough.

Ingredients

Euphorbia palustris

Scabiosa lucida

Nigella damascena
Persian Jewel Series

Cynoglossum nervosum

FLOWERS UNDER WATER

Ingredients

Rosa 'Blue Curiosa'

Allium stipitatum

Eustoma grandiflorum Heidi Series

Eustoma grandiflorum Heidi Series

Paeonia 'Red Charm'

Nigella damascena var.

APPEARING TO FLOAT in space, flower heads of rose, peony, eustoma, love-in-a-mist (*Nigella damascena* var.), and ornamental onion (*Allium stipitatum*) are here magnified and reflected underwater by an inverted pyramid of glass tumblers.

CREATING THE DISPLAY

• Decide how long you need the display to last. If longevity is required, omit the onion, which, although it looks superb, will cloud the water in a couple of days.

• Find a large "fish-bowl" vase, about 14in (35cm) tall, into which you can fit 10 or 11 tumblers, preferably ridged rather than plain to add to the refraction of light.

• Fill the vase with water to just over three-quarters of its capacity.

• Cut off the stems just below the flower heads and place one bloom inside each tumbler, facing toward the rim.

• Fill the tumblers with water.

• Invert the tumblers under the surface of the vase water, with their rims facing outward. Begin by wedging in the first three at the bottom, each one facing down at 45°, then pile on the others, positioning the flowers as you work.

• Float a selection of the remaining flowers on the surface of the water.

BASKET OF SWEET WILLIAMS

SWEET WILLIAMS have long enjoyed the reputation of being sweet-smelling, but I can only ever discern the faintest of perfumes from them. Here, a weathered terracotta basket plays host to several sweet williams (*Dianthus barbatus* Monarch Series) in a cheerful range of pinks and white, mixed with variegated leaves of *Euonymus fortunei* 'Silver Queen' and the pink-flowering *Escallonia* 'Donard Seedling'.

ARRANGING THE FLOWERS

• Terracotta is porous, so you will need to line the container with a plastic bowl or a sheet of plastic (*see p.308*).
• Wedge some soaked wet foam firmly into the bottom of the container.
• Nearly fill the container with water to which is added a few drops of bleach.
• Remove from the sweet williams all the green leaves that fall below the water level. Although it is difficult to get all the leaves off the stems, it is well worth the extra effort because they rot quickly in water.
• Arrange the sweet williams, euonymus leaves, and escallonia stems, encouraging them to extend wide of the container.
• Fill up the water level daily.

Alternative with *scarlet*

In this arrangement, I have mixed sweet williams in scarlet and salmon with silvery green euonymus foliage and the pink escallonia. Overall, the impact is much more pronounced than that of the original pink and white display. Red and green stand opposite each other on the color wheel (*see pp.30–31*), and this always has the effect of intensifying both colors.

Ingredients

Euonymus fortunei 'Silver Queen'

Dianthus barbatus Monarch Series

Dianthus barbatus Monarch Series

Dianthus barbatus Monarch Series

Escallonia 'Donard Seedling'

LEAF-COVERED BASKET

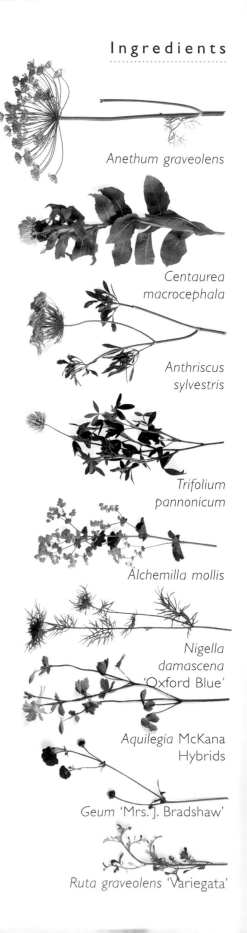

Anethum graveolens

Centaurea macrocephala

Anthriscus sylvestris

Trifolium pannonicum

Alchemilla mollis

Nigella damascena 'Oxford Blue'

Aquilegia McKana Hybrids

Geum 'Mrs. J. Bradshaw'

Ruta graveolens 'Variegata'

GARDENS ARE MOST COLORFUL in early summer. After the lull at the end of spring, a spectrum of colors begins to flush the garden – almost stealthily to begin with, then blatantly flooding in to cover every scrap of available space: the vivid greenish yellows of lady's mantle (*Alchemilla mollis*), the blues of love-in-a-mist (*Nigella damascena*), and aquilegias in a host of shades. Cradle a mass of these beauties in a lined basket covered with magnolia leaves, which glow with a light of their own.

COVERING THE BASKET

• You will need about 40 glycerined magnolia leaves (*see p.316*) to cover a 12 × 8in- (30 × 20cm-) basket.
• Run glue along the back of each leaf's spine; add a few dabs on the basket.

• Attach leaves at an angle, overlapping them to hide the basket. Attach a second row, overlapping the bottom of the first.
• As an alternative to glue, use floral wire pins, piercing the leaves behind each overlap to hide the wires.

FRAMED CENTERPIECE

WHILE CHANGING the frame of a painting one day, I thought that the frame could work as a table centerpiece with flowers and fruits arranged within it. It would last only a few hours – but long enough for a dinner party. Within the frame, on a bed of ferns, are roses (*Rosa* Dutch Gold®), yellow mariposa (*Calochortus luteus*), and some glistening redcurrants.

MAKING THE CENTERPIECE

- Choose a frame that complements the colors of the ingredients you plan to use.
- Stick a piece of dark cardboard to the back of the frame so that you can move the arrangement once it is done.
- Cover the cardboard with fern leaves, allowing tips to stray out onto the frame.
- Twist the petals off two roses to reveal their decorative calyces; place the whole rose, the calyces, and the loose petals on the ferns, along with the mariposa flowers.
- Fill in between the flowers, petals, and fern leaves with clusters of redcurrants.

Ingredients

Redcurrants

Rosa Dutch Gold®

Polystichum setiferum

Calochortus luteus

Alternative with *ivy*

A gilt picture frame has been used here to give a more ornate, Italianate look. The base layer is a delicate ivy (*Hedera nepalensis* 'Suzanne') on which are arranged campanula flowers, a eustoma (*Eustoma grandiflorum*) flower and petals, *Nectaroscordum siculum*, and pale pink *Lamium maculatum*. Luscious blueberries fill in the background.

ARTICHOKE BASKET

THIS BASKET of woven palm leaves is reminiscent of the globe artichoke (*Cynara scolymus*), its knobby texture conjuring up the tight layers of bracts that surround the "choke" or flowerhead. In the basket, I have combined seedheads of opium poppies (*Papaver somniferum*), flowerheads of sea holly (*Eryngium*), and artichokes in various stages of maturity to create a striking, low arrangement that is suitable as a table centerpiece.

MAKE A BASKET

- As the poppy leaves are short-lived, they can be replaced as they droop, or omitted.
- Artichoke heads are heavy, so it is best to use them in low displays, such as this one, for maximum stability.

- If left in the basket after the water has gone, all of the ingredients apart from the poppy leaves should dry successfully.
- *Papaver somniferum* 'Hen and Chickens' seedheads are great fun, and could be substituted for the opium poppy.

Ingredients

Cynara scolymus

Eryngium alpinum

Papaver somniferum

Alternative with *nightlight*

Take an almost open artichoke: remove the stem and hollow out from below, leaving enough flesh to hold the leaves in place. Pull out any leaves from the center that would overlap the candle flame, and slide in a tea light in a small glass holder.

PERFUMED PUNCHBOWL

TWO COUNTRY GARDEN PLANTS are used in this display: mignonette (*Reseda odorata*) and a pot marigold (*Calendula officinalis*). The toasted color of the marigold works well with the orange anthers of the mignonette, while a glass bowl shows off the slim stalks. This informal centerpiece will perfume any room with its mix of scents.

MAINTAIN THE DISPLAY

• Remove all the leaves from the stems of the mignonette: this is a fiddly job but, as they rot extremely quickly, it is worth doing.

• Change the water every day. The flowers are closely arranged, so it is quite easy to hold them with a hand just inside the bowl and tip the water away. Replace with water that has a few drops of bleach in it.

• Mignonette has a tantalizing scent that resembles a blend of violets, fresh hay, and sweet peas. Unlike most other flowers, the blooms retain much of this perfume even when they are dried, so it is worth preserving them when this arrangement is past its best. Simply snip off the flower heads and put them in a bowl with some other flower petals to dry: they will continue to release their perfume for many weeks.

• In the garden both pot marigolds and mignonettes grow readily from seed. Although the mignonette is not showy, it rewards with its delectable perfume. The marigolds help keep aphids at bay.

Alternative with *orchids*

A slightly wilder and more exotic display can be created by replacing the marigolds with one of the more delicate-looking orchids – here the little yellow blooms of the *Dendrobium* cultivar 'Golden Showers'. In this arrangement, the mignonette makes a low, tussocky surface close to the bowl, which is punctuated by the stems of orchids rising up out of the bowl and spraying out and down over the mignonette flowers.

Ingredients

Reseda odorata

Calendula officinalis 'Indian Prince'

FLOATING FLOWERS

WATER IS AN essential feature in any garden: in my London garden, I have a small pond, two water tanks, two old stone drinking troughs, and a couple of oil jars that I keep filled with water throughout the year. Every few days I pick some flowerheads, such as these rose-pink peonies (*Paeonia* 'Globe of Light'), and float them on the water's surface, to enchanting effect.

HOW TO MAINTAIN

• Float a couple of open-cup peonies on the surface of the water in a stone trough.
• Keep duckweed in check; otherwise, it will eventually take over the entire surface of water in troughs and ponds. For the best effect, try to allow at least a little clear dark water to show through at the surface.
• To maintain an attractive mossy exterior on terracotta or stone plant containers, spray them with water every day.
• Lean old oil jars at an angle, fill with water, and decorate with floating flowers such as yellow tuberous begonias, pale pink roses, or some geranium foliage.
• Remove floating flowerheads as they die, then replace with fresh blooms. If you don't have enough in your garden, you could always buy a few.

Alternative with *mortar*

This marble mortar has been relegated to the garden from the kitchen. It is small and elegant – measuring only 10in (25cm) in diameter – which makes it a perfect container for a few floating flowers. Here there are two 'Purple Tiger' roses, some deep red geraniums, and bright blue felicia flowers. Always keep the water fresh; flower petals and stems can very quickly produce rotting bacteria.

Ingredients

Paeonia 'Globe of Light'

PEONIES IN CHINESE LEAVES

LETTUCES AND PEONIES may at first seem an odd combination, but the leaves of Chinese lettuce (*Brassica rapa pekinensis*) are works of art: they are pale golden green, crisp, curling in at the tips, furled, and beautifully veined – and, when gently pulled apart, they make fascinating wraps for the peonies. Their texture is clearly visible through the glass vases, and the petals of the flowers merge with the frilly tops of the Chinese leaves to give the impression that the leaves and peonies (*Paeonia* cultivars) are one. These glass creations look best on a glass coffee table or as a group in the center of a dining table.

CHOOSING PEONIES

- Peonies are among the most beautiful of all flowers, with both simple single and frilly double forms; a range of reds, pinks, cream, and white is widely available in flower shops. If you grow them yourself, you can also have yellow flowers.

- Choose well-budded specimens that are just showing their color (*see p.310*).

Alternative with *chicory*

Many leafy vegetables can be of great value in displays. Chicory (both green and red), cabbages, chard (especially the red-stemmed ruby chard), curly kale, and rhubarb all have striking leaves or stalks that can be combined with bold flower heads. Here, red chicory leaves in a glass cylinder surround some deep red peonies that are fully open and nearly at an end – but still quite beautiful.

- Since these arrangements use peony blooms that are almost fully open, condition the flowers well (*see p.312*) and remove their leaves.

- Put a few drops of bleach into the water to help the Chinese lettuce last.

- All parts of peonies are mildly toxic.

Ingredients

Brassica rapa pekinensis

Paeonia 'Sarah Bernhardt'

TEATIME DISPLAYS

IT IS ALWAYS INTERESTING to adapt everyday household objects as containers for flowers. Here, a sleek modern kettle and old-fashioned china teapot act as perfect alternative vases on a side table. The highly polished kettle reflects the brightly colored poppies (*Papaver nudicaule* cultivars) that cascade around the rim: the opening is quite narrow, but the eccentric shapes of poppies can be chosen to fall in an attractive way.

HEAT TREATING POPPIES

• All types of poppies need to be heat treated (*see p.312*); re-treat the ends of bought poppies if cut.

• The simplest way to heat treat flowers intended for a kettle is to stand them in 1in (2cm) of almost boiling water in the kettle for about four minutes, then simply fill with cold water.

• If the poppies that you buy at a flower shop have been heat treated, this will probably be indicated on the wrapping. Such flowers should not be cut before arranging. If your arrangement requires that the stems be cut, then you will have to heat treat the flowers again yourself after cutting them to the length you need.

• Once they have been conditioned and arranged, poppies last surprisingly well – up to seven days. Their fragile looks belie a sturdy constitution.

Alternative with *teapot*

The same basic idea can be used to create displays of quite a different character. This nineteenth-century Staffordshire teapot is a more gentle affair than the ultra-modern kettle, and is home here to some beautifully scented sweet peas (*Lathyrus odoratus* 'Wiltshire Ripple'). Unlike the poppies, which hug the kettle, these sweet peas are arranged in an airy mound that floats up out of the teapot.

Ingredients

Papaver nudicaule 'Summer Breeze'

SHADES OF GREEN AND LIME

ALL-GREEN ARRANGEMENTS are rare, but green can be every bit as alluring as any of the other colors. It is ever-present in the landscape and is perhaps the most calm and restful of all colors. The fresh green of bells of Ireland (*Moluccella laevis*) and the chartreuse of a *Cymbidium* orchid cultivar are spiced up here by the touch of red of the *Ribes rubrum*, which serves to draw out the subtly different shades. This forward-facing display could be used to fill an unused fireplace.

Ingredients

Moluccella laevis

Allium aflatunense

Ribes rubrum

Cornus alba 'Elegantissima'

Cymbidium Thurso

Alternative with *green*

Removing the chartreuse cymbidium orchids tones down the fresh, springlike feel of the arrangement and produces a more muted, harmonious combination of shades. Green is on the cool side of the color wheel (*see pp.30–31*) but the natural tones of the worn copper bowl help to keep the overall feeling here refreshing but not cold.

FILL THE BOWL

• Because this bowl is low and wide, attach florist's prongs inside with adhesive clay and wedge in a low base of soaked wet foam.

• Add the branches of redcurrant (*Ribes rubrum*) last, so that the fruit is glimpsed through the foliage.

• This all-green arrangement would serve equally well for a special occasion or simply for everyday pleasure.

• Be sure that the bowl is kept filled with water as this is a thirsty arrangement.

• All the ingredients in this display should last for over a week, but remove individual orchid flowers as they die.

BLUE LAGOON

THE CONTAINER USED for this vivid display is a beechwood box with a wok wedged inside it to hold the water. An edging of hosta leaves provides a margin around the "pool," which is packed with bright blue irises. A solitary, dark red rose (*Rosa* THE DARK LADY 'Ausbloom') emerges from amid the irises, to great dramatic effect.

Ingredients

Hosta 'Frosted Jade'

Iris 'Professor Blaauw'

Rosa THE DARK LADY ('Ausbloom')

PREPARING THE POOL

- Make sure that the inner container is securely wedged in place. Attach a block of soaked wet foam to some prongs at its base to hold the arrangement in place.
- Cover the outer rim of the container with hosta leaves, and cram the inside with irises, pushing their stems into the wet foam at the base.
- Add a single flower in a contrasting color to the arrangement.

Alternative with *alchemilla*

The idea for this arrangement came to me as I considered the vivid green duckweed that appears on the surface of my water-filled troughs. Here a froth of alchemilla flowers covers the surface, while a lone 'New Dawn' rose floats serenely on the surface like a waterlily. This arrangement should be set at ground level, since it should be seen from above for the best effect.

CREATIVE WRAPS

INSPIRED BY Japanese presentation skills, this idea involves simply wrapping up vases so that the paper forms a ruff around the flowers. I think the best result is achieved with plain white textured paper, perhaps with some plant material woven into it, but you can use any type, from silky tissue or textured, handmade paper bound with ribbon, to crisp brown wrapping paper tied with string. These very easy creations are perfect for a lunch or dinner party, with single flowers in small glasses at each place setting and a larger arrangement for the center of the table.

Ingredients

Rosa 'Candy Bernice'

Rosa 'Hollywood'

Rosa 'Golden Gate'

WRAPPING THE GLASSES

- The best small glasses for this form of presentation are those with thick, heavy bases, since they are the most stable.
- Choose paper to match both the look of the flowers and the scale of the glass; small glasses are easier to wrap in soft papers.
- Cut or tear the wrapping paper into squares, making each side of the square about four times the height of the glass. Torn edges generally look best.

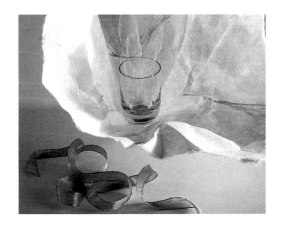

Alternative with *light*

To create a whole table setting, make a lamp by wrapping a goldfish bowl holding a tea light in the same paper used on the glasses. Tie the cord or ribbon just below the rim of the bowl, and flare the paper out horizontally so that it is not over the flame. Use a long taper to light the candle, and never leave burning candles unattended.

- Stand the glass in the middle of the square and pull the paper up around it, making sure that the base is flat and pleating the paper at the rim.
- Tie your chosen cord or ribbon around the paper wrapping just above the rim of the glass so that it cannot slip down, and flare the paper out slightly.

- To avoid getting the paper wet, use a baster or a funnel to fill the small glasses with water once they are in position.
- The shortness of the flower stems makes these displays particularly long lasting; they also provide a good way of extending the life of flowers that have been left over from fading larger displays.

Alternatives with *poppies*

A more vibrant effect can be achieved by using poppies, here the brilliant scarlet Oriental poppy *Papaver orientale* 'Beauty of Livermere', whose papery petals will suit your dining table setting. You could also have a different colored poppy or rose in each wrapped glass. The stems of all poppies must be heat treated (*see p.312*) after they are cut to length; they will then last for several days.

MEDITERRANEAN JAR

THIS TERRACOTTA jar, which is reminiscent of vessels from southern France with its burning lustrous colors ranging from almost black to a silvery gray, seems to be made for Mediterranean flowers and foliage. The arrangement, which would be perfect for a table or hanging in a garden, looks as if it is being blown by a strong breeze and mimics the appearance of plants from windswept coasts. Rosemary and ozothamnus make a good ruff for the flowers of lavender (*Lavandula*) and yarrow (*Achillea*).

ADAPTING THE JAR

• If you see a vase or pot that you like, it is always worth buying it even if it does not immediately seem ideal for flowers. This jar, for example, has a curved base and came in a hanging sling, but it is easy to keep it upright by supporting the base on a ring of braided raffia.

• Line porous jars with a plastic container or a plastic liner (*see p.308*); be careful not to pierce the plastic with woody stems.
• Wedge some soaked wet foam in the jar to hold the first few stems in place.
• To make this arrangement last as long as possible, remove all the leaves from the lower parts of the stems. Adding a few drops of bleach to the water that you use will also help prolong its life.

Ingredients

Rosmarinus officinalis

Ozothamnus rosmarinifolius

Achillea 'Hartington White'

Lavandula angustifolia

EXOTIC BASKET

A WOVEN PLASTIC shopping basket in gaudy hues is the humorous inspiration for this vivid arrangement. The hot colors of the basket have a South American or Mexican feel, so the sunny, papery flowers of satin flower or godetia (*Clarkia amoena*), which is native to those regions, seem appropriate. Their salmon and fuchsia pinks clash deliciously with the orange of the blood flower (*Asclepias curassavica*), which is also of South American origin. To achieve the best result, it is vital not to lose your nerve with the colors: think hot, hot, hot.

USING PLASTIC BASKETS

- Place a brick in the base of baskets such as these to ensure stability.
- Line the basket with plastic (*see p.308*), and wedge in soaked wet foam to about 2in (5cm) below the rim.
- Arrange the flowers standing straight up, to look as if they are almost growing out of the basket.
- Snip off the individual godetia flowers as they fade: this will encourage more buds to open farther up the stem.
- Check and fill up the water in the display frequently.

Ingredients

Asclepias curassavica

Clarkia amoena Grace Series

Clarkia amoena Grace Series

Clarkia amoena Grace Series

Clarkia amoena
Grace Series

Alternative with *celosia*

For another, slightly darker, combination, use bright crimson satin flowers, bright orange blood flowers, and some brilliant scarlet cockscombs (*Celosia argentea* Century Series). Remove most of the leaves from the cockscombs, as they have a tendency to droop.

TROPICAL HEATWAVE

THIS EXOTIC display, which looks particularly stunning against the sky blue wall, brings a touch of tropical sunshine to the coolest day. The flowers, fruit, and leaves are like vividly-colored parrots in oranges, pinks and yellows with beak, plume and crest shapes as well as soft, velvety textures and whorls of hard-edged, spiky leaves.

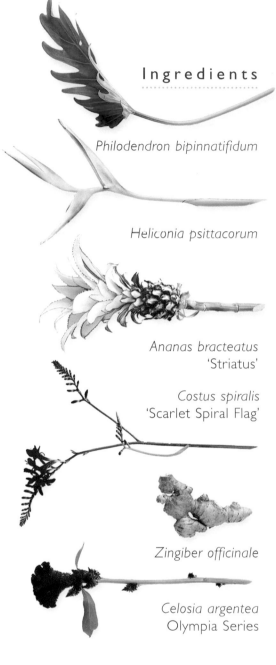

Ingredients

Philodendron bipinnatifidum

Heliconia psittacorum

Ananas bracteatus 'Striatus'

Costus spiralis 'Scarlet Spiral Flag'

Zingiber officinale

Celosia argentea Olympia Series

Heliconia marginata

Heliconia humilis

SUBMERGED GINGER

• Place a loose tangle of ginger roots in an elliptical glass container and three-quarters fill with water. Do not pack the ginger too tightly – the roots should support the stems without crushing them.

• Arrange the flowers and leaves in a broad fan shape so that they look as if they are growing naturally out of the ginger roots.

• Sweep upward from left to right, creating an almost straight line with the tips of the flowers and leaves. Allow a few of the leaves to hang downward to break the line.

• Place the largest item, the ornamental pineapple, slightly left of center to balance the arrangement.

• Change the water every three days to prevent the ginger roots from deteriorating. To avoid disturbing the arrangement, siphon off the water with a length of plastic tubing.

BLUES IN TERRACOTTA

TRUE BLUE FLOWERS are something of a rarity, but delphiniums, *Agapanthus* (African blue lilies), and gentians all bloom in the most glorious of shades. Blue and silver – here in the juvenile leaves of eucalyptus – make a superb combination, and this decorative terracotta windowbox intensifies the colors of these flowers because its shade is close to orange, the opposite color to blue in the color wheel (*see pp.30–31*). The flowers stand erect, almost as if they are growing, which fits the windowbox well. A long, narrow arrangement such as this is ideal for a side table, dresser or wide windowsill.

Ingredients

Delphinium Belladonna Group

Delphinium Belladonna Group

Agapanthus campanulatus

Gentian triflora

Eucalyptus gunnii

Alternative with *kniphofia*

In this alternative arrangement, the addition of a few stems of *Kniphofia* (red-hot poker) intensifies the effect already demonstrated in the main display, their fiery orange spires causing the blues to sing out even more joyously. If the agapanthus flowers in the main arrangement fade before the rest of the material, replacing them with *Kniphofia* or any other similar, intensely orange flower (*see Orange gallery, pp.454–457*) would be an excellent way of rejuvenating the whole arrangement. Only a very few flowerheads are necessary to achieve the desired effect.

BUILDING THE ARRANGEMENT

- Because terracotta is a porous material, it is important to line the windowbox with plastic or find a container that will fit inside it (*see pp.308–309*).
- Pack the trough with soaked wet florist's foam, filling the box to within 1in (2.5cm) of the rim.
- Arrange the stems of eucalyptus first, making a rough rectangular shape and making sure that they form a good three-dimensional structure.
- The first flowers to place are the strong spires of the delphiniums. Arrange them informally, keeping the tallest spire slightly out of the center.
- Remove most of the leaves from the stems of the gentians before inserting them: this will prevent the

leaves from obscuring the flowers and will also encourage the flowers to open farther up the stems.
- Last of all, arrange the agapanthus with their umbels of trumpet flowers; most of their flowerheads should be within the body of the arrangement.
- If the agapanthus are not commercially treated, they may perform variably and are likely to wilt a few days before the rest of the display.
- When your container is as ornamented and interesting as this one, it is best to see most of it; if the container is plain, however, it will often look better if it has a few flowers and leaves hanging down over the sides to provide interest.

TEACUP POSIES

THE SIMPLEST IDEAS are often the best: these crackle-glazed cups and saucers make perfect containers for a mix of cottage flowers and herbs to display on a windowsill. Little arrangements can be made with cuttings from the garden and look good with harmonious or clashing colors. Here, all the cups combine chrysanthemums with other flowers: on the left with goldenrod (*Solidago*) and China asters (*Callistephus*); in front with flowering mint (*Mentha*) and goldenrod; and on the right with cow parsley (*Anthriscus*) and sweet-smelling, shocking-pink freesias.

FILLING THE CUPS

• Because the cups' sides slope outward, the flowers need to be held in. Attach a prong to the inside base of each cup with florist's adhesive clay, then press onto it a disk of 1in (2.5cm) thick, soaked wet foam, shaped to fit the bottom of the cup.
• Fill the cups with water and arrange the flowers in the soaked wet foam.

• Choose flowers that complement each other: the chrysanthemums and asters have daisy flowers with dark centers, goldenrod and cow parsley lighten the arrangements, and freesias and mint have delicious scents.
• Ornamental cabbages (*Brassica*) provide interesting foliage but, if these are not available, any leaves can be used.

Ingredients

Chrysanthemum 'Tedcha'

Mentha longifolia

Freesia 'Pink Marble'

Callistephus chinensis Princess Series

Solidago 'Goldenmosa'

Anthriscus sylvestris

Ornamental *Brassica*

GLASS CYLINDERS

THIS STUNNING EFFECT is achieved by sandwiching yellow and orange lentils between two closely fitting glass cylinders. Erupting out of them are flowers in a close range of slightly clashing, piquant colors full of life and sunshine: cockscombs (*Celosia*), snapdragons (*Antirrhinum*), red-hot pokers (*Kniphofia*), and blanket flowers (*Gaillardia*). These shades of orange, apricot-pink, and carmine are particularly vibrant when used together: the leanings toward both blue and yellow produce excitement. Although creating this effect takes a little longer than using a simple vase, the finished result is well worth the effort.

Ingredients

Gaillardia × *grandiflora* 'Burgunder'

Antirrhinum majus Coronette Series

Kniphofia 'C.M. Prichard'

Celosia argentea Olympia Series

FILLING THE CONTAINERS

- Find two glass cylinders, one of which will fit inside the other, leaving a gap of approximately ½in (1cm).
- Fill the smaller of the two cylinders with water to 1½in (3.5cm) from the rim.
- Place a small piece of florist's adhesive clay on the bottom of the smaller cylinder,

and push it down into the larger vase.

• Using a funnel, pour lentils between the two glasses. Make a simple pattern by moving the funnel around as you feed two colors of lentils into it.

• To help these flowers last a week, add a few drops of bleach to the water and remove fading snapdragon blooms.

TROPICAL ANEMONES

Ingredients

Anemone coronaria
De Caen
Group

*Areca
lutescens*

THESE BRILLIANT RED anemones (*Anemone coronaria* De Caen Group) and fronds of areca palm (*Chrysalidocarpus lutescens*) look very elegant in their three glass vases, perhaps adorning a side table in a hall or living room. Anemones are naturally at their best in spring, but they can be found throughout the year in a range of stunningly intense colors.

ARRANGING THE ANEMONES

- Fill three glass vases with water and group them in an interesting and pleasing way. The vases could be identical or you may prefer to mix shapes.
- Arrange palm foliage in all three vases, aiming for a striking, full effect but without cramming in too many leaves.
- Shorten the stems of three or four anemone blooms, and submerge them at varying depths in the vases, taking care not to damage or fold the petals when pushing the blooms between the palm stems.
- Complete the display by carefully adding the upright anemone stems.

Alternative with *orchids*

Using the same three vases and palm foliage, you can create a softer, more diffuse effect by substituting yellow-flowered orchids, such as these *Oncidium flexuosum*. The feathery plumes last very well, but they are too small to be submerged in the water, as was done with the anemones in the original display.

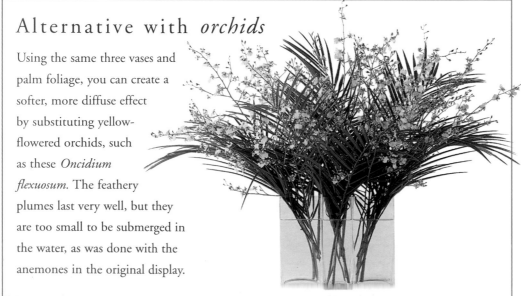

TRAILING LILIES

THE BEAUTY of these climbing lilies is breathtaking. Natives of the tropics, they are available for most of the year. The flowers of the most usually seen gloriosa lily have brilliant scarlet petals with yellow edgings and a lime-green base; the petals furl back and the ends of the leaves narrow to act as tendrils. Here the natural twining shape is used to hang down as well as to spray out of the basket, making a perfect display for either a low table or a wide windowsill. The lilies are complemented by the spiky looking flowers of *Centaurea montana* (a blue knapweed) and a scarlet cultivar of *Monarda* (bergamot or bee balm).

Ingredients

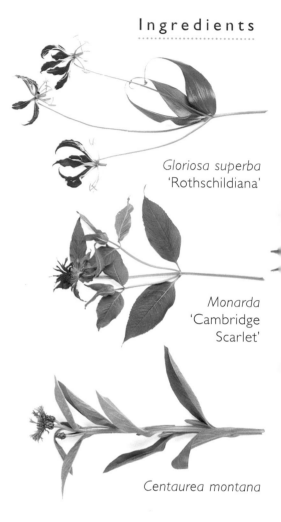

Gloriosa superba 'Rothschildiana'

Monarda 'Cambridge Scarlet'

Centaurea montana

PRACTICAL POINTS

- Always try to find a well-fitting, watertight container to fit inside any basket used in an arrangement. A plastic liner can be used (*see p.308*), but it may be pierced by the stalks of any woody stemmed flowers or foliage used in the arrangement, or even by the wicker itself.
- Gloriosa lilies have one drawback: all parts of the plant are extremely poisonous, so do not under any circumstances use their petals as food decoration.
- Bergamot is so named because its scent is similar to that of the bergamot (*Citrus bergamia*) used in Earl Grey tea: rub the petals occasionally to release the fragrance.

Alternative with *red and green*

The main arrangement is softened by the blue flowers. Remove them and the display becomes more potent, with a vibrant feel. The flowers of *Monarda* 'Cambridge Scarlet' have a green base and thin scarlet petals, and both leaves and flowers are aromatic. The wicker basket, with its warm red-brown tones, relates well to the reds of the flowers.

CABBAGE AND ROSES

THE BASIS of this rustic creation is Savoy cabbage (*Brassica*). The beautiful, heavily crinkled leaves, which have inspired a range of pottery imitations, are dark green on the outside, becoming lighter toward the pale yellow center. A circular terracotta casserole dish, glazed on the inside, makes a fitting container for the display of loosely arranged cabbage leaves, studded with rich, bright red roses. It is a creation that should be placed on a buffet or a dinner or coffee table, for it needs to be viewed from above.

ASSEMBLE THE DISPLAY

• Savoy cabbages are tricky to pull apart as each leaf is pleated closely into the one below. Cut each leaf at the base and pull it out from the bottom; it is unlikely to tear as it unfurls toward the outer edge, but

may break if pulled from the edge inward.
• Loosely layer the leaves in the dish, as if reassembling the cabbage, starting at the outside and working in.
• Add the flowers as each ring of leaves is

formed, making sure that the stem and leaf ends are in a good depth of water.
• The cabbage will decay very rapidly, but the roses can be reused in small glasses (*see pp.118–119*).

Alternative with *gentiana*

Many flowers can be used in conjunction with the strong textures of cabbage leaves, but they should be medium to small in size and of a color that stands out well. These brilliant blue willow gentians (*Gentiana asclepiadea*) look particularly attractive against the range of yellow-greens found in the cabbage leaves. For this alternative, a blue bowl complements and highlights the color of the flowers, while its shape makes a compact arrangement.

(see pp.118–119).

Ingredients

Brassica oleracea Capitata Group

Rosa 'Red Velvet'

ZINNIA BASKETS

BRIGHT AS BUTTONS and available in a range of vibrant colors, zinnias have appealingly simple, daisylike flowers, with the added attraction of a ring of tiny yellow starbursts around their central disk. They are such exuberant flowers that we can easily forgive them for being so short-lived; indeed, there is something particularly special about flowers that have a fleeting life. Single roses (*Rosa*), sweet peas (*Lathyrus odoratus*), lily-of-the-valley (*Convallaria majalis*), and gardenias are all the more marvelous for their transitory life.

Alternative with *dahlias*

The rustic qualities of this simple basket make it equally good for holding a range of other bright, cheerful flowers. The many single or semidouble dahlia cultivars are one possibility: these scarlet-splashed white blooms are especially striking. Dahlias will last for up to a week – and flower well into the autumn in the garden. As with the zinnias, line the basket and wedge in soaked wet foam.

Ingredients

Zinnia elegans

FILLING THE BASKETS

- Find containers to fit inside the baskets or line them with plastic, then wedge in a layer of soaked wet foam (*see p.308*).
- Arrange the flowers as if they are growing in the containers, using the bright green leaves to form an attractive layer from which the flowers can spring.
- These baskets give the overall appearance of plants in windowboxes and would make a fine display for a windowsill.

SHORELINE CENTERPIECE

A FLOWER ARRANGEMENT is really a still life: each time we create one it is like painting a picture. Shells were often used in seventeenth-century flower paintings, so it seems fitting to use them in displays. This beachscape for a dinner party table uses starfish, shells, and hydrangeas; many other flowers and foliage types would also work.

Alternative for a *wooden tray*

A rough wooden tray with rope handles makes an excellent container for a sandy display of shells and sponges but, of course, any collection in such a container must be a dry one. Fill up any holes or cracks in the box with adhesive putty, then fill it to about three-quarters of its depth with fine sand, forming gentle dunelike mounds on which to arrange the shells and sponges. Most of us collect shells and pieces of dead coral from the beach when we are on vacation, although it is worth noting that in some places this is illegal. You may wish to augment your collection with a few special purchases, but marine curios sold in gift shops are not always sustainably harvested and can include endangered species caught live. Try looking in second-hand stores for sales of old collections.

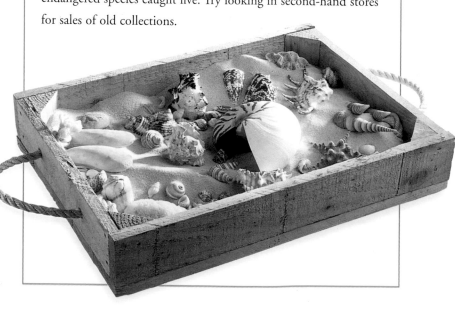

MOLDING THE SHORELINE

• Use a large, plain white ceramic platter – this one is about 16in × 12in (40cm × 30cm) – and make the arrangement in its final position, because the sand shifts if you try to move it.
• Mound sand from a builder's supply or craft shop in an arc to form a shore, then carefully pour in water.
• Scatter a few shells and starfish in a way that looks good from all angles. Position some of the smaller shells underwater.
• Place the flowers so that their stems are in the water. Sea holly (*Eryngium*) or any coastal plant would look appropriate.

Ingredients

Hydrangea paniculata 'Praecox'

SUNFLOWER JAR

SUNFLOWERS AND VAN GOGH are inextricably linked and for this project, which conjures up the breathtaking sunflower fields of southern France, I have chosen a part-glazed jar similar to one in which Van Gogh arranged his famous flowers. As well as the original sunflower (*Helianthus*), with its familiar ruff of bright yellow petals around a rich brown center, there are now many different varieties: tall and dwarf, single and double, in colors that range from creamy white to orange, red, rust, and chocolate brown.

PREPARING INGREDIENTS

• If the inside of the jar is not completely glazed, line it with plastic; you could find a watertight container to place inside the jar (*see p.308*), but this will need to fit very snugly to remain stable.

• Sunflowers are top-heavy and need to be well anchored; wedge in some soaked wet foam attached to a couple of prongs (*see p.304*). Using a narrow jar will help to keep the sunflowers together.

Ingredients

Fagus sylvatica f. purpurea

Helianthus annuus

Helianthus annuus 'Autumn Beauty'

• Remove most of the leaves from the sunflowers to make them last longer.

• Copper beech leaves (*Fagus sylvatica f. purpurea*) can be used fresh, in summer, when they are purple or when they turn a dark coppery color in autumn.

• Treat beech leaves (either plain green or copper beech) with glycerin (*see p.316*) before including in a fresh or dried arrangement. To prevent the leaves from turning a muddy color, add some natural dye to the glyccrin-water mix.

• Treated beech should not stand in fresh water for more than a week.

NOCTURNE IN BROWN

SOMETIMES IT IS THE FLOWERS that inspire an arrangement and sometimes it is the container. This dark brown jug with its old rose pattern cries out for an intense arrangement. The green and black of the kangaroo paw (*Anigozanthos*), together with alder twigs with catkins and cones (*Alnus glutinosa*) and little maroon-leaved "pineapples" (*Ananas nanus*), accentuate the luminous glow of the dark orange roses (*Rosa* 'Lambada') and mustard-colored orchids (*Arachnadendron*).

Ingredients

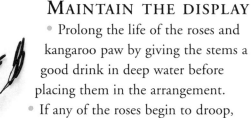

Alnus glutinosa

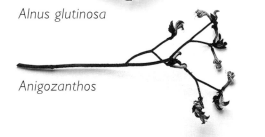

Anigozanthos

Arachnadendron

Rosa 'Lambada'

Ananas nanus

MAINTAIN THE DISPLAY

- Prolong the life of the roses and kangaroo paw by giving the stems a good drink in deep water before placing them in the arrangement.
- If any of the roses begin to droop, give the stems the hot water treatment (*see p.313*). This will encourage them to start taking up water again.
- Keep the jug filled with water, and once every three days replace the water in the vase completely.
- At the end of the life of the arrangement, retain and air dry the kangaroo paw and alder twigs. Then you can combine the two to create a simple but stunning new display.

Alternative with *old variety roses*

My favorite roses are the old varieties that are highly scented, very double, and with the darkest velvety red and purple petals, such as 'Cardinal de Richelieu', 'Tuscany Superb', and 'Souvenir du Docteur Jamain'. Here I have substituted roses with almost black petals for the dark orange blooms, to create an even more striking arrangement. A little sinister in appearance, it would make an ideal Halloween display.

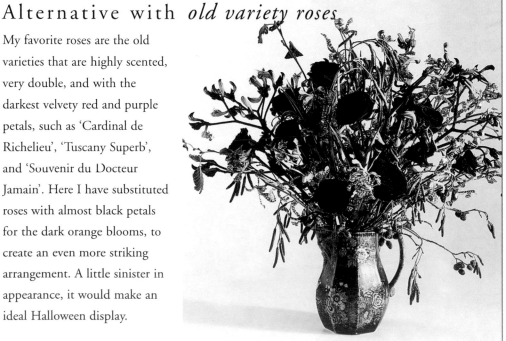

FRUITS AND FOLIAGE

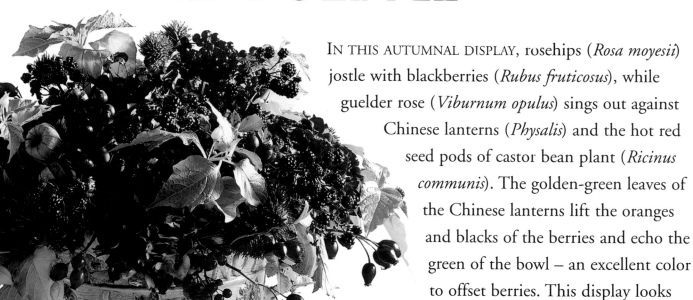

IN THIS AUTUMNAL DISPLAY, rosehips (*Rosa moyesii*) jostle with blackberries (*Rubus fruticosus*), while guelder rose (*Viburnum opulus*) sings out against Chinese lanterns (*Physalis*) and the hot red seed pods of castor bean plant (*Ricinus communis*). The golden-green leaves of the Chinese lanterns lift the oranges and blacks of the berries and echo the green of the bowl – an excellent color to offset berries. This display looks particularly good in a conservatory or on a garden table where it can be seen from indoors.

A NOTE OF CAUTION

• Although this display looks good enough to eat, all parts of castor bean plant are poisonous. Keep the arrangement out of the reach of small children.

• Castor bean plant can irritate skin; take care when arranging.

• Blackberries will stain when they drop – another good reason to keep this display outside. Indoors, be careful where you place it, or stand it on a tray.

Alternative with *red foliage*

Replacing the Chinese lanterns with red autumnal beech foliage creates quite a different effect. The colors are still lifted by the green of the bowl beneath, but now the tones within the tapestry of leaves and fruits are richer and more moody. The greener display suggests a sunny autumn morning; the rusty arrangement is like a dusky autumn evening.

Ingredients

Viburnum opulus

Hydrangea 'Preziosa'

Physalis alkekengi

Ricinus communis

Rosa moyesii

Rubus fruticosus

RURAL SCENE

FLOWER DISPLAYS, especially those composed of dried material, need not always be held in containers. Three flowering "trees," with a hedge and a bank below, provide a reminder of the countryside that you can hang on the wall. Because it is made from dried flowers, it lasts for months with hardly any attention; very gentle vacuuming will remove any dust that settles. When the display does begin to look a little tired, renew it using fresh material on the same frame.

MAKE THE STRUCTURE

- Make a frame of pencil-thick bamboo: three horizontal pieces 24in (60cm) long and three vertical pieces 18in (45cm) long. Bind with wire where they cross.
- Form two rectangular pillows of moss-filled chicken wire for the hedge, and three round pillows about 8in (20cm) across, for the trees (*see pp.326–327*). Be sure that the bamboo frame is completely covered.
- Take three pieces of bark about 10in (25cm) long for the tree trunks; attach the center trunk over the bamboo.
- Wire the two rectangular pillows and the three tree heads to the crossing bamboos.
- Wire on the other two trunks.

ADD THE COVERING

- Attach the sheet moss for the hedge using wire "hairpins" (*see p.320*) pushed through the pillows of sphagnum moss, then bent back on themselves.
- For each tree, spread out a mound of Spanish moss (*Tillandsia*), and wire onto the frame.

- Cut the stems of the curry plant (*Helichrysum*) and rose (*Rosa*) flowers to 1in (2.5cm) and poke into the trees.
- Wire in the hops (*Humulus*) and lavender (*Lavandula*).

Ingredients

Betula pendula (bark)

Sheet moss (dried)

Tillandsia usneoides (dried)

Sphagnum magellanicum (dried)

*Lavandula
angustifolia* (dried)

*Humulus
lupulus* (dried)

Helichrysum italicum subsp.
serotinum (dried)

Rosa 'Gabrielle' (dried)

VASE OF ANTHURIUMS

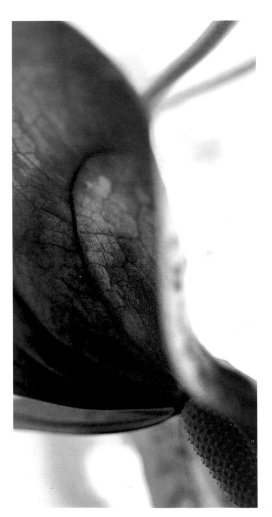

THE PART THAT A VASE PLAYS in a display can never be underestimated, and this vase is a winner in several important ways. It is striking in itself: the blue is reminiscent of tropical seas, while the fine red stripe adds interest and gives it an airy elegance. The narrow neck helps the flowers almost arrange themselves and means that a few flowers will fill the vase, making it useful for everyday displays as well as special occasions. In this display, green-and-crimson anthuriums float above pale-veined green and cream ornamental cabbage (*Brassica*) leaves: an exotic plant and a garden vegetable might seem an unlikely mix, but the result is stunning.

PREPARING THE MATERIAL

- Anthuriums need to be conditioned by standing in deep water for several hours before arranging (*see pp.310–313*).
- Cabbage stems can quickly begin to rot and smell unpleasant. To prolong their life, put a few drops of bleach in the water before you create the arrangement.
- After two or three days, empty out the water in the vase and replace with fresh: it is quite easy to grip all the flowers in the vase together while you do this.

- Since the anthuriums last for a fairly long time, remove the cabbage when it begins to wilt and replace with other foliage – maybe some tropical philodendron leaves or a spiky grass leaf.
- The shape of this vase makes arranging easy, the narrow neck holding the stems in position without the need for foam or additional support. Do check, however, that a vase is heavy enough to balance a top-heavy arrangement.

Alternative with *nerines*

Here the same anthuriums have had their stems cut so that they huddle close to the rim of the vase. They are interspersed with nerines, whose intense scarlet petals possess a beautiful crystalline quality. Set off by the translucent blue of the vase and picking up its red veining, the combination is electrifying. Another variation might be to use hosta or bergenia leaves instead of the cabbage.

Ingredients

Arthurium andraeanum 'Trinidad'

Brassica Northern Lights Series

CAPE GREENS

IN THE RUGGEDLY BEAUTIFUL Cape peninsula in South Africa, over 9,000 species of the vegetation known as fynbos grow, despite the difficult terrain, poor soil, and harsh weather. Bunches of these Cape greens are exported all over the world, together with proteas, heathers, and banksias. Made with a mixture of these plants, this wild-looking arrangement in a mellowed, copper pan looks particularly good in a relaxed, rustic setting.

Ingredients

Rumex obtusifolius

Berzelia abrotanoides

Leucadendron laxum

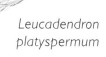

Leucadendron platyspermum

Leucadendron laxum

Erica bicolor

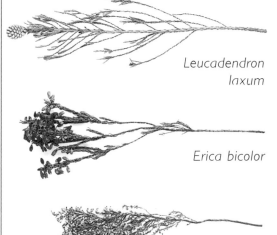

Erica baccans

FILLING THE BOWL

- Fynbos lasts extremely well, but with so much plant material in the arrangement it will use up a great deal of water. As a precaution, add a few drops of bleach to the water and fill the bowl regularly.
- Wedge a layer of soaked wet foam into the bowl; because the material is arranged standing upright, it needs some support until most of it is in place.
- Keep most of the stems almost vertical, just slightly bending some of the flowers and greens outward toward the edges to give the rim of the container a softer look. You need to get a good balance of groups of textured greenery, with some of the more imposing flowers, cones, and foliage interspersed.
- This could be arranged as an all-around display to go on a coffee table, or as a three-quarters display for a side table, where the front and sides will have more importance than the very back.

Alternative with *yarrow*

For some extra color in this alternative arrangement, I have added yarrow (*Achillea*), which, together with the rust-colored dock seed spires (*Rumex obtusifolius*), seems to have a "rough-and-tumble" affinity with the scrubby South African plants. The flat heads of the yarrow work particularly well with the intricate textures of the other plants.

AUTUMN PURPLES

BROWN AND GOLD are the predominant colors of autumn, but plum, purple, mauve, and black also play a part. Hydrangeas that start out as bluish pinks (such as the *Hydrangea* 'Preziosa' shown here) turn a much deeper color as they dry on their bushes, while many shrubs bear berries of purple and black. A group of soft raffia baskets here makes an interesting and unusual setting for flowers and berries in related colors, including the spires of *Aconitum carmichaelii* and the purple flowers of *Limonium sinuatum*.

CHOICE OF MATERIALS

• There are many dramatic autumn fruits: the violet berries of *Callicarpa*, pinky white snowberries (*Symphoricarpos*), and the blue laurustinus (*Viburnum tinus*).
• Statice (*Limonium*) and hydrangeas will often dry if placed in soaked wet foam and left to dry out. Monkshood (*Aconitum*) can be air dried, but it will darken.

• Line the baskets with plastic and fill them with soaked wet foam (*see p.308*) or stand containers in them; the latter gives flowers more access to water and makes it easier to fill up. In a soft basket, such as the pink one, foam helps to hold its shape and keep it steady; if using a container, surround it with crumpled paper.

Ingredients

Viburnum tinus

Aconitum carmichaelii 'Barker's Variety'

Clerodendrum trichotomum

Hydrangea 'Preziosa'

Limonium sinuatum Pacific Series

Ligustrum lucidum

EXOTIC CASCADE

THIS TOWER OF DANGLING exotic flowers makes an imposing floor display for a grand occasion. The tall basket allows heliconias and love-lies-bleeding (*Amaranthus caudatus*) to hang down without obstruction. The heliconias have extraordinary green and orange bracts, like a series of parrots' beaks, that last for a couple of weeks. Love-lies-bleeding, with its tassels spilling out, is a perfect partner. Papyrus heads (*Cyperus papyrus*), palm fronds (*Dypsis*), and golden-green, velvety kangaroo paw (*Anigozanthos*) complete the striking show.

BUILD THE TOWER

• Good containers to consider for an arrangement like this are galvanized florist's buckets or even elegant umbrella stands, suitably lined (*see p.304*). The whole display comes to some 5ft (1.5m) in height when completed.

• The tall, narrow shape is inherently unstable, so it is vital that the container is weighted well at the bottom: here, a tall, cylindrical vase of just about the same diameter as the basket and two-thirds the height of it sits on top of four bricks in the bottom of the basket.

• Take care to keep the arrangement balanced as you build it: if all the heavy, dangling heliconias were to one side, the basket would fall, even with the bricks.

• Start with the longest heliconia dangling lowest in the display and gradually build the display upward.

• These tall palm fronds had to have nearly 2ft (60cm) of their leaflets removed to give them long "stalks" for arranging.

• The love-lies-bleeding leaves will die first. Remove them, and the rest of the display will last for another ten days.

Ingredients

Amaranthus caudatus

Heliconia nutans

Anigozanthos flavidus

Cyperus papyrus

Dypsis lutescens

BAMBOO TRIPOD

THIS STRIKINGLY SIMPLE arrangement is reminiscent of a Japanese water garden. A graceful bamboo tripod supports a dark copper-glazed bowl containing a floating amber-colored chrysanthemum and pine twigs (*Pinus nigra*). Standing beside it, a larger, similar bowl echoes the composition of the first. The scale of the tripod and bowl can be adjusted, and the plant material can be varied to suit the season.

CREATING THE DESIGN

• To create the tripod for a bowl that is about 10in (25cm) in diameter, you will need three bamboo stakes measuring ½in (1.5cm) across and 17in (43cm) long.

• With a small saw, cut one end of each stake at an angle, cutting at a joint to prevent the bamboo from splintering. Cut the other end of each stake straight across.

• Tie the stakes together with fine-gauge wire, 8in (20cm) from the bottom, with the angled ends positioned to form a stable base. Splay the canes out so that each one is at right angles to the others,

then bind them securely in position.

• Paint the bamboo to suit the bowl and location: I sprayed this tripod with cranberry-colored paint, applied a light coat of gold, then high-lighted the joints with more cranberry.

• Bind the joint with ribbon to conceal the wire.

• Choose flowers that will float, such as chrysanthemums, begonias, camellias, roses, dahlias, and anemones.

Ingredients

Pinus nigra

Chrysanthemum 'Tom Pearce'

WATSONIA SPRAY

ORANGE AND LIME GREEN are a particularly luscious combination; lying close to each other on the color wheel (*see pp.30–31*), they are both harmonious and uplifting. Here, orange watsonias (*Watsonia pillansii*) appear almost luminous against a chartreuse chrysanthemum cultivar (*Chrysanthemum* 'Green Spider'). Great swathes of watsonia grow in the fynbos habitats of southern Africa – a wonderful source of many extraordinary blooms. The flowers form an elegant fountain, rising from a froth of spider chrysanthemums in a tall, bronze-based glass vase, and are perfect for a side table.

COMBINING FLOWERS

• Watsonias, which originate from South Africa, are sometimes hard to find. However, both montbretia (*Crocosmia*) and gladioli belong to the same family and many forms of these could be substituted, if necessary, to achieve the same effect.
• The larger flowered chrysanthemums can be difficult to use as they sometimes appear heavy and clumsy. One solution is to treat the flower heads almost like foliage, as here, keeping them close to the vase, with more delicate flowers springing from them. This is both easy and effective.
• Be careful not to damage the base and largest petals of the chrysanthemums when arranging them; once a chrysanthemum starts to disintegrate, all the other petals quickly follow suit.

Alternative with *purple*

To achieve a more muted effect, combine the watsonias with deeper, richer colors, such as the plum of the chrysanthemum 'Sentry' used here. This, or the main arrangement, could also look good with an orange gladiolus such as 'Little Darling', which is bright orange with a yellow throat, or the frilly, brilliant orange 'Firestorm'. There are also magnificent *Crocosmia* cultivars, such as 'Firebird' and 'Lucifer', both bright red, that make a strong impact.

Ingredients

Watsonia pillansii

Chrysanthemum 'Green Spider'

SCENTED BOWL

A BUFF-PINK ROSE on the inside of this Chinese bowl provided the inspiration for my choice of flowers in this arrangement, its color suiting the bowl so perfectly. Lilac (*Syringa*), roses (*Rosa*), and laurustinus (*Viburnum tinus*) all have delicious scents, and the rosemary (*Rosmarinus*) is aromatic too. This is a wonderful display for a low table.

Alternative with *yellow*

The main arrangement is warm and slightly subdued, yet substituting clear yellow carnations (*Dianthus* 'Golden Cross') for the pink picoteed 'Rendez-vous' alters the look completely. Yellow stands out more than any other color, and this faintly green-yellow shade, in particular, freshens and intensifies the colors of the flowers surrounding it.

PREPARE THE BOWL

• Old bowls such as this are often slightly damaged; any bowl or vase that is chipped or cracked should have a watertight container placed inside it (*see p.308*) to prevent it from leaking.

• Attach prongs to the base of the container with adhesive clay, having made sure that the inside is completely dry. Secure a block of soaked wet foam on the prongs to hold the stems in place.

SELECT THE FLOWERS

• Remove all the leaves from the lilac to help prolong the life of the flowers; this is often already done with lilac from florists.

• If possible, seek out the older varieties of carnations (*Dianthus*), which tend to have the most delicious clovelike scent.

Ingredients

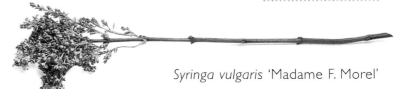

Syringa vulgaris 'Madame F. Morel'

Rosa 'Metallica'

Hedera helix 'Congesta'

Viburnum tinus

Dianthus 'Bookham Fancy'

Rosmarinus officinalis

WOOD ON WOOD

MY COLLECTION of wooden kitchen implements had been sitting untouched for many months, and I was thinking of putting them away; then it occurred to me that they might make an interesting display in front of a little-used fireplace. Other woody things included in the creation were pinecones, pieces of palm frond, lengths of bamboo, and some old cinnamon sticks. The result is jokey but demonstrates how any objects can make a great display.

ARRANGING THE ITEMS

- Select a container that looks right and fits comfortably in the place where you will keep the display.
- Look for wooden objects, such as a mallet, a pepper grinder, a citrus squeezer, or a spoon from Africa, which have special interest in terms of their shape or texture.
- Cover the base of the container with cones. These will keep the ends of the items wedged in place when you position them in the container.
- Place the larger, longer items, fitting in the largest ones at the back and angling all the pieces against each other. This can be like a game of jackstraws, so use more cones to keep things from moving around.
- Wedge in all the smaller bits and pieces, dividing the objects leaning to left and right at a point off-center in the container.

Ingredients

Dried palm frond

Bamboo

Cinnamon

Pinecone

Fir cone

CALLA LILY FAN

WHEN USING GLASS containers, consider not only the shape that the flowers and foliage make above the water but also how the stalks look under water. In this arrangement of apricot calla lilies (*Zantedeschia*), gold-splashed elaeagnus, and golden holly berries (*Ilex verticillata*), the stems come together at the bottom in a fan shape. The result is a dramatic display, perfect for a narrow side table or a windowsill.

ARRANGE THE STEMS

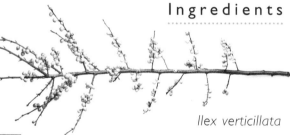

- Take particular care when handling elaeagnus – its spines are sharp.
- If possible, fill the hollow stems of the calla lilies with water (*see p.312*) to prolong their display.
- Start by arranging the calla stems on the right-hand side, propping them up against the side of the vase.
- Next place more callas on the left, with a long stem extending to the base of the vase on the right.
- Now place the berried stems in a curve below the callas, with the elaeagnus in a curve below these.

Ingredients

Ilex verticillata

Alternative with *roses*

In the main arrangement, the color of the berries echoes that of the calla lilies, creating a harmonious effect. Here, some small, bright red roses have been added to give more vibrancy. They have all been kept to much the same length, shorter than the callas and berries but longer than the elaeagnus, to create distinct bands of color across the width of the fan.

Zantedeschia 'Dusty Pink'

Elaeagnus pungens 'Maculata'

STRIPED FLOWERS

THIS ELEGANT ITALIAN vase has a fluted mouth, which makes it easy to arrange flowers in. It may be a little on the large size for everyday use, but it is ideal for a party. In this display, a glorious variety of material – striped flowers in orange, peach, pink, and yellow, together with apricot-colored berries – cascades outward.

Ingredients

Ilex verticillata

Hippeastrum 'Masai'

Tulipa 'Flaming Parrot'

Rosa 'Minuette'

PREPARE AND CHOOSE

• Place the largest flowers and stems first to achieve a good balance in the vase.

• The hippeastrums have particularly thick stems; fill them with water before arranging (*see p.312*), to prolong their life.

• Striped, dappled, picoteed, and spotted flowers have long been valued for their distinctive looks. The most interesting examples include carnations and pinks, but there are also camellias, dahlias, ranunculus, zinnias, primulas, and auriculas. Among my favorite striped roses are the red and white 'Roger Lambelin', white and raspberry-pink 'Ferdinand Pichard', and Purple Tiger ('Jacpur'), which is purple and ivory.

LENTEN ROSES

THE BEAUTIFUL NODDING flowers of Lenten roses *(Helleborus orientalis)* enliven the dark days at the close of winter. The garden hybrids look wonderful in the garden, but their amazing colors and spotted markings are best appreciated when facing upwards and floating in a shiny bowl. With their stems cut short, they will give pleasure for a week.

USING HELLEBORES

• Hellebores are available in an enormous range of colors: my favorite is intense green. All flower from the middle of winter to the middle of spring.

• Neither the Lenten rose nor the other related hellebores, such as the Christmas rose *(Helleborus niger)*, will last well if the flowers are left on the full stems. Before arranging them in lukewarm water, pierce each stem with a pin a few times just below the heads; this may give them a life of three or four days.

• It is best to cut the stems very short – to no more than ½in (1cm) – and float the flowers on water, as in this arrangement; then they should last for a week.

• Remember that all parts of the hellebore are mildly toxic, and the sap that bleeds from the stems can irritate skin.

• Hellebores are quite variable, and there are many different cultivars and hybrids. Those shown here are from my garden. If you want to grow your own hellebores, go to your local nursery to see what is available.

Ingredients

Helleborus orientalis hybrid

Helleborus orientalis hybrid

Helleborus orientalis hybrid

Helleborus orientalis hybrid

Alternative with *hyacinths and forsythia*

The main arrangement is elegant and restrained, in shades from cream to purple. A fresher feel can be achieved by adding other spring colors. Here, single flowers cut from a pale Delft-blue hyacinth and a stem of sunny yellow forsythia replace some of the deeper-toned Lenten roses. Another alternative would be to include white or pink camellias, whose waxy blooms resemble those of floating waterlilies.

CHILI CANDLES

PICTURE AN ALFRESCO dinner in the dying warmth of a summer's evening; just the soft scent from pots of lilies and tobacco plants and the gentle light from a group of fragrant candles. Old terracotta pots make decorative and safe containers for candles: surround them with crimson amaryllis flowers (*Hippeastrum* 'Liberty'), glistening red chilies, and moss, and they will help create a magical atmosphere that is guaranteed to make the evening a stunning success.

Ingredients

Red chili

Hippeastrum 'Liberty'

Sheet moss

FITTING THE CANDLE

● Cut a piece of soaked wet foam just large enough to fit inside a 4in (10cm) diameter terracotta pot. Cut a 9in (22cm) circle of plastic liner, place it over the pot, then push the foam down over it to wedge the plastic into the pot.

● Tuck some fresh sheet or sphagnum moss between the sides of the pot and the plastic liner, then trim off any visible plastic. Push a fat, 1³/₄in (4.5cm) candle into the center of the foam.

● Cut four or five amaryllis flowers, retaining as much stem as possible.

● Wire the stalk ends of nine 3in (7.5cm) chilies (*see pp.318–321*), leaving 1½in (4cm) of spare wire. Push the amaryllis and chilies into the foam so that they spread out from the center. Fill in with damp moss.

AUTUMN BOUNTY

A SYMBOL of thanksgiving for the Earth's bounty, this cornucopia is made to hang on the wall, its mouth spilling out hydrangeas (*Hydrangea* 'Preziosa'), globe artichokes (*Cynara scolymus*), holly berries (*Ilex verticillata*), and fruit-laden branches of date palm (*Phoenix dactylifera*). The horn has a covering of green sheet moss, garlanded with Spanish moss.

CREATING THE HORN

- Cut two rectangles from a 12in- (30cm-) wide roll of chicken wire: one 14in (36cm) long, the second 8in (20cm) long. Twist the first into a cone with a radius of 4in (10cm) at the end. Twist a second cone, closed to a point at the end.
- Place the smaller cone into the larger one and join them with fine gauge wire.
- Stuff the inside with dry sphagnum moss, leaving a space large enough to insert a large, watertight container.
- Pin sheet moss to the frame with floral wire hairpins (*see p.320*).

- Wire three lengths of Spanish moss to the front of the horn so they appear to spiral around, but leave the back clear.
- Suspend the horn on a screw or picture hook, choosing a point near the top where it will be well balanced. Protect the wall from any water damage by inserting some cardboard or plastic.
- Wedge soaked wet foam into the container and fill with water, then place the container inside the horn, using moss to keep it firmly in position.
- Arrange the flowers, dates, berries, and artichokes to spill out of the horn.

Ingredients

Cynara scolymus

Phoenix dactylifera

Hydrangea 'Preziosa'

Ilex verticillata

CORNCOB BASKET

ADAPTING A CONTAINER to be part of a display is very rewarding. For this creation, which would look superb as a centerpiece, cover a circular basket with dried moss, then attach a ring of dried corncobs, their husks drawn up to create a ruff. Inside, a mound of gold and orange roses (*Rosa* 'Rhumba') and purple sage (*Salvia*) echo the colors in the cobs.

MAKING THE DISPLAY

• Start by wiring fairly large pieces of reindeer moss to the basket. Push floral wire "hairpins" through the moss and the weave of the basket, then back through the basket, leaving no sharp ends inside.
• Attach the dried corncobs over the moss in the same way, twisting the wire tightly around the cob just where the husks join, then pushing the ends through the moss and basket and back through the basket.
• Find a plastic container that fits inside the basket, or you can line the container with plastic (*see p.308*).
• Wedge soaked wet foam into the container or lined basket.

• Draw on the colors of the cobs when choosing the flowers: here, yellow roses flecked with orange are combined with a violet sage to make a low, informal mound of flowers flanked by the drawn-up corn husks.
• The rose stems are cut short for this display, which helps the flowers last well, but the stem ends must still be cut at a sharp angle and scraped (*see p.312*).
• This container will last for months and also looks good holding dried flowers.

Ingredients

Rosa 'Rhumba'

Salvia viridis 'Claryssa'

Zea mays 'Strawberry Corn'

Reindeer moss

PUMPKIN DISPLAY

GOURDS LOOK GREAT just as they are: small ones are beautiful, simply piled into a basket and will often last all winter, but they also make extraordinary containers. Here, a medium-sized pumpkin holds chilies (*Capsicum*), pink Japanese anemones, vibrant *Leonotus leonurus*, and lime-green chrysanthemums within an edging of ornamental cabbage (*Brassica*). For a perfect Halloween display, set the pumpkin and some candles alongside a turkscap squash, with its magical combination of glowing orange, green, and white skin, and strangely beautiful shape.

SQUASH CANDLES

• For candle holders, remove the tops of small squashes and just enough flesh to fit in a tea light. Cut the bases of the squashes so that they are level and stable.

• To hollow out a large squash, cut straight down in a circle around the top. Pry out the top and scoop out a substantial amount of the flesh. Line with plastic (*see p.308*) or fit a container inside, wedge in foam, and arrange the flowers.

Ingredients

Capsicum frutescens

Chrysanthemum 'Shamrock'

Anemone x hybrida

Leonotis leonurus

Brassica oleracea 'Tokyo'

BRIMMING BASKETS

WHEN PLANT arrangements are grouped together, interesting relationships develop between the containers. Here, a picnic basket and a wicker wine carrier are displayed together. Each basket would be fine on its own, but I like the way the smaller one adds depth to the display. The large basket is filled with bittersweet (*Celastrus*), crabapples (*Malus*), and euonymus, the smaller one with rose-hips and bittersweet.

Ingredients

Rosa rugosa hips

Celastrus orbiculatus

Malus x robusta 'Red Sentinel'

Malus 'John Downie'

Euonymus alatus

Ilex verticillata

ARRANGING THE BASKETS

• Line the picnic basket with thick plastic liner and tape up the sides.

• Pack the base of the basket with a layer of soaked, wet foam bricks, then arrange the crabapple boughs by pushing the stems into the foam. Start with upright branches on the left, with subsequent branches leaning over to the right.

• Place four tumblers of water in the wine container and arrange the rose-hip stems in them, making slightly uneven mounds.

• Add some trails of bittersweet – one twisting around the handle, and another trailing out at the far right-hand corner of the arrangement.

AUTUMNAL SWAG

Ingredients

Physalis alkekengi

Hydrangea 'Preziosa'

Helichrysum italicum subsp. serotinum

Humulus lupulus

THE COLORS OF AUTUMN speak of the setting sun, of golden and red ripening apples, and of the glowing embers of bonfires. Autumn is a great time of year for dried flowers, which seem to epitomize the season with their tapestry of warm colors. This dried flower swag, which includes Chinese lanterns (*Physalis alkekengi*) and hops (*Humulus lupulus*), would be perfect for a Thanksgiving or bonfire party, draped over a mantelpiece or on a dresser shelf.

MAKING THE SWAG

- Make the swag on a rigid, 1¹/₂in (4cm) diameter chicken-wire tube, filled with dried sphagnum moss (*see pp.324–325*).
- If the tube is well stuffed, most of the dried material can be simply poked in between the wires into the moss. If you glue the stems first, they will definitely not fall out, but be sure to remove any shiny glue strings that remain. You can also wire the dried material (*see pp.318–321*) before inserting it into the chicken-wire tube.
- To maintain the green color of the hops (*Humulus lupulus*), keep them in low light, out of direct sunlight.

Alternative with *yellow bows*

If using the swag as a garland, you may like to add some decorative bows along its length. Here, I've used rich yellow paper ribbon, which has an affinity with the dried flowers in both color and texture. However, burlap or linen ribbon in shades of brown, rust, orange, gold, or yellow would also look attractive. Make the individual ribbons (*see p.335*) and wire into position.

OPULENT TAZZA

THIS LAVISH LOW ARRANGEMENT in a tazza (a glass wine bowl) makes an ideal centerpiece for the dinner table since it does not obscure the diners' views. To an exotic melange of orange *Ranunculus asiaticus*, pink *Eustoma grandiflorum*, fragrant *Polianthes tuberosa*, deep orange *Euphorbia fulgens*, lotus seedheads (*Nelumbo nucifera*), and fig leaves (*Ficus carica*) is added black grapes, tumbling voluptuously from the glass bowl.

CREATE THE FRAMEWORK

• Attach a florist's prong to the base of the tazza with adhesive clay. Attach a piece of soaked wet foam 2in (5cm) square and 3in (7.5cm) high. Fill the tazza with water.

• Tie a bunch of grapes to each end of a length of wire and lay over the tazza. Add two more pairs of wired bunches.

• Weave in an inner circle of wire, about 2in (5cm) in from the rim. The foam and the spider's web of wires will help hold the flowers in place as you arrange them.

Ingredients

Ficus carica

Euphorbia fulgens

Eustoma grandiflorum Heidi Series

Nelumbo nucifera

Polianthes tuberosa 'The Pearl'

Ranunculus asiaticus Turban Group

Vitis vinifera

CLUSTERS AND STRIPES

AUTUMN IS FULL of surprises, and the beauty berry (*Callicarpa*) is one of the oddest, its myriad of lilac berries clustering like beads on the stem after the flowers have gone. In this light, floating, airy arrangement, the beauty berry is joined by deep red and yellow gerberas, gloriosa lilies (*Gloriosa superba* 'Rothschildiana'), the domed, rusty heads of coneflowers (*Echinacea purpurea*), and a spray of rich green leaves (*Hakonechloa macra* 'Aureola'). Echoing the flowers, the clear glass vase is striated with orange – the stripes look as if they have trickled down from the gloriosas and gerberas.

Ingredients

Hakonechloa macra 'Aureola'

Gerbera jamesonii

Echinacea purpurea 'Robert Bloom'

Gloriosa superba 'Rothschildiana'

Callicarpa bodinieri var. *giraldii*

FORMING THE DISPLAY

• Begin by placing the stems of beauty berry to create a zigzag top to the arrangement. Follow with a fountain of *Hakonechloa* leaves around the base.

• Next add the gloriosa lilies. These flowers are very poisonous, so be careful when handling them and wash your hands after finishing the arrangement.

• Before adding the coneflowers to the arrangement, support their heads (which are prone to drooping) by inserting a short length of floral wire from the flowerhead down the stem of each flower.

• Finally, place the different colored gerbera flowers to give an informal but balanced composition.

Alternative with *gladiolus*

The stunning *Gladiolus* 'Novalux' has yellow flowers with rich red throats. When mixed with the *Callicarpa* it produces a dense display that would glow if placed against a rich dark background. The colors of the plants combine in an interesting way, with the lilac-violet of the berries vying with the intense yellow and clashing with the orange-red of the gladioli.

CHRISTMAS FAN

THIS SILVER VASE in the shape of a squashed sphere with a slice taken from the top seemed to call out for a dramatic treatment: I arranged a dense curve of umbrella plant (*Cyperus alternifolius*), like a Mohican haircut, interspersed with tiny, glossy red chili peppers (*Capsicum*). With its exciting textures (*see pp.44–45*) and the startling contrasts of red and green (*see pp.30–31*), this would make this an ideal candidate for a Christmas display.

HOW TO ARRANGE

• Crumple some chicken wire and insert it carefully into the vase – this will make it easier for you to arrange the umbrella plant leaves so they follow the wedgelike curve of the vase mouth. Alternatively, you can use a pin holder or some soaked wet foam attached to the base of the vase.

• Insert the leaves into the chicken wire or foam, keeping the shape compact and even. Once you have established the basic fan shape, trim away any straggling leaves.

• Insert the pepper stems, fitting them so that they sit flush with the overall fan shape. Use the most vivid red variety available: a red that exactly opposes the green in the color wheel (*see pp.30–31*) will emphasize the greenness of the leaves and the redness of the chilies.

• Fill the vase with water.

• This striking arrangement will look its best in simple, contemporary, even minimalist surroundings.

Alternative with *twigs*

To increase the size of the arrangement without destroying the simple, uncluttered shape, I have added a tracery of lichen-covered twigs of larch (*Larix decidua*) with little cones on them. Once the cyperus leaves and chili peppers are in place, you can simply push the twigs down through them, keeping the radius of the larch ends parallel to that of the grassy fan.

Ingredients

Cyperus alternifolius

Capsicum
Fasciculatum Group

CHRISTMAS FANTASY

ARRANGEMENTS THAT BRING a smile seem especially appropriate for the festive season, and this concoction of lights and winter greenery provides a humorous slant on the traditional Christmas tree. This "tree" has a trunk made from a hurricane lamp filled with fir (*Abies*) and the ribbon-like leaves of sedge (*Carex*), topped by lights. The effect is stunning, but simple to create; it is also absolutely safe since no water is involved. Displays with lights look wonderful in windows or on a hall table.

MAKING THE TREE

• Tape the wire of a set of 50 lights down the back of a pot that is about 5in (12cm) wider in diameter than the hurricane lamp glass. Pack dry foam into the pot.

• Pass the lights through the glass from the bottom to the top. Embed the glass in the dry foam in the pot.

• Fill the glass with long-lasting fir, sedge, and dried hibiscus lanterns.

• Pile the lights on top of the glass to form the crown of the "tree." If necessary, support them on twigs anchored in the top of the hurricane lamp.

• Surround the tree with dried sheet moss (*Mnium hornum*) and a few hibiscus lanterns.

Ingredients

Mnium hornum

Abies procera

Hibiscus sabdariffa

Cryptomeria japonica 'Cristata'

Carex oshimensis 'Evergold'

MIDWINTER TWIGS

A VASE THAT RESEMBLES a piece of bark with twisting ridges is the inspiration for this mix of lichen-covered twigs, which includes Austrian pine (*Pinus nigra*), European larch (*Larix decidua*), noble fir (*Abies procera*), and common alder (*Alnus glutinosa*). I have added some silver-leaved *Leucadendron argenteum* as its wintry color seems to match so well. The old nest, found in my garden, makes a natural partner.

HOW TO FORM

- This is a display that can be viewed with pleasure from all sides. However, if you wish to display it on a mantelpiece, side table, or shelf, you could arrange it so that it has just one main side.
- Unless you add holly, as suggested in the alternative, this display requires only a little water and can be kept through the winter season while it dries.
- Since the twigs of lichened larch are particularly brittle, remove any smaller, lower offshoots and add them last.
- After trimming the nest and edging it with reindeer moss, I placed a few small larch cones inside.

Alternative with *holly*

An even more seasonal display can be created by adding holly. The variegated holly that I found had no berries; I included a few twigs of deciduous holly with berries. If necessary, you can twist some realistic, wired plastic berries onto fresh holly stems. Holly curls up and browns very quickly if dry, so be careful to replenish its supply of water in the vase.

Ingredients

Alnus glutinosa

Pinus nigra

Larix decidua

Abies procera

Aspalathus sp.

FESTIVE CHANDELIER

STUDDED WITH CRABAPPLES *(Malus)* and hung in a hallway, this two-tier fir-decked chandelier welcomes visitors at the front door. It is lit with candles, but could just as easily be garlanded by white fairy lights. The chandelier consists of one large and one smaller ring with fir-covered holders containing low candles in glass tumblers. Hanging in the center of the rings, just below the larger one, is a mossy sphere spiked with mistletoe *(Phoradendron)*: all who pass underneath must honor tradition!

MAKING THE CHANDELIER

- Construct two moss-filled chicken-wire rings, one 9in (23cm) and one 15in (38cm) in diameter *(see pp.324–325)*.
- Push stalks of grand fir *(Abies grandis)* into the rings, all pointing in the same direction; bind them in with fine wire.
- Make six smaller, moss-filled rings to act as holders for the glass candle tumblers. Attach three to each ring, spacing them equidistantly; wire securely in position.
- Stud the rings and candle holders with wired crabapples *(see p.320)*.
- Attach the ends of three 34in (85cm) chains to points midway between the candle holders on the larger ring, securing them with floral wire hairpins pushed through the chicken wire and chains.
- Attach the smaller ring to the chains,

10in (25cm) from the larger one, making sure that the rings are parallel.
- Make a 4in (10cm) diameter sphere from chicken wire and wet foam. Cover with mistletoe sprigs; attach a chain.
- Join the four chains at the top, letting the sphere hang within the lower ring.

Ingredients

Abies grandis

Malus 'Crittenden'

Viscum album

CHRISTMAS SHOPPING

THE BRILLIANT orange-red of a felt shopping bag complements to perfection this spectacular winter display. Rich, dark green holly (*Ilex*) and magnificent red stems of dogwood tower above the rim of anthuriums (*Anthurium veitchii*), whose ivory spathes darken to red at their edges, while their jaunty spadices almost match the color of the basket.

PREPARING THE BASKET

- Having chosen a suitable bag or basket for your arrangement, find a bucket or watertight container to fit inside it.
- Stuff rolled newspaper around the base of the bucket; this will help to support the bag or basket and give it a good shape.

- Wedge a block of soaked wet foam at the base of the bucket to help keep the stems in position, especially when you are beginning to create the display.
- First place the dogwood twigs, slightly taller in the center than at the sides.

Next, arrange the holly, aiming to create a three-dimensional arrangement. Finally, add the anthuriums around the rim, taking care not to make them too even.
- Fill with water as necessary, adding a few drops of bleach each time.

Ingredients

Ilex × meserveae 'Blue Prince'

Cornus alba 'Sibirica'

Anthurium andraeanum 'Fantasia'

Alternative with *hydrangea*

Not as startling in their effect as the anthuriums, the *Hydrangea macrophylla* are none the less an attractive alternative with their green-tinged red, mauve, and pink flowers. Whereas I simply edged the bag with the anthuriums, I have mounded the hydrangea flowers from the front to the back of the bag. They will dry on the stem, and the display will last for several weeks as long as the dogwood and holly stems are in water.

TROPICAL SPLENDOR

IN A BREAK with tradition, this fir tree is decorated with fresh tropical flowers. The large lime-green orchids (*Cymbidium* Thurso) dangle seductively from the branches, while the scarlet-and-yellow parrot flowers (*Heliconia stricta* 'Fire Bird') resemble flickering flames. A garlanding of gypsophila, lit by small white lights, adds an icy frosting.

DECORATING THE TREE

- Cut the orchids and parrot flowers to leave a ¾in (2cm) stem on each. Push a rose wire through each stem near the join with the petals and wind it around the stem. Twist the wire ends around a fir branch to attach to the tree.
- Wire a ring of *Heliconia* flowers to the top ring of branches on the tree to make a ruff around the stem.
- To make the gypsophila garland, first cut some 39in (1m) lengths of white thread. Make a slipknot at one end and attach a 2in (5cm) sprig of gypsophila by twisting the thread through the offshoots; add another gypsophila sprig so that it overlaps the first by about ½in (1.5cm), then wind the thread through that.
- You will need to make about ten of these garlands for a 8ft (2.5m) tree.

Ingredients

Heliconia stricta 'Fire Bird'

Cymbidium Thurso

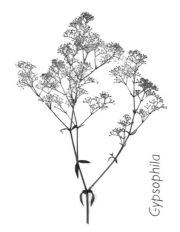

Gypsophila

MAGNOLIA WREATH

FREQUENTLY THE SIMPLEST of things work out to be the best. This wreath, shaped like the ancient Greek and Roman headdresses, consists of nothing but the leaves and fruit of Southern magnolia (*Magnolia grandiflora*). The evergreen leaves of what I think is one of the most beautiful of all trees have glossy, rich green tops and brown felty backs, making a very special contrast. The fruits look like fleshy pinecones and drop rich red seeds as they ripen – in winter the trees have both leaves and fruit. This wreath lasts very well and can be hung traditionally on the front door or on an inside door to welcome people into a room.

MAKING THE WREATH

- Cut a strip of chicken wire about 3½ft (112cm) long and 4in (10cm) wide, stuff it with dry sphagnum moss (or wet moss if the wreath will hang outside), and form it into a tube about 2in (5cm) in diameter (*see pp.324–325*).
- Bend the tube into the wreath shape, or a circle if you prefer, and use fine-gauge wire to join the ends at the apex; attach a stub wire hanging loop at this point.
- Cut some 4in (10cm) medium-gauge

wires and fold them into a "U" shape.
- Use these to wire together groups of three leaves each in a fan shape, placing some green side up and some brown.
- Lay the moss-filled tube on a flat surface with the top end away from you. Starting at the top, arrange the trios of leaves by layering them down the sides of the wreath with their tips pointing toward the top. Attach the leaves by pushing the ends of the wires through the moss, then bending them back. Finish off the base of the wreath with a "rosette" of overlapping leaves, radiating out from a central point.
- Wire in some fruits, keeping the best for the center of the "rosette." Conceal any exposed wire tube with wired single leaves.

Ingredients

Magnolia grandiflora

GLITTERING SWAG

Pinus sylvestris cones

Pinus strobus cone

Larix decidua

LICHEN-COVERED twigs of European larch (*Larix decidua*) are just right for swagging a window, doorway, or a fireplace that will not be used for fires over the Christmas holidays. I have sprinkled the twigs with tiny silver star spangles to make them glitter, and decorated them with glittering dried heads of the opium poppy (*Papaver somniferum*), plus a mixture of pinecones and some large turquoise and blue glass spheres.

Papaver somniferum (dried)

FESTIVE FIREPLACE

• To attach the swag to a stone or marble fireplace, fit a long wire loop tightly around the length of the mantelshelf (*right*). You can then tie the swag to the wire. For wooden fireplaces, use the same method, or attach with small tacks.

• Make the two side drops by binding larch branches together with dark-colored fine-gauge wire. The branches should be long enough to reach two-thirds of the way down the sides of the fireplace.

• Spray-paint the poppy heads and pine cones in blue and silver to complement the color of the glass spheres.

• Randomly wire some of the poppy heads and pinecones onto the larch side drops.

• Take the completed side drops outside

and spray them with photo mount, then immediately sprinkle them with the tiny glittering silver stars. They are now ready to hang from the fireplace wire.

• Repeating the technique used for the side drops, make two larger twig sections for the top of the fireplace, each just over half the length of the mantelshelf. Select the branches by holding them in position and appraising their shapes before making up the sections.

• Secure the twig sections to the wire, placing them top to top, so that they fan upward and intertwine attractively at the center of the mantelpiece.

• Add the glass spheres, using their hooks to wire them into the twigs and placing them so that each side looks different.

HANGING CHRISTMAS TREE

SEVERAL YEARS AGO, when our front living room was being redecorated, I ordered a perfect small Christmas tree. The tree, when I went to pick it up, was perfect, but large. Of course I was seduced into taking it home, but the problem then was where to put it. The solution – to hang it upside down in the stairwell. Now this has become a house tradition, and each year our second tree is suspended by four ropes from the upper banisters. The tree is then decorated so that it looks equally good from the ground floor and from the floor above.

SUSPENDING THE TREE

- Choose a tree that does not drop its needles, such as *Abies nordmanniana*.
- Cut two ropes long enough to pass down from one hanging point, loop through two lower branches at the base of the trunk, and back to another support.
- With two helpers, attach one end of each rope to hanging points with a non-slip knot, then thread each rope around two different base branches of the tree.
- Pulling on the untied ends will raise the tree, with one person guiding the tip, until the loose ends can be tied off securely.

ADDING DECORATIONS

- Prepare the Chinese lanterns (*Physalis alkekengi*) by opening each one and splitting them into four or five "petals" with the fruit in the center. The "petals" need to be turned inside out so that they splay open like a flower.
- Wire the opened Chinese lanterns (*see pp.318–321*) then attach them to the tree branches with fine-gauge wire, checking that they look right from where they will be viewed on the hanging tree.
- Develop the color theme by adding traditional gold decorations such as stars, suns, and moons, and tying in some bows of glistening gold or orange ribbon.

Ingredients

Physalis alkekengi

SILVER TRUMPET

SPRINGING FROM the bell of this matte silver vase – whose simple shape is one that seems to encourage flowers to fall into place all by themselves – are crimson *Hippeastrum* 'Liberty' (amaryllis) flowers, whose trumpet-shaped flowers echo the shape of the vase. These are complemented by the bold leaves of *Dracaena surculosa*, *Alocasia macrorrhiza*, and palm.

Alternative with *peppers*

In this arrangement, tall stems of scarlet peppers (*Capsicum*) replace the crimson amaryllis flowers. While still providing a satisfying shot of color, they allow the leaves in their wide variety of shapes, and dark green or light green and golden tones to take center stage. I have arranged the large palm leaves (*Chamaerops fortunii*) so that they spray out around the edges of the vase, producing beautiful fan shapes both in their own right and as a grouped whole.

Ingredients

Alocasia macrorrhiza 'Variegata'

Dracaena surculosa

Hippeastrum 'Liberty'

Capsicum frutescens

Chamaerops fortunii

ARRANGING THE TRUMPET

- Use a tall, flaring, narrow-based vase such as this only if the base is heavy enough to balance the weight of the flowers arranged in it; otherwise there is a danger that it will topple over.
- Half-fill the vase with water.
- To prolong the life of the amaryllis flowers, cut the ends of the hollow stems, hold each plant upside down, and fill the stem with water. Place a thumb or finger over the cut end and immediately upend it into the vase water. Alternatively, plug the filled stem with some moist cotton before placing in the vase (*see p.312*).

- Arrange the dracaena, alocasia, and palm leaves in and around the amaryllis stems, positioning leaves of contrasting color against each other.
- Encourage the production of more amaryllis buds by removing any wilting or dead flowers as they appear.

SUGARED FRUITS

A GLOWING, cranberry-red candle giving off a gentle herbal scent, surrounded by glistening sugared fruits and flowers, creates a festive Thanksgiving centerpiece. Around the candle are piled sugared persimmons, plums, oranges, lychees, pomegranates, pineapple, and nectarines. The rich sugared orange roses, added as a sweetly sumptuous finishing touch, will last for several days when crystallized like this, the fruits and their skins even longer (*see p.316*). Once the arrangement has served its purpose, the fruits can be carefully washed and eaten.

Ingredients

Rosa 'Rodeo'

Lychees

Fruits

Alternative with *narcissus*

As a contrast to all the reds, golds, and oranges in the bowl, I have replaced the roses with sugared paperwhite *Narcissus* to give an almost snowy effect. This narcissus, which can be forced to flower from autumn to early winter, has a clear, sharp-sweet perfume and is one of the delights of winter. For displays of a different character, other lasting flowers to use are carnations, violets, primroses, or members of the *Primula* Wanda Supreme Series.

CREATING THE DISPLAY

• Brush the fruits and flowers all over with lightly beaten egg white, then use a sieve to sprinkle coarse sugar over them.
• Put the sugared fruits and flowers to dry in a warm place before arranging them.
• Position the candle. You may find it easier to create a pleasing arrangement if you place a block of dry foam under it.
• Build up a balance of the fruits and flowers around the candle.
• Avoid using any poisonous alternatives to roses (such as hellebores) in case they are eaten by mistake.

TABLETOP TREES

TWO CHRISTMAS TREES and some snowballs provide an unusual display for the festive season. The trees are made from long-lasting noble fir (*Abies procera*) bedecked with the scarlet berries of winterberry (*Ilex verticillata*) while the snowballs are made of reindeer moss. After a few days the berries will dry out a little, but they still look attractive. The trees could also be decorated with bunches of artificial berries, tiny Christmas ornaments, limes or kumquats wired with floral wires (*see p.318*), or tiny low-voltage lights. These flat displays would be perfect for a mantelshelf or perhaps a side table.

Ingredients

Abies procera 'Glauca'

Ilex verticillata

Reindeer moss

CHOOSING PLANT MATERIAL

• The best greenery to use for these trees is *Abies procera* 'Glauca': the needles of the noble fir last well, and this cultivar is a wonderful frosty blue. It is widely available during the festive season.
• Red berries are always the first to spring to mind at this time of year, but there are also many forms of holly with beautiful orange or yellow berries.

MAKE THE FRAMES
- Bind bamboo stakes together with wire to form two triangles, the larger one 18in (45cm) high and the smaller 14in (35cm) high.
- Wrap the triangles with chicken wire, leaving one side open. Stuff the space with dried sphagnum moss to form a pillow (*see p.327*).

COVER THE TREES
- Working up from the base of each triangle, layer with sprigs of fir, pointing them down in the center, out at the sides, and up at the top.
- Add berried holly twigs wired in with floral wires.

MAKE THE SNOWBALLS
- To form each snowball base, crumple a piece of chicken wire around a handful of dried sphagnum moss, tucking in the ends of the wires.
- Cover the bases with reindeer moss held in place with medium-gauge floral wires bent double to form "hairpins" (*see p.320*).

WINTRY BASKET

IT IS ALWAYS A PLEASURE to give and receive flowers in winter, and this basket, decorated with seasonal greenery and containing flowers that evoke the beauty of winter's snow and ice, would make a glorious gift. The blooms in this woven grapevine basket are the exquisite white *Anemone coronaria* 'The Bride', framed by willow and feathery twigs of the Austrian pine (*Pinus nigra*). As a gift, this basket is simplicity itself.

BUILDING UP THE BASKET

- Weave twigs of twisted willow into the spaces between the vine stems of the basket to make it look a little wilder.
- Line the basket with a firm, waterproof container – it will not show, so do not worry about its appearance.
- Wedge a 1in (2.5cm) layer of soaked wet foam into the base of the basket to hold the flowers in place and to help prolong their life.
- Insert the flowers, letting them crowd one another but without damaging their petals.
- Place the pine twigs in the container, saving a few to tie into the outer edge of the basket, along with wired pieces of reindeer moss.

Ingredients

Reindeer moss

Pinus nigra

Anemone coronaria 'The Bride'

Alternative with *holly*

I have taken out some of the anemones and replaced them with red-berried holly, making the basket more appropriate for the Christmas season. The dark, glossy leaves and red berries provide an excellent foil for the delicate anemones. Remember that the holly needs to be in water or inserted into the foam. If its ends become dry, it will brown in a short time.

TINSELED VASE

A VASE OF FLOWERS, arranged and ready to display, makes a perfect present – especially at Christmas time. To give the gift an extra festive touch, I have wound a length of gold-tinted tinsel into the vase before arranging the flowers, which are white lilac (*Syringa vulgaris* 'Jan van Tol'), some brilliant small parrot flowers (*Heliconia stricta* 'Fire Bird'), snow-on-the-mountain (*Euphorbia marginata*), and tea tree (*Leptospermum scoparium* 'Gaiety Girl').

PREPARING THE GIFT

• Choose the vase with care – for a gift, the vase is as important as the flowers. This one is so well shaped that flowers seem to position themselves without effort.

• Wind a generous amount of tinsel into the vase, checking that the effect is pleasing from every angle.

• Half-fill the vase with water, then all the recipient need do is fill it up.

• Insert the flower stems into the vase, taking care not to spoil the effect of the tinsel. You may find that it helps to hold back the tinsel against the edge of the vase with a long knife or piece of bamboo while you arrange the first stems. Once you have placed all the flowers, gently tease out the tinsel if necessary.

• Take another length of tinsel, tuck the end into the arrangement, and wind the rest around the top of the vase, looping it over one or two stems near the edge, so that it forms a ruff around the flowers.

Alternative with *roses*

The combination of peach and red has a special appeal, achieved by replacing the parrot flowers with peach-colored roses and holly berries. The sweetly perfumed roses and little branches of berries are particularly attractive in this arrangement. A touch of red among green always announces the Christmas season, but I'm not averse to using some summery flowers as well as seasonal ones.

Ingredients

Heliconia stricta 'Fire Bird'

Syringa vulgaris 'Jan van Tol'

Euphorbia marginata

Leptospermum scoparium 'Gaiety Girl'

TOMATO SWAG

IMPRESS YOUR PARTY GUESTS at Christmas by adorning the buffet table with an unusual tomato and rose swag. You can make the swag up to 24 hours in advance of the occasion if the room is kept cool during that period. Choose slightly unripe tomatoes, and add the parsley just two hours before the guests arrive. The everyday vegetables and evergreen foliage used in the swag make it an inexpensive decoration that can be made at any time of the year.

Ingredients

Rosa 'Nikita'

Vine tomatoes

Hebe brachysiphon

Parsley

Eggplant

FORMING THE SWAG

- Shape a series of moss-filled chicken-wire tubes, each approximately 4ft (120cm) long (*see pp.324–25*) into inverted Gothic arches, with their ends approximately 3ft (1m) apart.
- Wire the ingredients (*see pp.318–321*) and insert them so that they point down toward the apex of each arch.
- Start by covering the base thickly with sprigs of hebe, then add the vine tomatoes, eggplants, roses, and, finally, the parsley.

ATTACH THE SWAG

- Hammer small pins through the cloth and into the table edges. (For this reason, use an old table or inexpensive trestle.)
- Secure the swag to these nails with fine wire and decorate with large paper bows (*see p.335*) at each of the top ends.
- If you make the swag in advance, spray-mist the flowers and foliage before guests arrive.

CATTAIL WREATH

NOTHING IS more welcoming than a door bedecked with a festive wreath of dried flowers, fruit, and leaves. Here, the soft, earthy tones of cattails (*Typha latifolia*) and oak leaves (*Quercus macrocarpa*) act as a foil for the intense red of pomegranates (*Punica granatum*), vivid scarlet-flowered *Celosia argentea* (cockscomb), and the yellow thistleheads of knapweed (*Centaurea macrocephala*).

PREPARE THE INGREDIENTS
- For the wreath, use the flower heads from stems of air-dried cockscomb and knapweed (*see pp.314–315*).
- To keep the cattails intact, spray with hair spray and dry upright in a vase.
- Cut a 1in (2.5cm) hole in the base of each of four pomegranates and carefully scoop out the seeds with a teaspoon.

COMPLETE THE WREATH
- Stuff each pomegranate with wax paper, then push a wire hairpin (*see p.320*) through each one, from top to bottom.
- Using raffia, tie bundles of cattails and their leaves to a wreath base of twisted wicker "rope." Wire in the pomegranates around the wreath, then push the dried flower heads between the wicker strands.

Ingredients

Quercus macrocarpa

Punica granatum

Typha latifolia

Centaurea macrocephala

Celosia argentea Olympia Series

Flower creations for church and synagogue;

bouquets, posies, hoops, and headdresses

for brides and bridesmaids; flowers,

garlands, and table arrangements for

receptions: all are featured in this section.

WEDDING AND CHURCH

✳ availability of ingredients   ✱ longevity of display

✱✱ level of difficulty

PEW CORNUCOPIA

THIS CURVING cornucopia is designed to adorn the end of a traditional church pew, but it would grace any form of wedding ceremony with its simple, relaxed, natural, and informal mood. At the head of the cornucopia is a profusion of fresh blue irises, pink *Chamelaucium uncinatum*, *Eustoma grandiflorum* 'Mariachi', and *Limonium sinuatum*. The tail is a swathe of sweet-scented silver wattle (*Acacia retinodes*). Decorations like this can be made in advance, then brought in and arranged over the ends of the pews on the day.

GETTING STARTED

- Allow yourself plenty of time to create this decoration, especially if you are making a number of them. The frames can be made two days in advance of the event, the flowery heads one day in advance, but the wattle must be applied to the tails on the actual day or they will soon dry out.
- Begin by constructing the gently curving tails. Each consists of a tube of chicken wire filled with barely damp sphagnum moss. The tube narrows from a diameter of about 3in (8cm) at the top to almost a point at the bottom. Its length depends on the size of the pew for which it is intended – the tail of the example shown is 27½in (70cm) long.
- Conceal the wire with Spanish moss.

Ingredients

Acacia retinodes

Iris 'H.C. van Vliet'

Eustoma grandiflorum 'Mariachi'

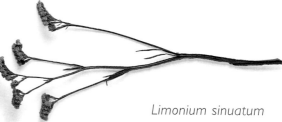

Chamelaucium uncinatum

Limonium sinuatum

COMPLETING THE DISPLAY

• To make the head of the cornucopia, first wrap a rectangular block of soaked wet foam in chicken wire.

• Cut off the lower crosspiece of a wire coat hanger, leaving just the hook and two arms; straighten the arms and poke them through the wrapped foam block.

• Bend the arms back up around the wire and into the foam, so that the block can hang securely from the hook of the hanger, which you can now twist by 45°.

• Hang the block at a convenient height against a wall and, on the day before the event, arrange all the flowers by poking their stems into the foam. On the day, wire sprays of wattle (all facing upward) into the tail sections.

• Carry the heads and tails to the pews and join them in situ using wire hooks.

• Hang each cornucopia over a pew-end, covering any gaps with flowers or moss.

RESPLENDENT IN WICKER

THESE TRUMPET-SHAPED wicker baskets are ideal for tall, floor-standing church displays – perhaps on either side of the altar or by the entrance. Deliciously perfumed silver wattle (*Acacia retinodes*) provides a contrast of yellow flowers and green foliage to a host of pink flowers, including lilies (*Lilium* 'Côte d'Azur'), pink waxflower (*Chamelaucium uncinatum*), *Eustoma grandiflorum* 'Mariachi Pink', and statice (*Limonium sinuatum*). The same flowers could be arranged in a large urn or vase and raised close to eye-level by a tall pedestal.

Ingredients

Acacia retinodes

Lilium 'Côte d'Azur'

Eustoma grandiflorum 'Mariachi Pink'

Chamelaucium uncinatum

Limonium sinuatum 'Art Shades'

Alternative with *iris*

Without removing any of the acacia or pink flowers from the wicker vase, I have enlivened the display by adding some pale blue highlights. Some stems of a light blue iris (look for *Iris* 'Pickwick', for example) have added a fresh, springlike touch, or you could achieve the same effect by adding white flowers such as lilac (perhaps *Syringa vulgaris* 'Mme Lemoine'). The white blooms of an ornamental cherry are another possibility.

MAKING THE DISPLAY

• Place two bricks in the base of the basket to prevent it from overturning.

• Line the basket to make it watertight, and then wedge in blocks of soaked wet foam to within 4in (10cm) of the top.

• Arrange the flowers in a fan shape. To make sure that the display stays three-dimensional, arrange some flowers and foliage facing toward the back.

• Add the lilies last, aiming for balance but without becoming too regimented.

• Fill up the wet foam daily because the flowers will drink up the water rapidly.

SPRING BLOSSOMS

Ingredients

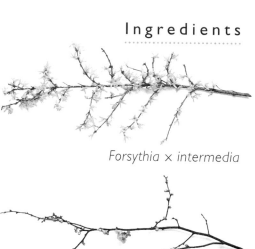

Forsythia × intermedia

Prunus avium

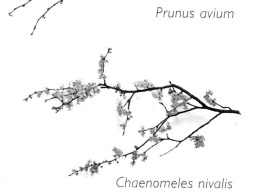

Chaenomeles nivalis

JUXTAPOSING THE DELICACY of spring blossoms with a heavy lead vase may seem odd, but in fact, the flowers seem to float up out of the silvery gray container. The delicate wild cherry (*Prunus avium*), white ornamental quince (*Chaenomeles*), and clear yellow forsythia look ethereal against a pale wall or against the sky on an upstairs windowsill.

Alternative with *viburnum*

This more eye-catching effect is achieved by adding flowers of the snowball bush, *Viburnum macrocephalum*. Its pompoms of spring-green fading to white make the display look very fresh. Remove all the leaves from the snowball bush stems, since they would detract from the airiness of the bare twigs. For a softer alternative, replace the bright yellow forsythia with the pale lemon of *Forsythia suspensa* or *Forsythia* 'Spring Glory'.

FORM A TWIG OUTLINE

• Use the shapes of the branches to form the structure of the arrangement: forsythia tends to grow quite straight, but the stems of the other ingredients offer more interesting and intricate lines.

• Avoid using too many branches: the arrangement should have an airy feel and not appear too crowded.

• Stand back frequently to check the overall shape and keep rearranging the branches until the balance is just right: if too many of the twigs cross, the tracery will look busy rather than lacy.

• All of this material has a good vase life, particularly the forsythia; the delicate cherry blossoms will be the first to fade, but even these last reasonably well.

BASKET OF POSIES

A RUSTIC GARDENING BASKET lined with moss and filled with posies of seasonal flowers makes a novel alternative to a bridal bouquet. Bridesmaids could carry smaller versions, with perhaps little baskets holding a tiny posy for the very young. After the ceremony, the bride can throw not just one but all the posies to relatives and friends.

LINE AND FILL THE BASKET

• Line the basket with a layer of sheet moss, using a glue gun to attach it. This can be done well in advance.

• The day before the wedding, create each posy from a different mix of pretty, sweet-scented flowers. Edge the posies with a ruff of galax leaves, tie with colored cord, and stand them in water.

• At the last moment, dry the stems and place the posies in the basket.

Ingredients

- Lathyrus odoratus
- Eustoma grandiflorum Heidi Series
- Narcissus 'Silver Chimes'
- Tulipa 'Picture'
- Tulipa 'Angelique'
- Anthriscus sylvestris
- Myosotis sylvatica
- Freesia 'Blue Heaven'
- Galax urceolata

WILD SCENTED POSY

PERFUMED POSIES, known as tussy mussies, were carried by both men and women in the seventeenth and eighteenth centuries, when their scent was held to be as therapeutic as it was refreshing. The scent of this wild-looking, contemporary posy is absolutely delicious, combining the pervasive perfumes of mock orange (*Philadelphus*), freesias, aromatic herbs, and delicately sweet-smelling tea tree (*Leptospermum*). This gentle dome, broken by spires, is perfect for a bride or her bridesmaids.

FORM THE POSY

• Take the conditioned flowers and foliage and remove all leaves below the point where the tie will be. Bind in the material, stem by stem, with thin twine or fine-gauge wire (*see pp.330–331*).

• For a natural-looking tie, wrap three or four strands of raffia around the stems to cover the binding. Leave enough at the ends to tie in a raffia bow made from 10 or 15 strands. Leave the stems uncovered or bind with ribbon (*see p.334*).

• If the posy is made in advance, leave the stems a little long and place in some water in a tumbler; at the last minute, cut off the excess from the stems and wipe dry.

Ingredients

Philadelphus x lemoinei

Freesia 'Elan'

Leptospermum scoparium

Rosmarinus officinalis

Thymus vulgaris

ROSE-PETAL COCKTAILS

TO ADD A TOUCH of glamour to a special lunch, dinner, or reception, simply stand petal-filled cocktail glasses at each place setting, next to the wine glasses. I like it if each of the "cocktails" is different, but they could just as easily all have the same flowers and colors. For a frothy topping, finish with a spray of lime-green lady's mantle (*Alchemilla mollis*).

Ingredients

Rosa 'Enigma'

Rosa 'Vicky Brown'

Rosa 'Valerie'

Rosa 'Anne Marie'

Alchemilla mollis

Black olive

FILLING THE GLASSES

• Simply twist off enough flower petals to fill the cocktail glasses and pile them in — either randomly or arranged to resemble a layered drink or an exotic flower.

• If you wish, place a silver cocktail stick with a black olive in each glass.

• These petal "cocktails" can be made a couple of hours in advance. If kept in a cool place, such as the salad crisper in a refrigerator, they will keep longer. Once out, they will last for an evening.

• Gypsophila can be used as an alternative to alchemilla as a frothy topping.

• To continue the theme, sprinkle some rose petals on the salad — they taste as good as they look. Other edible flowers are nasturtiums, tuberous begonias, and borage. In spring try apple, cherry, and pear blossoms, primroses, and other colored polyanthus and violets.

FRESH GREEN AND WHITE

SIMPLICITY OF LINE and color defines this display. Tall, elegant, pure white lilies and delphiniums, exotic emerald arums (*Zantedeschia aethiopica* 'Green Goddess') and anthuriums, and fresh green larch (*Larix decidua*) branches are arrayed in a large, hand-built pot with a lichenlike finish. The delphiniums were chosen because their near-black centers stand out so well. Place vases on either side of an altar, or use them as an imposing floor-standing arrangement at a reception.

USING LILIES

• Madonna lilies (*Lilium candidum*) can be found for only a limited period, but *L. longiflorum* is available all year round in flower shops and can be substituted.

• Lilies are noted for their scent, but this varies from one kind to another: Madonna lilies have a very sweet fragrance, while others have a more spicy note, and some are even unpleasant.

• Be sure to remove the flowers' pollen anthers if they are likely to be brushed up against: lilies have strongly colored yellow pollen that stains fabric immediately. As the flowerbuds open and before the pollen develops, grasp all the anthers and gently pull them toward you: they will easily detach from their green stamen filaments. Leave the central stigma intact.

• All these cut flowers, but especially the lilies, take up copious amounts of water.

Alternative with *foxgloves*

Foxgloves (*Digitalis*) are at the height of their flowering season at the same time of year as Madonna lilies. There are pure white foxglove cultivars that would look ravishing with the other white flowers used in the main arrangement. To give the arrangement a different, more countrified feel, include a few spires of the more familiar pink foxgloves with purple-spotted throats. These also relate well to the finish of the vase.

Ingredients

Anthurium 'Midori'

Delphinium 'Sandpiper'

Lilium candidum

Zantedeschia aethiopica 'Green Goddess'

Larix decidua

CRIMSON FEATHERS

FLOWER PETALS and feathers are an unusual and exciting combination: I have mixed the two in this vibrant bridal bunch of sweetly scented crimson peonies (*Paeonia officinalis* 'Rubra Plena') and matching feathers. The result is dramatic and opulent, and could be carried by an extrovert, adventurous bride or her teenage or adult bridesmaids. A matching crimson bow completes the posy.

Ingredients

Paeonia officinalis 'Rubra Plena'

MAKING THE POSY

- Keep the flowers in deep water while they open, removing them just before you wish to prepare the bunch.
- Group together seven peonies in peak condition, tying just below the flowers.
- Wire some single and double feathers, cut from a length of feather trimming, and thread them down through the flowers, leaving about 3in (7cm) protruding.
- Swirl a 10in (25cm) length of feather trimming around the bunch, tying in with wire attached to each end.
- Finish the posy with a crimson bow (*see p.335*) overlaying the tie.

WEDDING AFTERGLOW

THE HEAT OF THE SUN has subsided, leaving guests to enjoy an alfresco dinner on a balmy summer's evening following a perfect country wedding. A memory of the sun stands at the center of each table: a luscious, golden orange display of calla lilies (*Zantedeschia*), butterfly weed (*Asclepias*), and galax leaves radiating around a glowing candle, which is protected from the breeze by a hurricane lamp.

Ingredients

Asclepias tuberosa

Zantedeschia elliottiana

Galax urceolata

ARRANGING THE CANDLE

- Fill a 4in (10cm) deep, round aluminum can with soaked, wet foam blocks set onto florist's spikes.
- Sink a candle onto a central prong then place the glass over it.
- Fill the container with water and arrange galax leaves around the glass shield, slightly overlapping them.
- For a warm, golden effect, choose callas in pale yellow, gold, and pale orange.
- Cut each calla stem at a sharp angle and push into the foam around the glass, facing outward and overlapping the leaves.
- Fill in between the callas with butterfly weed (*Asclepias tuberosa*) and galax leaves.

FLORAL ICE BOWL

ONE OF THE MOST striking ways of presenting flowers is to capture them in ice. The simplest method is to freeze a single flower in an ice cube, but the more adventurous can make an iced flower bowl or a champagne bucket to keep in the freezer, ready for a special occasion. The effect of vibrantly colored flowers, trapped in a glasslike bowl, is enchanting, while the transience of the display adds to its allure. Here, I have used feathery cilantro leaves and the flowers of a vivid blue iris (*Iris* 'Professor Blaauw').

Ingredients

Iris 'Professor Blaauw'

Coriandrum sativum

MAKING THE BOWL

• Take two glass bowls: one just over 1in (2.5cm) smaller in diameter than the other. Half-fill the larger bowl with water.

• Place the smaller bowl in the larger one, and fill it with water until its base is floating approximately ³/₄in (2cm) above the bottom of the larger bowl.

• Dry the sides of the outer bowl and the rim of the inner. Hold the inner bowl in place by placing two pieces of tape at right angles over the two bowls.

• Carefully insert flowers and foliage between the bowls, using a skewer to gently push them into position. Leave the bowls overnight in the freezer.

• To unmold the ice bowl, float the two glass bowls in cold water and add cold water to the small inner bowl. After a minute or two, gently lift out the inner bowl. Invert and remove the larger bowl.

Alternative with *champagne bottle*

You can make a champagne ice bucket in exactly the same way as the ice bowl, using two small bucket-shaped vessels as molds, one slightly larger than the other. Avoid using any poisonous flowers or leaves, in case someone decides to break off a piece of ice and eat it.

SUMMER BOUQUET

THIS ELEGANT WEDDING bouquet, which can be cradled in one arm, comprises a combination of clear pink lilies, peach roses edged with pink, white gladioli flowers with dark throats, and ruscus leaves. Then there is the added allure of the subtle perfumes of both the lilies and the roses. Peach and pink work well with most white fabrics and are quite ravishing with ivory and cream.

USING WIRE

• From a selection of lilies, roses, gladioli, and ruscus, wire about 12 individual flowers (*see pp.318–321*).

• Lay down a wired lily bud and fit two lily stems on either side of it. Wire these three lilies together 10in (25cm) from the top, leaving 7in (18cm) of wire for end binding. Cut the stems to leave a 6in (15cm) handle below the tie.

• Bind in more wired flowers and stems of foliage. Lay in two more stems of lily near the binding, then add the other flowers and foliage. Bind all the flowers together securely with the wire.

• Overbind the wire tie with ribbon and attach a matching bow (*see p.335*).

Ingredients

Rosa 'Lovely Lady' ('Dicjubell')

Lilium 'Metrostar'

Gladiolus 'Halley'

Ruscus hypophyllum

CLASSICAL URN

THE COLORS of this gorgeous arrangement are in the pink, purple, and cream range, all mixed with the feathery green of *Sorbus aucuparia* (rowan). With the foliage forming a fan-shaped, three-dimensional arrangement that looks good from the front and sides, the addition of foxtail lilies (*Eremurus × isabellinus*) and gladioli fills out the curve so that the whole display down to the base of the urn nearly forms a circle.

Ingredients

Sorbus aucuparia

Hydrangea paniculata 'Praecox'

Eremurus × isabellinus

Gladiolus 'Violetta'

Lilium 'Ascari'

MAKING THE DISPLAY

• To avoid the possibility of staining clothing or furnishings, remove the pollen from the lilies before placing them in the arrangement (*see p.313*).

• Line the urn with a watertight bowl. Mound soaked wet foam blocks into the bowl, cutting them to fit the curve of the base, and piling them three high.

• Attach the foam blocks inside the bowl, using chicken wire stitched with fine-

gauge wire. Place the bowl in the urn.

• Arrange the foliage to give a fan-shaped, three-dimensional effect. Fill in the curve with gladioli and lilies.

• Place large heads of lilies, with as many as four flowers out on a stem, to give a good balanced effect. Finally, add the green-white flowering hydrangea stems.

• Large arrangements can easily become top-heavy, but a substantial iron urn such as this solves the problem.

BOUQUET WITH SHELLS

WHITE SPRAY BOUQUETS have long featured in weddings. In the past, bouquets often flowed down to the floor, but the size of the bouquet should be in proportion to the height of the bride. This elegant bouquet is composed of white and pink-tinged flowers, including fragrant stephanotis, set off by little pink-tinged white shells.

FORM THE BOUQUET

- Drill a small hole in each shell where it tapers to a point. Use a small masonry bit, and support the shell on a piece of wood. Thread a medium-gauge floral wire through the hole and wind it back tightly on itself.
- Wire the plant material (*see p.318*) – some of the pittosporum as single sprigs and some in little bunches. Wire the stephanotis and three or four heads of alstroemeria in bunches of three or four flowers and the rest as single flowers.
- Start by making a circular posy (*see p.330*), binding in the flowers, foliage, and shells one by one.
- Next make a tail (*see p.330*), relating it to the height of the bride, and bind this into the posy to form the spray shape.

- Bind the handle with ribbon, winding it down the stem then up again, and finish by using the ends to tie in a bow.
- Keep the bouquet in a cool but not icy place – outside, under cover, in cool weather, or in a cooler in summer.

Ingredients

Pittosporum tenuifolium 'Silver Queen'

Alstroemeria 'Capri'

Scabiosa caucasica 'Miss Willmott'

Rosa 'Emerald'

Stephanotis floribunda

ROSE TREE

THIS STANDARD ROSE tree is quite easy to make and a group of them would look wonderful at a wedding reception. The roses (*Rosa* 'Nostalgia') are pale pink with a deeper pink flush on the outer petals – they remind me of the scene in *Alice in Wonderland* where three gardeners are trying to color the flowers on a white rose tree red; these roses look just as if they have been painted. You could use any colored rose, maybe matching them to the bride's or the bridesmaids' bouquets. The tiny pink buds of *Skimmia japonica* provide contrasting texture and interest.

MAKING THE BASE

- For the base you will need a basket about 12in (30cm) across; a plastic flower pot to fit inside it; a straight branch 3ft (1m) long; cement; soaked wet foam and chicken wire with which to make the head.
- Cover any holes in the base of the pot with newspaper. Drive a nail through the bottom of the branch to help anchor it. Set the branch in the pot with cement.
- Form the head of the tree with chicken wire and foam (*see p.326*). Push the head onto the branch once the cement has set.

Ingredients

Skimmia japonica 'Rubella'

Rosa 'Nostalgia'

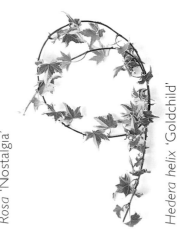

Hedera helix 'Goldchild'

DRESSING THE TREE

• Place moss around the base of the trunk
and wind ivy around the branch, tucking
the ends into the moss and under the
chicken-wire-and-foam head.

• Arrange the roses and skimmia in the
foam of the head, aiming to keep the
overall shape slightly uneven to produce
a more realistic appearance.

• To prolong the life of the roses and
skimmia, make sure that the foam forming
the head of the tree is kept moist.

CONE FOUNTAIN

THE GLORIOUS FORMS and textures of the flowers dictated the overall shape of this arrangement. Tall hollyhocks (*Alcea rosea*) extend the line of the container on the left, while a foam of lady's mantle (*Alchemilla mollis*) spills out on the right. Between these, bursts of color radiate out in a half-wheel, from the hub of an enormous protea (*Protea cynaroides*).

Ingredients

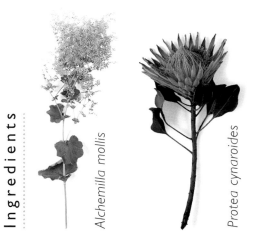

Alchemilla mollis

Protea cynaroides

Lilium 'Rosita'

Alcea rosea 'Chater's Double'

Consolida ajacis

Spiraea douglasii

Centaurea hypoleuca

Alternative with *centaurea hypoleuca*

Creamy pink foxtail lilies (*Eremurus*) and a few hollyhocks (*Alcea rosea*) on the right are again set off by lady's mantle. This time, a deep carmine knapweed (*Centaurea hypoleuca* 'John Coutts') takes upper center stage, together with a few plum-colored poppies. At the center of the display, nestling beside a large, almost ice-pink protea, is a group of deep pink and green-white proteas.

ARRANGING COLORS

• Arrange the flowers so that they are seen from the front and sides in groups of single colors. Strong colors look best towards the center of the display.

• Place the long hollyhock stems at the front left, where they will best be seen.

• Balance the almost upright angle of the hollyhocks with a spray of lady's mantle cascading out of the vase on the right.

• Fill out the center of the display with bunches of pink larkspur (*Consolida ajacis*), centaurea, and spiraea.

• Finally, place a large, open protea low down to the left of center.

• Check this arrangement from all sides to be sure that it has good front-to-back depth: it should not look one-dimensional.

WATERMELON VASES

FOR A SPLASH OF BRILLIANCE at a summer cocktail party or buffet, simply take a slice out of a watermelon and have some brilliantly colored godetias (*Clarkia*) cascading out of its juicy flesh. With a skin that can be mottled with markings like a lizard's back, and sumptuous red flesh, the watermelon is unsurpassed where coloring is concerned. Continue the theme by serving watermelon margarita cocktails, and a nonalcoholic melon punch.

Ingredients

Clarkia amoena

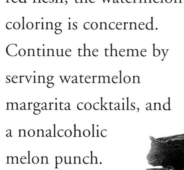

Clarkia amoena

Watermelon

PREPARING THE MELON

- Find the side of the watermelon on which it will sit most steadily. Remove a slice that amounts to about one-fifth of the fruit – this is for you to eat!
- Choose flowers with fairly stiff stems to push easily into the melon flesh. Godetias work well with their brilliantly colored, papery flowers that look almost artificial.
- You can use other melons apart from watermelons – those with yellow, ribbed

gray-green, or beige skins, for example, but I think that they look best with autumnal arrangements.

- Other flowers that you might consider using instead of godetia are scarlet and pink freesias, roses in mauves and creams, gypsophila, eustoma (especially the ice pink ones), gaillardias, sweet peas, small flowered orchids – the brilliant purple ones are terrific – or poppies.

LATE-SUMMER HARMONY

A FROTH OF PALE, delicate colors shimmers above an opaque white glass vase with cerulean blue decorations. Icy pink nerines, clear blue delphiniums, white phlox, yellow marigolds (*Tagetes*), and pale green foliage – how harmoniously these springlike colors mix, even with late-summer flowers. The trumpet shape of the vase makes arranging the flowers easy – it is simply a matter of balancing colors, shapes, and textures in an informal look. A few tall delphiniums stand up out of the arrangement, while the nerines cluster below the center.

MIXING THE COLORS

• Remember to use appropriate amounts of the different colors: softer shades of blue will retreat while the stronger pink and yellow will stand out.

• An arrangement composed entirely of pastel colors will have a very soft look: here, the addition of just a small amount of bright orange butterfly weed (*Asclepias*) significantly sharpens the look.

• Spread the various colors so that they are well balanced but do not make patterns. It is all too easy to produce a straight line of one color within an arrangement; break it by simply moving just one flower.

• Remove any leaves that would be under water: those that are overlooked will quickly decay and start to affect all the other flowers (*see p.311*).

• When using a tall, narrow vase, make sure that it is heavy enough to balance the weight of the arrangement.

Ingredients

Delphinium 'Cressida'

Tagetes Antigua Series

Nerine bowdenii 'Alba'

Phlox 'Kelly's Eye'

Phlox paniculata 'Fujiyama'

Curcuma aeruginosa

Lysimachia vulgaris

Asclepias tuberosa

ROSE BOWL

A RICH GOLDEN BROWN marble bowl makes an elegant container for this display of just one type of flower – a melange of roses (*Rosa* cultivars) in peach, yellow, and pink, with just enough color clash to add interest. The boiled-sweet hues of the roses are mouthwatering, and their scent is intoxicating too. This sumptuous display would be perfect for a church christening, placed on the floor close to the font.

FILL THE BOWL

• It is often best to arrange heavy containers like this in situ.
• Attach several prongs to the base of the bowl with adhesive clay and push on a 1½in (4cm) layer of soaked wet foam.
• Fill the bowl with sufficient water to cover the top of the foam layer.

• To prolong their lives, cut each rose stem at an angle and scrape each end (*see pp.312–313*). Treated in this way, the flowers should last for a week.
• Arrange the prepared rose stems in the bowl, taking care to achieve an even but seemingly random mix of colors.

• Flowers for special occasions need to be perfect for only a few hours; buy or cut roses on the point of opening a few days ahead so that they peak for the event.
• In summer, this arrangement would look stunning with full-blown peonies (*Paeonia*); in autumn, try a mix of hydrangeas.

Ingredients

Rosa 'Vivaldi'

Rosa 'Bo'

Rosa 'Candy Bianca'

Rosa 'Gold Strike'

Rosa 'Pistache'

TOWERING POTS

IN MY GARDEN I sometimes plant annuals and trailing plants in one pot standing on top of the soil of another. Here, I have extended the idea to a set of three graduated terracotta pots to create a tower of cut flowers. To complement the color of the pots, I filled them with early autumnal dahlias in glowing shades of red and pink, set off by the shiny leaves and lime green flower buds of *Skimmia × confusa* 'Kew Green', with pale blue echinops and trails of ivy (*Hedera*). Dahlias are not long-lived flowers, but their forms and colors are stunning.

Ingredients

Dahlia 'Ruby Wedding'

Dahlia 'Rhonda'

Dahlia 'Wootton Cupid'

Skimmia × confusa 'Kew Green'

Echinops bannaticus

Hedera helix 'Goldchild'

MAKING THE TOWER

• To make the tower, you will need three terracotta pots in the following sizes: 14in (35cm); 11in (28cm); 8in (21cm).
• First fill the largest pot with enough dry foam to bring the inner level to about 4in (10cm) below the rim. Instead of dry foam, you might like to use crumpled newspaper, but make sure that it is packed firmly into the pot to provide a stable base.
• Terracotta is porous, so each layer needs to be lined. Cut two pieces of plastic liner 10in (25cm) wider than the diameter of the pot. Gather one piece around the outside of the middle-sized pot and secure with adhesive tape. Place the other piece of plastic over the rim of the large pot and tuck it down onto the surface of the dry

foam or crumpled newspaper.
• Place the medium-sized pot in the center of the plastic-lined large pot, then wedge pieces of soaked wet foam between the two layers of plastic. Trim the plastic level with the wet foam around the inner pot.
• Line the smallest pot with plastic; wedge it into the middle pot with soaked wet foam. Repeat the lining process for this pot inside the middle-sized pot. Fill the smallest pot with soaked wet foam.
• Before arranging the dahlias, condition them (*see pp.310–313*).
• Arrange the flowers and foliage in the soaked wet foam in the top pot and around the other two pots. Finish with trails of ivy around the largest pot.

GOLDEN BRIDAL POSY

MOST FLOWERS can now be obtained at almost any time of the year, but it is more natural sometimes to allow the seasons to dictate at least the colors in an arrangement, if not the flowers themselves. In this bride's posy for an autumn wedding, rich golden-yellow and orange lilies (*Lilium*) are mixed with yellow-flushed red Peruvian lilies (*Alstroemeria*), orange hips from the wild rose *Rosa eglanteria,* and a golden variety of scarlet plume (*Euphorbia fulgens*).

PREPARE THE POSY
• Carefully remove the thorns from the rose stems and the barbs from the tree asparagus (*Asparagus myriocladus*).
• Pluck off the pollen-bearing anthers of the lilies because they produce a yellow stain that is particularly difficult to remove from clothing and furnishings (*see p.313*).

• The ingredients need to be wired in advance (*see p.318*) and then tied in, one by one, to form the posy (*see p.332*).
• All the ingredients are reasonably long lasting once wired and out of water, but keep the bouquet in a cool, but not cold, place until it is needed.

Alternative with *hair combs*

Small cuttings of the ingredients in the posy can be used to make matching hair combs for the bridesmaids (*see p.332*). Prepare these at the last possible moment, binding the flowers and foliage onto the comb with fine florist's wire. Take care not to make the combs too heavy or bulky, or they will not stay in place.

Ingredients

Lilium Golden Clarion Group

Lilium 'African Queen'

Lilium 'Escapade'

Lilium 'Grand Paradise'

Asparagus myriocladus

Euphorbia fulgens

Rosa eglanteria

Alstroemeria 'Victoria'

ORCHID HOOP

THIS ELEGANT RING of orchids and berries is designed as an alternative to the simple posies of flowers that are usually carried by bridesmaids. Little jewel-like orchids (*Dendrobium*, *Vanda*, and *Arachnis*) in lime green, fuchsia pink, and purple are interlaced with sprigs of winter berries and ruscus foliage on a circle of birch twigs (*Betula pendula*) to create a delicate but stunning hoop. The berries give it a wintry appeal, but without them the hoop could be made at any time of the year and would still make an impact. A striped ribbon of red and creamy yellow, bound around the twigs to form the handle, culminates in a double bow.

Alternative *headdress*

The headdress base is made of plastic-covered floral wire (*see p.330*) rather than twigs, making it easier to produce an even circlet of the correct size for the bridesmaid's head. The elements are wired on and include lengths of birch to disguise the base and to match the hoop.

Ingredients

Ilex verticillata

Betula pendula

Ruscus hypoglossum

Dendrobium 'Madame Pompadour'

Dendrobium bigibbum

Vanda tricolor

Arachnis flos-aeris

MAKING THE HOOP

- Adapt the size of the hoop to the height of the bridesmaids: a 14in (35cm) hoop is about right for an adult bridesmaid.
- Take four lengths of birch twig and wire the tip of each to the base of the next; bend into a hoop, wire the ends together, and tuck in any stray tips (*see pp.332–333*).
- Mark the position for the handle and finishing bow with a piece of string, but leave making the handle until last to avoid getting glue on the ribbon.
- To cover the hoop, use small-leaved greenery that lasts well: ruscus is excellent and smilax can also be used, but it does not last as long. Attach the leafy sprigs to the hoop with wire or a glue gun.
- Attach wired orchid flowers and berries to the hoop with wire or a glue gun.
- Bind ribbon around the carrying gap and finish with a bow (*see p.334*).

GARLANDED COLUMN

THE SOARING RANKS of church pillars are majestic, but they will look even more beautiful when garlanded with flowers for a special occasion such as a wedding. Scale is the key to success: delicate strands will be lost on large columns. Making substantial garlands, like this rope decorated with fat roses (*Rosa* 'Polar Star') and tulips (*Tulipa* cultivars), requires a major effort, but even two beautifully decorated pillars near the altar and some matching pew ends will look magnificent.

Ingredients

Tulipa 'Generaal De Wet'

Rosa 'Polar Star'

Tulipa 'Purissima'

Cryptomeria japonica 'Elegans'

Alternative with *red*

Flowers used to decorate a church usually look best if they echo colors that are already present, perhaps in the vivid shades of stained-glass windows or in the wall hangings and vestments. Here, the bright red tulips have replaced the orange flowers of the main garland to give a rich, sparkling effect. This color combination would be perfect for a dramatic church setting, such as a large wedding or a baptism.

MAKE THE GARLAND

- The garland base is a thick cord wrapped with fine-gauge wire (*see pp.318–319*).
- First wire on the cryptomeria, cut into 6–7in- (16–18cm-) pieces. Tree asparagus (*Asparagus myriocladus*) could also be used, but remember – it bears vicious thorns.
- Wire the other ingredients to the garland, making sure that the flowers face the front; distribute them evenly along the length.
- Attach the cord securely at the top of the pillar and wind around tightly, keeping the back against the pillar. If any gaps show up, tuck more plant pieces behind the cord: it should hold them firmly in place.
- Store the garlands in a cool place until needed. Cryptomeria and roses will last a couple of days, tulips just a few hours.

HOLLY-FILLED URN

THE ASSOCIATION OF red and green has always been part of the festive season: this lead urn holds just such a combination for a winter wedding or Christmas service. Plain green holly (*Ilex*) usually has plenty of berries but variegated holly is often not so well endowed: add color with the tiny, red, starlike flowers of scarlet plume (*Euphorbia fulgens*).

Alternative with *green and white*

For a more restrained and elegant arrangement, simply remove the scarlet plume to leave a combination of green and white in the two forms of holly, the white lily (*Lilium* 'Pompeii'), and the sweetly scented Amazon lily. Although the lilies are expensive in midwinter, they will last very well if the water is filled up regularly.

USING AN URN

• Metal containers such as this often leak. Line with plastic or, if the edges are sharp, find a container to fit inside (*see p.308*).

• Wedge soaked wet foam into the lined urn or inner container and cover it with chicken wire to help hold the heavier stems in position.

• Take care with the holly and euphorbia, which can irritate skin. Remove flowers from the Amazon lily as they fade.

Ingredients

Euphorbia fulgens

Lilium 'Pompeii'

Ilex aquifolium 'Madame Briot'

Eucharis amazonica

Ilex aquifolium 'Golden van Tol'

FLORAL PLACE SETTING

BEAUTIFULLY DECORATED place settings help make a wedding reception feel special. Here I have used a charger plate with a simple leaf design, encircling it with small posies of deliciously aromatic rosemary, bay, thyme, sage, asparagus, and heather. The rolled napkin is tied with a rough linen bow, into which is tucked one of the herbal bunches.

ARRANGING THE HERBS

* Decide on the chargers you wish to use. They do not need to be the same design as your service but need to work with it in terms of color and style.
* Using a matching ribbon, tie small posies of sage (*Salvia officinalis*), thyme (*Thymus vulgaris*), bay (*Laurus nobilis*), baby asparagus (*Asparagus officinalis*), rosemary (*Rosmarinus officinalis*), and some heather (*Erica carnea* 'Vivellii') for good luck. If you want to make the posies well in advance, omit the relatively short-lasting sage.
* Tuck the posies under the lip of the charger with the leaf tips all pointing out counterclockwise to create a full circle.
* Tie the linen bow loosely around the napkin and tuck in a sprig of herbs.

Alternative with *yellow*

The yellow and orange border of this charger is matched by the colors of the primula polyanthus and pansies, whose snipped-off heads are tucked into a ring of ivy sprigs arranged around the rim. As the flower heads are short-lived, cut and arrange them just before use.

Ingredients

Erica carnea 'Vivellii'

Salvia officinalis

Asparagus officinalis

Thymus vulgaris

Laurus nobilis

Rosmarinus officinalis

Fresh ideas for posies, bouquets, baskets, and flower-decorated gifts to inspire you when you wish to give something special for a birthday, anniversary, or dinner party, or just a simple, everyday offering.

FLOWERS FOR GIVING

✷ availability of ingredients ✷ longevity of display
✷✷ level of difficulty

VALENTINE HEARTS

IT SEEMS ALMOST **mandatory** to use the heart-shaped flowers and leaves of anthuriums in a Valentine's Day arrangement. Here, I have used a clear glass vase to display the rich pink spathes of *Anthurium andraeanum* 'Lunette' and the dark green leaves of *Anthurium crystallinum* and *Colocasia esculenta*.

Ingredients

Colocasia esculenta

Anthurium andraeanum 'Lunette'

Anthurium crystallinum

Alternative with *red*

While I would say that pink anthuriums are more beautiful than the red, it is undeniable that red has become the color most associated with Valentine's Day. For those people who are sticklers for tradition, here is the red version, for which I have used *Anthurium andraeanum* 'Tropical' with its deep red spathes and green spadices. The display looks good on a glass, stone, or pale wood surface, or even standing against a mirror.

DISPLAYING THE HEARTS

• Cut one leaf of *Anthurium crystallinum* and one spathe of *Anthurium andraeanum* 'Lunette' and submerge them in the water-filled glass vase. They will not last as long under the water as above, but it is fun to arrange them like this, and they will look fine in the water for three or four days.

• Take the large green leaf of *Colocasia esculenta* and twirl its tip into the mouth of the vase. The stem pokes down into the water at the back of the arrangement.

• Arrange the heart-shaped flowers and leaves above the water in a loose, asymmetrical style. The spathes have a tendency to settle upside down – the plant world has no concept of Valentine's Day.

• Remove the submerged leaf and spathe after three or four days, and substitute clean water. The display above the water will last for another ten days or so.

PRETTY IN PINK

EARLY AZALEAS AND rhododendrons provide a welcome bridge to summer. This gift basket of pink-flowering plants makes a beautiful indoor display, after which the plants can be grown outside in a flower bed or in pots. Below the standard azalea (*Rhododendron* 'Sweetheart Supreme') are the ice-pink *Rhododendron yakushimanum* 'Isadora', lovely pink winter heath (*Erica carnea* 'Vivellii'), and ivy (*Hedera*).

ARRANGING THE BASKET

- Line your chosen basket with plastic.
- Assemble the plants in their pots, then pack enough sphagnum moss into the base of the basket to raise the rims of the pots to just below the top of the basket.
- Water all the plants thoroughly by immersing them in cool, not cold, water for about ten minutes.
- Drain the pots before placing them in the basket. Keep an eye on the azalea: the first 2in (5cm) of stem should be black after watering, and the plant will need water when the stem reverts to brown.
- Position the plants to your liking, concealing the pots with more moss.
- Tie a pink ribbon around the basket when the flower arranging is complete.
- These acid-soil-loving plants can be left outside in pots of acidic soil mix, but bring them in when they flower again.

Ingredients

Rhododendron 'Sweetheart Supreme'

Rhododendron yakushimanum 'Isadora'

Hedera helix

Erica carnea 'Vivellii'

EASTER NEST

A MOSSY NEST filled with eggs and sweet-scented spring flowers makes a very special Easter gift. Surrounding the little pile of blue hen's eggs are flowers in soft pastel shades, including white and pink hyacinths (*Hyacinthus orientalis* 'White Pearl' and 'Lady Derby'), the narcissus cultivar 'Cragford', pale pink Persian buttercups (*Ranunculus asiaticus* Turban Group), ornamental cabbage (*Brassica oleracea*), Christmas roses (*Helleborus niger*), and golden-yellow polyanthus (*Primula*).

ARRANGING THE NEST

- Find an oval plastic container deep enough to hold and conceal soaked wet foam, and large enough to accommodate the eggs and all the flower stems.
- Using chicken wire, construct a firm, oval base for the container to sit on.
- Make a chicken-wire tube and fill it with sphagnum moss; the tube must be long enough to form into a ring around the container and the chicken-wire base (*see pp.324–325*). Attach the ring to the base with wire.
- Attach enough sheet moss and reindeer moss to completely cover the outside of the chicken-wire and moss ring.
- Fill the container with soaked wet foam.
- Place the eggs in a pile, on the foam, slightly off-center.
- Arrange the flowers in the soaked wet foam, placing the taller ones in groups at the back of the container. Fill in between the flowers and the eggs with a layer of moss.

Alternative with *yellows*

In this sunny alternative, the pink hyacinths and ranunculus have been omitted, and only yellow, cream, and white flowers are used. There are creamy yellow hyacinths, as well as the white ones, and white narcissus. Sprigs of fragrant yellow mimosa (*Acacia*) add to the delicious spring scents of the display.

Ingredients

Reindeer moss

Sphagnum moss

Hedera helix

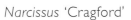

Narcissus 'Cragford'

Hyacinthus orientalis 'White Pearl'

Hyacinthus orientalis 'Lady Derby'

Ranunculus asiaticus Turban Group

Brassica oleracea

Helleborus niger

Primula Polyanthus Group

THREE POSIES

IDEAL AS A DINNER PARTY or anniversary gift, posies need just a few flowers from the garden or a florist bound into a bunch. They may be soft or bright, pale or rich, but should always be simple. An attractive tie or bow of ribbon, raffia, or strands of ivy, as here, finishes them off perfectly.

PURPLE AND SILVER

• This posy is a poem in mauve, lilac, and silver – always a magical combination.

• Pale lilac iris (*Iris* 'H.C. van Vliet') and mauve hyacinths (*Hyacinthus* 'Anna Liza') provide the main colors, with the hyacinths also adding their sweet scent.

• Spires of silver leaves and spikes of soft pussy willow (*Salix*) are used to offset the blue-purple tones of the flowers.

• A strand of raffia is tied around the stems of the posy, then over-wound and finished off with a trail of ivy.

• Stand the posy in a container of water to keep it fresh until it is presented.

INTENSE PERFUMES

• Here an unusual combination of flowers, both with rich, heady scents, produces an intoxicatingly beautiful posy.

• The clear yellow roses (*Rosa* 'Simba') are round and soft with a fruity scent.

• The enchanting, mustard-and-brown widow iris (*Hermodactylus tuberosus*) has a velvety texture and an exotic shape that is a perfect foil to the round roses, plus the added bonus of a rich, sweet scent.

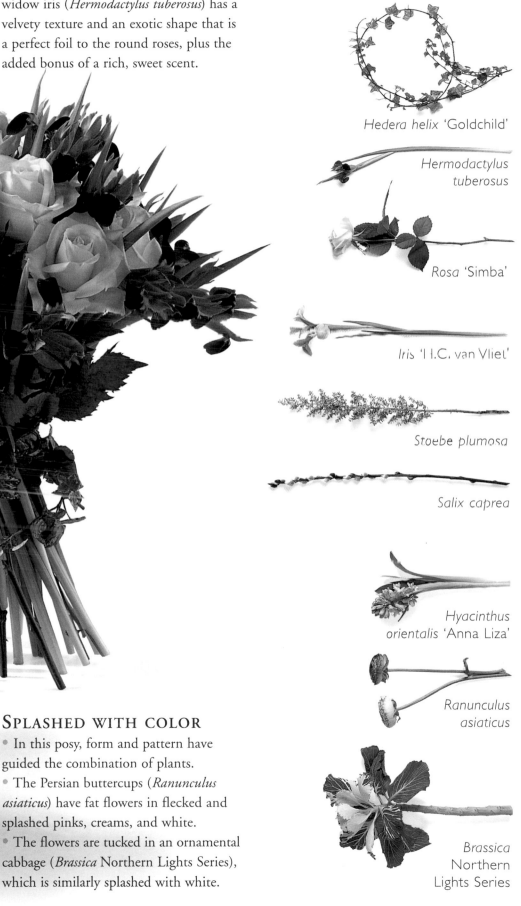

Ingredients

Hedera helix 'Goldchild'

Hermodactylus tuberosus

Rosa 'Simba'

Iris 'H.C. van Vliet'

Stoebe plumosa

Salix caprea

Hyacinthus orientalis 'Anna Liza'

Ranunculus asiaticus

Brassica Northern Lights Series

SPLASHED WITH COLOR

• In this posy, form and pattern have guided the combination of plants.

• The Persian buttercups (*Ranunculus asiaticus*) have fat flowers in flecked and splashed pinks, creams, and white.

• The flowers are tucked in an ornamental cabbage (*Brassica* Northern Lights Series), which is similarly splashed with white.

BOX OF SPRING BULBS

SNOWDROPS (*Galanthus*), the first harbingers of spring, push up even through frost and snow to show their shining white, nodding flowers. Blooming later in the garden, but available in shops from early winter, are sweet-scented hyacinths (*Hyacinthus orientalis*), in delectable fresh colors, and diminutive perennial daisies (*Bellis perennis*). Combine these three plants to make a growing gift that epitomizes spring. When they fade, plant them out in the garden for a display next year.

Alternative with *muscari*

The snowdrops will be the first to fade, but there are several other spring flowers that can be substituted. Try primulas in a vast range of colors, little irises in yellow or purple, or these blue, butter-scented grape hyacinths *(Muscari)*. If they are not available potted, use cut flowers in glass holders concealed in the moss.

Ingredients

Hyacinthus orientalis 'Lady Derby'

Galanthus nivalis

Bellis perennis cultivar

PLANTING UP

- Plant the bulbs in pots well in advance; have a few more than you will need to allow for variations in flowering times.
- Line the box with plastic (*see p.308*) and stand the pots in it, arranging them in groups with the tallest at the back and the smallest clustered to one side at the front.

- Tuck fresh sphagnum moss between and over the pots to conceal them.
- The hyacinths may need some support as the flowers open and become top-heavy.
- This display lasts best in a cool place; it should last for up to three weeks if it is placed outside, perhaps on a table, where

the flowers can easily be enjoyed from a kitchen or living-room window indoors.
- If standing the box outside, make drainage holes in the liner to prevent the plants from becoming waterlogged; if you bring the box indoors, stand it on a tray to catch any drips.

PEACHES AND CREAM

WHEN TRYING TO THINK of a present that is just right, flowers can usually provide the answer. Best of all is an arranged basket of flowers, which requires no effort on the part of the recipient apart from filling with water. Here, nestling among the leaves of *Hosta* 'Francee', I have arranged peonies (*Paeonia* 'Baroness Schröder'), roses (*Rosa* 'Champagne Cocktail'), astilbe, and eustoma (*Eustoma grandiflorum* Heidi Series) in peaches, cream, and champagne – a color mix that is elegant and always easy to place.

MAKING UP THE BASKET

• Buy peony and rose buds that are just showing color: if the buds are too tight, they may not open (*see p.310*).

• Condition the roses (*see pp.310–313*) and remove most of their leaves.

• Place the astilbe in hot water for a few minutes, then leave in cold water for several hours before arranging.

• Place a piece of soaked wet foam inside a bowl that fits snugly inside the basket. Prop the foam up at a slight angle with some crumpled newspaper.

• Starting with the longest stems, push them into the foam across one end of the basket. Layer in the rest of the flowers and foliage to create an asymmetrical display. Leave the handle of the basket visible.

• Attach a decorative bow (*see p.335*).

Ingredients

Eustoma grandiflorum Heidi Series

Hosta 'Francee'

Rosa 'Champagne Cocktail'

Paeonia 'Baroness Schröder'

Astilbe 'Irrlicht'

PETAL PAPER

ATTRACTIVE WRAPPING paper is often hard to find and very expensive. A simple way to create an individual look is to use flower petals held between two sheets of cellophane over a wrapping of plain paper. Just a couple of flowers should suffice: the best are roses (*Rosa*), carnations (*Dianthus*), poppies (*Papaver*), or others with fairly thin and flattish petals. Add a gauzy bow, and in just a few minutes you'll have produced a stunning wrapping.

MAKE THE WRAPPING

• Cut two sheets of cellophane and one of plain paper to the right size for the box.
• Lay one sheet of cellophane on a flat surface covered with newspaper and spray evenly with a clear spray adhesive. Lay the petals on the paper, using fewer where there will be folds. Spray again with adhesive, and lay the second piece of cellophane on top.
• Wrap the gift with the plain paper and the glued cellophane. Bind with ribbon in a harmonizing color and attach a bow.

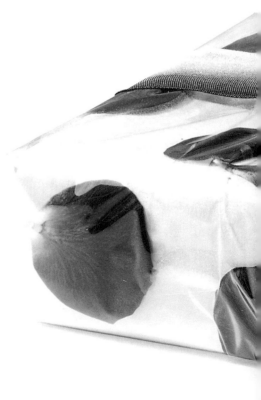

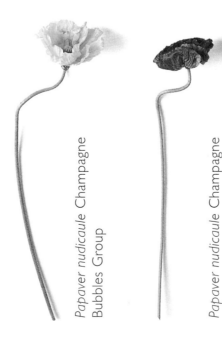

Ingredients

Anemone coronaria De Caen Group

Rosa 'Prima Donna'

Papaver nudicaule Champagne Bubbles Group

Papaver nudicaule Champagne Bubbles Group

PINK POSY

A BEAUTIFULLY PERFUMED posy is a very special present to give; make it even more so by including some flowers from your garden. Grow as many scented plants as possible – flowers like jasmine (*Jasminum*), lavender (*Lavandula*), and honeysuckle (*Lonicera*), as well as herbs such as mint (*Mentha*) or rosemary (*Rosmarinus*). These flowers could convey a message: pinks (*Dianthus*) are for boldness, chrysanthemums for love, and ferns for fascination – but lavender is for mistrust.

Alternative with *white*

White *Dianthus*, rosemary, phlox, gypsophila, and chincherinchee make up another perfumed gift. 'Mrs. Sinkins' is perhaps the best fragrant white pink, but 'Haytor White' has a delicious clove scent. The perfume of phlox is highly individual, and gypsophila has a strong honey fragrance. This posy could be carried by a bridesmaid at an all-white wedding.

COMBINING ELEMENTS

• Try to use a variety of different scents that smell delicious when they are brought together: spicy pinks, heady lavender, and aromatic chrysanthemums.

• This perfumed posy subtly combines a range of colors from pale mauve to deep pink, as well as variations in texture from the flat-headed pinks to the winged lavender and spiky chrysanthemums, giving it great depth and interest.

• Surround the flowers with a unifying ruff of fern (here *Rumohra*) leaves, rather than their own foliage.

• To build the posy, bind in the flowers one by one using thread (*see p.328*), and cover the binding with a ribbon.

• Advise the recipient to snip the stems and put the posy into water as soon as it is received. It can be left as it is or rearranged at a more convenient time.

• A small posy like this is perfect for a bridesmaid to carry.

Ingredients

Rumohra adiantiformis

Dianthus 'Cranmere Pool'

Dianthus 'Valda Wyatt'

Lavandula stoechas

Chrysanthemum "Pink Bigou"

AUTUMN BOUQUET

FLOWERS MAKE welcome gifts for hosts, but they can take time to unwrap and arrange. This bouquet of red cockscombs (*Celosia*), pink zinnias, and scented cream carnations (*Dianthus* 'Terra') requires just a quick snip of the stems before placing in a simple container, so that the flowers can be enjoyed right away.

MAKING THE BOUQUET

- Condition the flowers (*see pp.310–313*) well in advance, but try to compose the bouquet just before presenting it.
- Gather the conditioned flowers one by one into a round bunch and tie with string, wire, or raffia (*see p.332*).
- Cut the stems (at an angle) so that they are all roughly the same length.
- Remove all lower leaves that would

otherwise be below water level.
- Pleat a length of colored crepe paper into 1in (2.5cm) vertical folds. Gather the paper around the bunch so that the top forms a ruff just overlapping the flowers. Squeeze the lower half of the pleated crepe paper into a tube around the stems.
- Tie where the paper flares out (roughly over the tie of the flower bunch) and finish with a ribbon or bow (*see p.335*).

Ingredients

Rumex sanguineus

Dahlia 'John Prior'

Callistephus chinensis Princess Series

Celosia argentea Olympia Series

Dianthus 'Terra'

Zinnia elegans

ANNIVERSARY BASKET

BASKETS OF FLOWERS make wonderful presents to celebrate anniversaries, and it is easy to choose appropriate flowers at any time of the year for ruby, sapphire, coral, silver, and golden wedding celebrations. This gift for a silver wedding anniversary is held in an oval, rustic basket and consists of a mixture of country flowers, such as Queen Anne's lace (*Anthriscus sylvestris*), Michaelmas daisy (*Aster novi-belgii*), and China aster (*Callistephus chinensis*) together with the seedheads of montbretia (*Crocosmia*) and exotic little *Dendrobium* orchids. A silvery white bow completes the arrangement perfectly.

Ingredients

Callistephus chinensis Princess Series

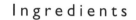

Dendrobium bigibbum

Anthriscus sylvestris

Crocosmia sp.

Aster novi-belgii 'Mount Everest'

MAINTAINING THE DISPLAY

• The basket is best lined with a plastic bowl but, if you cannot find a suitably sized one, use a plastic lining (*see p.308*). Wedge well-soaked wet foam into the container or plastic lining, and fill with water before you arrange the flowers.
• Check frequently to make sure that there is plenty of water in the container; this is a particularly thirsty arrangement.
• To water a densely packed, small display like this, drop ice cubes between the flowers, so that they melt into the foam.
• Remove individual flower heads from the orchid stems as they fade.
• The montbretia (*Crocosmia*) seedheads are particularly long lasting.

Alternative with *red*

The same basket here holds an arrangement for a ruby wedding anniversary: wonderful rich red, perfumed freesias mingle with striped red-and-white dahlias, velvety celosias, and sprays of scarlet *Crocosmia* 'Lucifer'. The flowers of this montbretia will not last as long as the seedheads, but they can easily be removed from the display as they fade.

FLORAL GIFT WRAPS

HALF THE FUN OF GIVING and receiving presents is in their presentation – the excitement and anticipation of receiving a beautifully wrapped present is tremendous. Black and white wrappings are always extremely stylish: here I have used black and white papers and black-edged gold ribbons to wrap and decorate a bottle of champagne and a gift box. These sophisticated presentations are enhanced by tucking a few white-tinged green roses into the paper folds and under the ribbons.

WRAPPING THE GIFTS

• To wrap a champagne bottle, take a sheet of wrapping paper measuring 13in × 20in, making sure that it is the same color or design on both sides. With a pencil, lightly mark points A–J as indicated on the diagram (*right*).

• Fold the bottom left-hand corner of the paper forward along line B–E.

• Turn the paper back along line A–D.

• Fold the right-hand end of the paper forward along line I–F.

• Turn the paper back along line J–G.

• Place the bottle on the folded paper with its top close to the peak at point C.

• Wrap the right-hand end of the paper loosely around the bottle, then fold the left-hand, triangular-shaped paper over this. Secure in place with adhesive tape.

• Attach a ribbon bow at the front of the wrapped bottle (*see p.335*).

• Fold the excess paper under the bottom of the bottle and secure with tape.

• Tuck four roses with a few leaves on the stems into the fold at the left-hand side of the bottle, so that their heads curve around its neck.

• Wrap a gift box in the usual way, neatly folding in the end paper and finishing with with a ribbon tie. Lay two roses across the point where the ribbons cross, then attach a matching bow, using the ribbon ends to secure the roses and the bow.

Ingredients

Rosa 'Emerald'

0in   6in   10in

C   I   J

8in B

3rd fold over

4th fold back

1st fold over

5in A

2nd fold back

0in   D E   F G   H

0in   8in 10in   13in 14in

If our plant materials are
to realize their peak potential, we
need to treat them with care and
consideration. Lasting quality can
be achieved by simple conditioning, which

PRACTICAL TECHNIQUES

is clearly explained in this section. Here,

too, are ways to preserve plant material,

how to make garlands, wreaths, and

special displays, and how to wire flowers

and foliage for them.

TOOLS AND EQUIPMENT

UNLIKE MANY CRAFTS that demand the acquisition of expensive pieces of equipment before you can get started, arranging flowers requires very few tools. In fact the simpler projects often require little more than a pair of florist's scissors and some wet and dry foam. If you decide to try some of the slightly more advanced projects, then the other tools and props illustrated below may prove useful. Flowers and containers are your main ingredients, of course, and having a good supply of vases to choose from will be your greatest asset. Before starting a project, always make sure that everything you need is on hand.

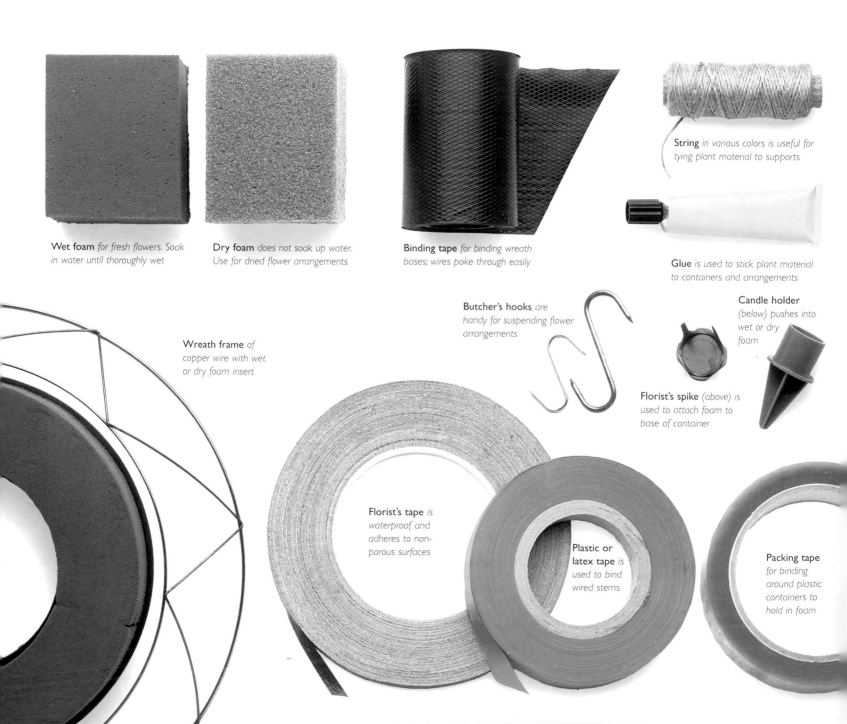

Wet foam *for fresh flowers. Soak in water until thoroughly wet*

Dry foam *does not soak up water. Use for dried flower arrangements*

Binding tape *for binding wreath bases; wires poke through easily*

String *in various colors is useful for tying plant material to supports*

Glue *is used to stick plant material to containers and arrangements*

Wreath frame *of copper wire with wet or dry foam insert*

Butcher's hooks *are handy for suspending flower arrangements*

Candle holder *(below) pushes into wet or dry foam*

Florist's spike *(above) is used to attach foam to base of container*

Florist's tape *is waterproof and adheres to non-porous surfaces*

Plastic or latex tape *is used to bind wired stems*

Packing tape *for binding around plastic containers to hold in foam*

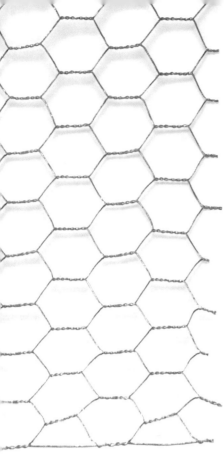

Chicken wire *can be bought in 1in (2.5cm) and ½in (1.25cm) gauges*

Heavy-gauge floral wires *are needed for wiring larger flower heads and plant material*

Medium-gauge floral wire *is used for wiring medium-weight material*

Thin-gauge floral wires *are ideal for wiring small single flowers and leaves*

Spool wire *is used for fine work such as wiring single flowers to floral wires*

Rose wire *is fine silver wire for wedding work*

Florist's scissors *are useful for cutting stems and removing leaves and thorns*

Sheet moss *provides useful background material*

Pruners *are essential for cutting heavier woody stems*

Sphagnum moss *is used for filling chicken-wire bases*

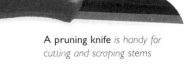

A pruning knife *is handy for cutting and scraping stems*

Spanish moss *is available dyed (left) or natural (right)*

Glue gun and glue sticks *provide a neat method of attaching materials to containers. Cool-melt models are safest to use, but hot-melt is stronger*

Bun moss *can be used fresh and preserved*

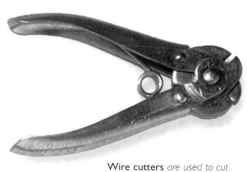

Wire cutters *are used to cut floral wires and chicken wire*

CONTAINERS

AN ESSENTIAL REQUIREMENT in the flower arranger's supply cabinet is a few basic, well-shaped containers. Vases with rectangular or trumpet profiles are the easiest to use, as these shapes hold flowers without the need for foam, pinholder, or wire support. For everyday use, I find that glass containers are the most adaptable; a group of three rectangular glass vases, similar to those used on pp.132–133, can be used either singly or in combination, according to how many flowers you are displaying.

TYPES OF CONTAINER

Glass, metal, ceramic, terracotta, stone, and basketware receptacles have long been the traditional containers in which to display flowers, but I like to use a variety of "found" objects, such as old boxes, saucepans, kettles, cups, and drinking glasses, as well as conventional vases. What you should always look for are containers that work together with the flowers to produce arrangements that look both natural and inevitable. Of course, practicality must also be borne in mind: stone, for example, can be heavy to move, while containers that require plastic liners – such as those made of wicker and terracotta – could possibly spring a leak and damage a valuable piece of furniture.

GLASS provides an extremely sympathetic material for vases, and I love to see flower stems in clear glass vases. Since glassware surfaces are shiny, however, the material is less appropriate for rustic arrangements.

METAL containers, such as those made of brass, copper, bronze, pewter, aluminum, iron, and lead, work particularly well for larger displays. However, small silver or copper beakers and jugs also make elegant receptacles.

TERRACOTTA, with its warm, earthy look, is ideal for rustic arrangements. One of my favorite materials is weather-distressed terracotta, when minerals have leached through the surface and moss has taken hold.

CERAMIC is, along with glass, the most popular medium for vases. Stoneware can carry exceptionally beautiful glazes, but the lower-fired, more porous pieces need to be well glazed to prevent them from leaking.

BASKETWORK containers made of wicker, vine, and twigs are the most rustic of all containers. If you are using them for fresh flowers, they must be lined with either a rigid or flexible plastic liner (*see p.308*).

ADAPTING CONTAINERS

INCREASING HEIGHT

Flower stems do not always come in just the lengths that we require, which may be a problem when creating large-scale projects or using deep containers. As an alternative to using flower funnels (*right*) when longer lengths are required, I sometimes improvise by using the tubes that orchids come in, pushing a stem into a tube filled with water, then attaching the tube plus flower to a strong stem or stick higher up in the arrangement. An alternative to raising the inner base of a deep container (*below*) is to increase the length of stems by wiring them to floral wires (*see pp.318–319*). This was done with the violets on pp.76–77, to charming effect. These last two methods are, of course, possible only when the container being used is opaque rather than translucent.

FLOWER FUNNELS can be pushed straight into the soaked wet foam in which you are arranging flowers or, if you need even more height, they can be wired to lengths of bamboo inserted into the arrangement. Make the funnels invisible by smothering them in foliage.

RAISE THE BASE of a deep container, such as the rhubarb forcer shown here, by placing two bricks inside it, then placing a vase on top of the bricks so that its rim comes to just below the rim of the outer container. This reduces the length of flower required by some 9–10in (23–25cm).

RIGID LINERS FOR CONTAINERS

The best way to line any container that is likely to leak is with a rigid inner plastic liner. This is particularly true for very large arrangements, where you should always use a rigid liner. Florists usually stock a range of liners in various sizes, but you may be able to improvise with a plastic or glass bowl from the kitchen.

1 SELECT A RIGID liner that either fits or is slightly smaller than the cavity in your container. Here a plastic utility bowl is a good fit for a terracotta garden urn.

2 MAKE SURE THAT the liner is securely wedged into the container by packing any space between them with tightly crumpled newspaper or wedges of dry foam.

PLASTIC LINERS

If you are unable to find a suitable rigid liner to fit a small- or medium-sized container, and are concerned that it may not be watertight, line it with a strong piece of plastic. Plastic garden bags provide an inexpensive source of lining material but must be used double to give adequate protection.

1 CUT THE PLASTIC to line the container, leaving a generous overlap that will be trimmed away later. Tuck the plastic loosely down around the sides of the container. In this case a double layer of plastic bag is being used to line a woven basket.

2 WEDGE SOAKED wet foam into the plastic-lined container. Trim away the excess plastic to just below the container rim. If the liner is likely to be visible through the weave of the basket, line it first with moss.

3 WHEN ARRANGING the flowers, be careful not to pierce the plastic with their stems. Lining the basket with moss before inserting the plastic will help prevent it from being punctured by sharp ends of wicker.

ADAPTING UTENSILS

Large, decorative flower containers can be prohibitively expensive, especially if they need to be heavy enough to stabilize a large arrangement. One way of keeping down the costs is to adapt an everyday household utensil, such as a bucket. The bucket shape is particularly good for the type of large flower arrangements that are required for churches or concert halls. Although it is not particularly attractive in itself, once it is wrapped with moss or hay, as here, the humble bucket is transformed into an interesting and appropriate container. This technique can, of course, be applied to any usefully sized container in need of disguise or adaptation. Large terracotta or plastic flowerpots, for example, are relatively inexpensive and could be dressed up in this way for a grand occasion.

THE HAY-WRAPPED container lends a countrified air to this arrangement and works well with the 3ft- (1m-) high fountain of lilies, roses, and chestnut leaves.

1 IF THE HAY contains long strands, it will be easy to lay out as a long rectangle and roll around the container in one piece. If it consists of smaller pieces, cover the bucket section by section, securing each piece temporarily with lengths of raffia tied around the container.

2 ONCE THE BUCKET is covered, tie three lengths of raffia tightly around the container so that the hay is held securely in place. Tie the raffia ends in decorative bows. Remove any temporary raffia underties that were used to hold the hay sections in position.

WOODY STEMS

The branches of flowering shrubs such as lilac and mock orange (as well as of much foliage) have woody stems that take up water with difficulty. To assist the process, remove the lower leaves from each stem and cut the end at a sharp angle. Hammer about 1in (2.5cm) of the stem end and scrape the stems a little above the crushed sections. This will help increase the surface area for water uptake.

MILKY-SAPPED STEMS

Flowers such as milkweed, spurge, and poppies, whose stems contain milky sap, are best heat-sealed before arranging in water. After removing the lower leaves, cut straight across the stems with a sharp knife and hold the bottom 1in (2.5cm) in a flame until it starts to burn. Do not cut the stems again after burning – the flowers are now ready to be arranged in water.

HOLLOW STEMS

Some flowers, such as amaryllis, lupine, delphinium, and calla lily, have large, hollow stems that can be filled with water to help them last longer in arrangements. Once the stems are filled and plugged, leave them to stand in a bucket of water to take up water in the usual way. As an alternative to plugging the stem with cotton, after filling with water, place your thumb over the end and upend the stem into a vase filled with water.

1 HOLD THE FLOWER upside down and fill the hollow stem with cold water. Note that the stem has been cut at an angle to create a larger surface area for water uptake.

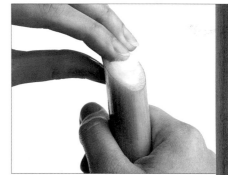

2 SEAL THE STEM with a moist cotton plug to keep the water in and still allow water uptake once the flowers have been arranged.

STRAIGHTENING TULIP STEMS

It is possible to improve the condition of forced tulips, whose weak stems often droop in an awkward way. Remove some of the leaves, then cut the stems at an angle with a sharp knife. Make a vertical slit in the stem to further increase the area capable of taking up water, then follow the techniques described below.

PRICK THE STEM
If tulips have been out of water for some time, air may have become trapped in the stems, preventing water uptake and causing the flowers to wilt prematurely. To release trapped air, carefully prick the stem of each tulip with a fine, sterilized needle just below the flowerhead.

1 AFTER PREPARING THE STEMS, wrap the tulips in waxed florist's tissue, which will retain its rigidity in water. You could also use brown paper or newspaper.

2 STAND THE TULIPS in cold water for several hours. To assist the straightening process and to strengthen the stems, add flower food to the water.

HOT WATER TREATMENT

To counteract drooping, place the prepared flowers in a deep, supportive holder containing about 2in (5cm) of very hot (not quite boiling) water. Leave for five minutes, then fill with cold water. Allow the flowers to recover before arranging them.

REMOVING POLLEN

Many lilies carry pollen that can stain badly. Although they look best with their pollen intact, it is wise to remove it, especially if the flowers are to be placed in a position where someone could brush against them. It is best to remove pollen before it develops; it is then easy to grasp all the stamens between two fingers and pull off the pollen sacs in one quick movement.

COLD WATER TREATMENT

It is sensible to prepare all flowers before embarking on any arrangements. Simple measures, such as adding flower food to the vase water or refreshing flowers in deep, cool water, may add considerably to the longevity of your arrangements.

FLOWER FOOD
To revive drooping blooms, wrap the flower heads in paper, stand the flowers in warm water, and add a package of florist's flower food. Leave for several hours while the warm water eliminates air locks.

MAINTAINING FRESHNESS
Place flowers that are ready to use in a bucket or other large container part-filled with cool water. Leave for two hours or so before beginning an arrangement.

PRESERVING MATERIAL

PRESERVED FLOWERS and leaves have a unique, muted beauty that is reminiscent of the colors in old tapestries. Use their unique qualities to create quietly glowing creations, rather than trying to emulate fresh flower arrangements. Do resist the temptation to keep preserved flower arrangements for too long: after three months, light exposure causes them to lose their color, and they will begin to look tired and dusty. Of the three methods of preserving plant material that are described here, air drying is the easiest and, I think, the most successful.

AIR DRYING

DRYING IN A VASE

Many flowers will air dry if simply left to stand in a vase. After conditioning the flowers (*see pp.310–313*), place them in a vase filled with about 1in (2.5cm) of water and leave them while the water dries out. Baby's breath, sea thistle, globe thistle, yarrow, strawflower, larkspur, grasses, and beech leaves are all suitable for this drying method. Roses and delphiniums dry this way too – as I find sometimes by default. Although air drying plant material in a vase is not as effective as hanging bunches up to dry, it is a simple technique and can be successful with the right flowers.

Good Air-drying Material   V=Vase H=Hang

Acanthus (Bear's breeches)	V/H		*Fagus* (Beech)	V/H
Achillea (Yarrow)	V/H		*Gypsophila* (Baby's breath)	V/H
Allium (Onion)	V/H		*Lavandula* (Lavender)	H
Astilbe (Astilbe)	H		*Moluccella* (Bells of Ireland)	H
Calendula (Marigold)	H		*Monarda* (Bergamot)	H
Centaurea cyanus (Cornflower)	H		*Nigella* (Love-in-a-mist)	V/H
Consolida (Larkspur)	V/H		*Paeonia* (Peony)	H
Cortaderia (Pampas grass)	H		*Physalis* (Chinese lanterns)	V/H
Delphinium (Delphinium)	H		*Rosa* (Rose)	H
Echinops (Globe thistle)	V/H		*Salvia viridis* (Clary sage)	H
Eryngium (Sea thistle)	V/H		*Solidago* (Golden rod)	V/H

HANGING BUNCHES

This very effective method of air drying requires a cool, dry, airy, dark place, such as a mudroom or cellar, in which to hang the bunches while they slowly dry. The best time to pick flowers for drying is late morning on a dry day.

1 REMOVE ALL LOWER leaves from the flowers; squashed leaves lead to rotting, which will ruin your dried flowers. Flowers need to be just opening, in good condition, and with dry stems.

2 TIE SMALL BUNCHES of the flowers together, making sure that they are not rubbing against each other and that there are no leaves caught in the tie. Leave a long length of string free to hang up the bunches.

3 CHOOSE A SUITABLE drying place and hang the bunches from a rail so that they do not touch. Leave for between one and three weeks until the flowers are thoroughly dry.

OTHER TECHNIQUES

PRESERVING PLANTS WITH GLYCERIN

Many flowers can be preserved using glycerin, but the best results are obtained with foliage. Condition the material (*see pp.310–313*), then place it in a large container in a solution of 40 percent glycerin to 60 percent hot water. When beads of glycerin show on the flowers or leaves, the material is ready. Plants tend to lose color when preserved; to remedy this, add some natural dye to the solution, matching the color of the flowers or leaves.

Stand stems in a glycerin solution

Good Plants for Glycerin

Acer (Maple)
Choisya (Mexican orange blossom)
Fagus (Beech)
Eucalyptus (Gum)
Fatsia (Japanese fatsia)
Ferns (various)
Gaultheria shallon (Salal, Shallon)
Hedera (Ivy)

Hydrangea macrophylla (Hydrangea)
Liquidambar (Sweetgum)
Moluccella laevis (Bells of Ireland)
Prunus sargentii (Sargent cherry)
Quercus robur (Common oak)
Quercus ilex (Holm oak)
Selaginella kraussiana (Spikemoss)
Senecio 'Sunshine' (Senecio)

PRESERVING PLANTS WITH DESICCANTS

A number of desiccants (drying agents) can be used to dry flowers that are not too fleshy petaled or stemmed. The best results are obtained with silica gel, but this must be handled with great care, using a mask and rubber gloves. Dried borax or alum with fine sand will also coax the moisture out of flowers and leaves, but the process is slower than with silica gel.

Good Plants for Desiccants

Alstroemeria (Peruvian lily)
Convallaria (Lily-of-the-valley)
Dahlia (Dahlia)
Eustoma (Lisianthius)
Freesia (Freesia)
Gerbera (Gerbera)
Gladiolus (Gladiolus)

Lilium (Lily)
Narcissus (Daffodil)
Paeonia (Peony)
Ranunculus (Buttercup)
Rosa (Rose)
Tulipa (Tulip)
Zinnia (Zinnia)

USING SILICA GEL

Buy silica gel as very fine crystals (larger ones mark petals). Be sure the gel is dry by putting it in a low oven for several hours. Place a thin layer of gel in an airtight box, lay the flowers on the gel, adding more until the flowers are submerged. Cover for two days only, since flowers will crumble if overdried.

PRESERVING PLANTS WITH BORAX AND ALUM

Mix three parts of either borax or alum with two parts fine sand. Be sure that the mixture is dry (but not hot) before use by placing in a low oven for several hours. Follow the same procedure as for silica gel, but wait at least ten days before checking whether the plant material is dry.

STEAMING FLOWERS

Revive dried flowers that are squashed or crumpled by holding them in the steam from a boiling kettle. The petals will start to flop down with moisture within minutes. When this movement begins, hold the flowers away from the steam and upside down. Blow gently up into the petals to separate them out. Keep blowing until the petals are set in their new, refreshed shape.

Flagging petals are revived

STORING DRIED FLOWERS

The cardboard boxes that flowers are sold in at markets are ideal for storing dried flowers, and these should be obtainable from your local florist. Layer bunches of flowers into the boxes, supporting the flower stems just below their heads with crumpled tissue or waxed paper. Make sure that the flowers are not crushed or overcrowded, since they are quite brittle when dry. Replace the lids and store the boxes in a cool, dry place.

SUGARING FLOWERS

Edible sugared flowers are very simple to make and provide delightful cake decorations that will keep for up to three days. The prettiest flowers to use are violets, roses, and primroses; tuberous begonia flower petals can also be prepared in this way. Because the process uses raw egg white, these sugared flowers should not be eaten by pregnant women or elderly people.

As a cake decoration, arrange petals to resemble flowers

1 LIGHTLY BEAT an egg white in a small bowl until the egg is broken down but not frothy. With a fine paintbrush, coat the petals on both sides with the beaten egg white.

2 USING A STRAINER, sprinkle the petals with granulated sugar. Place gently on a fine mesh cake rack or waxed paper and leave in a warm, dry place until dry.

WIRING CONES AND FRUITS

Most plant material is straightforward to wire in the ways already described (*see pp.318–19*). Pinecones (which I like to use in autumn and winter arrangements) and fruits require a different approach, however. Many fruits can be wired by pushing a floral wire through from the stalk end; when it comes through the other end, bend the top into a short "U" shape and draw the wire back through the fruit. This works well with small citrus fruits, apples, and crabapples. Wiring a cone is described below.

Sweet chestnut

Pinecone

Red apple

1 **PASS A PIECE OF FLORAL WIRE** of a suitable weight to bear the pinecone across the stalk end of the cone, just where it starts to curve in. Wedge the wire into the first band of woody scales, leaving 2in (5cm) jutting out.

2 **WIND THE FLORAL WIRE** around the cone, pulling it in toward the center, underneath the woody scales. Continue winding the wire around, under the scales, until the short and long ends overlap.

3 **TWIST THE TWO ENDS** of wire together for several turns, then pull the long end of the wire down under the cone so that it appears to emerge from the base of the cone. Snip off the short end of the wire.

USING WIRE HAIRPINS

Made from sections of floral wire, "U"-shaped pins are useful for attaching moss or other covering materials to chicken-wire frames, to florist's foam, or for holding pieces of plant material in position on frames or bases. They are also invaluable when creating swags or wreaths. As with all wiring techniques, choose the lightest possible wires to do the job efficiently.

Moss pinned around candle base

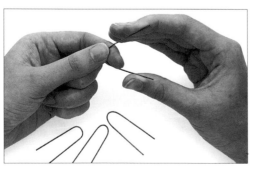

1 **CUT LENGTHS OF WIRE** so that they are long enough to push deeply into your frame once they are bent into a "U" shape or, for heavier attachments, will go through the frame with enough length to be bent back.

2 **LAY PIECES** of covering material, such as moss, against the frame and pin them in with the pins. Attach single plant or flower stems to frames or bases with two pins.

WIRING FOR SHAPE

Although it is always best to choose flowers and foliage for their natural shapes, it can sometimes be useful to give very straight stems more character by wiring them into different shapes. Bear in mind, however, that only the gentlest curves look convincing. If the stem will not be seen, simply twist a floral wire or spool wire in a spiral down its length and then gently bend it into a curve.

GLUEING MATERIAL

A glue gun is useful when creating dried flower arrangements, though it can also be used for attaching fresh flowers – to twigs or sapling branches, for example. There are two types of glue gun: they look the same, but one type operates at a high temperature and gives a very firm bond; the other works with a cooler melting glue and is therefore safer to use, although the bond is not as secure.

USING A GLUE GUN
Preheat the glue gun. Clean the surfaces to be glued, then apply a small amount of glue to each surface. Hold the surfaces together for about one minute until the glue has set.

HOLLOW STEMS
Flowers with hollow stems, such as snapdragons and larkspur, simply require a floral wire pushed up the stem as far as it will go. You can then gently ease the stem into a natural-looking curve to suit your arrangement.

REPAIRING STEMS
Repair a broken stem by inserting a length of floral wire into each end of the break and pushing the pieces together. For the flower to survive, however, the broken stem must be below water level so that the flower can continue to take up water.

A wired, hollow stem can be bent into a gentle curve

Repair a broken stem with a wire reinforcement

Attach plant material with glue gun

MAKING BASES

IF YOU PLAN TO MAKE A GARLAND to frame a window or doorway, to hang in swags against a wall or table front, or to spiral around a column or pole, it is best to assemble it on a flexible base. Wire, heavy twine, light cord, or soft rope are all suitable materials for constructing flexible bases for dainty, lightweight garlands of fresh flowers. Garlands of heavy plant material or solid-shape designs, however, are best made on a rigid base constructed from chicken wire and moss (*see pp.324–325*).

FLEXIBLE BASE

The basic technique for making a flexible garland base is fairly straightforward, but when you set out to make one, bear in mind that it can take several hours to complete a long garland. Much of a project's success will depend on the initial selection and preparation of the flowers and plant materials that you use. Choose a mixture of flowers and plant materials that will blend well together along the length of the garland, and check that you have all the tools and equipment that you will need on hand. Cut flowers and leaves into 3in (7cm) lengths, then wire thin stems with floral wires (*see pp.318–319*). Separate out combinations of the material to bind into the small, individual bunches that will make up the garland.

Fine floral wires

Spool wire

Ivy sprigs

Florist's scissors

Wired spray chrysanthemums

Wired grape hyacinths

Wired anemones

Wired spray carnations

Heavy twine

A fine turn of the wire holds the bunch in place

1 HAVING MADE UP small individual bunches of the prepared flowers and leaves for the garland, place the first bunch near one end of a length of heavy twine. Bind some spool wire two or three times around the bunch and the twine to secure them firmly.

2 TO PREVENT the wire from unraveling, pass the wire spool back up between the individual flower bunch and the twine, then pull it down firmly on the other side. Form a hanging loop at the end of the wire to suspend the garland once it is completed.

3 PLACE A SECOND prepared bunch with its head overlapping the stems of the first. Attach to the twine as described in Steps 1 and 2. Continue adding bunches to the end of the twine. Reverse the directions of the final bunch so the garland has flowery ends.

Trailing variegated ivy is always a good choice for combining with flowers in garlands

The bright blue flowers of grape hyacinth have a sweet buttery scent

RIGID WREATH BASE

MAKING THE BASE

The most versatile type of rigid base is a tube made of chicken wire rolled around a solid stuffing of dry sphagnum moss. Such a base should be used for wreaths and for heavy garlands and swags. To make a rigid base for a wreath, cut a length of 1in- (2.5cm-) gauge chicken wire, 2in (5cm) longer than the desired circumference of the finished wreath and about 8in (20cm) across. Once you have rolled the moss-filled wire into a tube (*see Steps 1–2, below*), secure it along its length with the wire ends. To cut down on preparation time, you may like to consider using the pre-made rigid base wreaths that are available from good flower shops and garden centers.

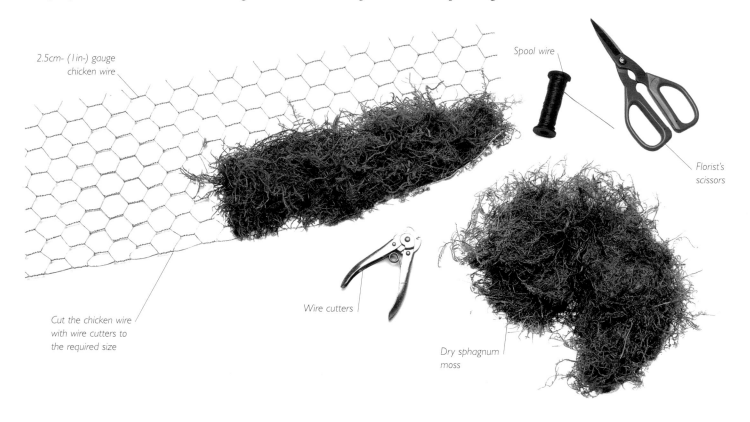

2.5cm- (1in-) gauge
chicken wire

Spool wire

Florist's
scissors

Cut the chicken wire
with wire cutters to
the required size

Wire cutters

Dry sphagnum
moss

Press the roll
into shape as
you go

Bend the tube
until the two
ends meet

Lace the ends
of the ring
together with
spool wire

1 SLIGHTLY FLATTEN the chicken wire and lay it on a firm surface. Place the moss along one side, distributing it evenly. Starting from one end, roll the moss-filled wire into a firm tube, molding it into shape as you go.

2 SEAL THE TUBE by bending the cut ends of the chicken wire into the moss. Hold the tube with both hands and, working from one end, bend it around so that the two ends fit together to form a ring.

3 COMPLETE THE RING by running spool wire back and forth from one end of the tube to the other and pulling gently until you achieve a seamless join. Neatly tie off the ends of the wire so that none is protruding.

COMPLETING THE WREATH

After constructing the rigid base, the next step is to cover it with more moss to obscure the chicken wire. Choose from Spanish moss, which has delicate, threadlike fronds in natural gray-green or dyed dark green colors; bun moss, whose cushionlike mounds retain their fresh green color so well; or sheet moss – a variety with a natural color that makes a good background material for busy arrangements. Use wire hairpins (*see p.320*) to secure the moss to the base.

Moss-filled chicken wire base

Heavy floral wire for loop

Florist's scissors

Floral wires for hairpins

Dried peonies   Wired cones   Dried wired roses   Dried strawflowers   Spanish moss

Hanging loop

1 BEND MEDIUM FLORAL WIRES into "U"-shaped hairpins with which to secure the moss to the base. Push the pins through the moss into the base, bending the pin ends back into the base on the other side of the wreath.

2 TWIST A STRONG FLORAL WIRE in the middle to form a hanging loop. Push the wire ends through the base from back to front. Bend the wire ends back into the base to secure.

Spanish moss

3 PREPARE THE PLANT MATERIAL, wiring fruit or cones (*see p.320*) and refreshing dried flowers (*see p.317*) as necessary. Arrange the background elements (here wired cones) in a well-balanced but informal pattern.

4 PIN IN the next layer (here wired bunches of preserved ivy, strawflowers, and dried roses), keeping the colors evenly distributed. Finish with the largest flower heads – here single heads of dried peonies.

WRAPPINGS AND TRIMMINGS

THE SECRET OF MAKING a special gift even more special lies in the presentation. I am always amazed at the difference some attractive wrapping paper or cellophane and a bow can make: even the smallest posy takes on a jewel-like quality when beautifully wrapped. I keep a supply of ribbons, papers, and cellophane so that I can quickly wrap flowers that I have bought or picked to give as a present.

CELLOPHANE WRAPPING

PLEATED RUFF

This is a very simple but attractive method for wrapping a posy. A sheet of cellophane is pleated along its length, then drawn up around the bunch of flowers. The cellophane is then fanned out to form a pleated ruff surrounding the flowers.

1 FOR A BUNCH of flowers that is approximately 12in (30cm) high, cut a sheet of cellophane about 3ft (1m) long and pleat it roughly into 3⁄4in (2cm) folds along its length.

2 PLACE THE BUNCH of flowers in the middle of the pleated cellophane and draw the two ends of the sheet around them. Scrunch the cellophane in at the tops of the stems and tie tightly. Fan out the pleats around the flowers. Finish with a ribbon tied in a bow.

POINTED FOLDS

In this equally simple method of wrapping flowers, cellophane sheeting is folded up over the flowers to form pointed ends with the flowers at the center. For a posy approximately 12in (30cm) high, you will need a 2ft- (60cm-) long sheet of cellophane.

1 LAY THE POSY diagonally on the cellophane, from the center to the top left-hand corner. Fold the cellophane so that the bottom right-hand corner is over the flowers.

2 DRAW THE TWO POINTS of the cellophane on either side of the posy up around the flowers and tie in at the top of the flower stems with ribbon. Ruffle out the cellophane so that it surrounds the bunch evenly. Attach a ribbon bow to finish.

RIBBONS AND BOWS

Each year brings a wider choice of ribbons made of fabric, paper, and plant material. Of the fabric ribbons, I always favor those with wired edges because they can be formed so easily into perfect shapes. Paper ribbons have to be unfurled before use, and bows made with them need to be reasonably large. Raffia works well with more informal bunches, as do single bows. For a more elaborate display, make a double bow (*see below*) or a multiple bow with several ribbons. To complete, leave the long ribbon ends to trail and curl down the length of the bouquet.

Ribbon multiple bow

Raffia single bow

Paper double bow

1 UNROLL some of the ribbon and loop one end forward and back over itself. Hold the loop in place with your thumb and forefinger. Trim the ribbon end in an inverted "V" shape.

2 AFTER UNROLLING more ribbon, form a second loop, the same size as the first, by bringing the rest of the ribbon back over the first loop in an "X" shape.

3 FORM A THIRD LOOP by bringing the remaining length of ribbon up and over the front of the two loops of the bow that have already been formed.

4 WITH THE REST of the ribbon, form a fourth loop, bringing the end back over the middle of the bow in a second "X" shape. Trim the ribbon end in an inverted "V" shape.

5 PLEAT THE RIBBON at the center, where it crosses, working outward in both directions. Secure the center of the bow by binding with a length of fine spool wire.

6 IF YOU LIKE, cover the wire binding at the center of the bow with a length of narrow ribbon. Open up the loops of the bow and arrange the trailing ends.

A visual feast of all the plant material in the book, the Directory provides essential information, such as Latin and common names of all the plants, the season in which they are at their best, when they may be available in

DIRECTORY

flower shops, and the length of each plant sample shown. This is followed by a short description of how best to care for each plant and flower, and finally how long it will last provided that it starts off fresh and in good condition.

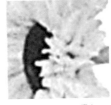

CHRYSANTHEMUM

PRODUCING SHOWY flowers in every color except blue, chrysanthemums (the national flower of Japan) are mostly hardy perennials and half-hardy annuals. The predominant colors for the perennials are autumn shades, which is fitting since they flower during that season. The cut flower trade produces "spray" chrysanthemums all year round: these have many flower heads to a stem and are either single flowered, like daisies, or double flowered, like pompoms, in colors ranging through green, yellow, orange, red, purple, and white. In some varieties, known as "spider," the petals are very fine; others have quilled petals. In autumn the large-flowered varieties become available: some of these can be over 8in (20cm) in diameter and are produced by disbudding flowering stems, leaving only the main, top flower bud to develop and flower.

The annual or biennial chrysanthemums hailing from Mediterranean countries are mostly single daisies such as marguerites, with varieties in yellows, reds, pinks, and white. These varieties are now named *Leucanthemum*. The large-flowered hardy perennials have now been renamed *Dendranthema*. Chrysanthemums are long lasting, particularly spray chrysanthemums, which should last for two weeks once cut.

Chrysanthemum 'Delaware'

Chrysanthemum 'Emerald'

Chrysanthemum 'George Griffiths'

Chrysanthemum 'White Spider'

Chrysanthemum 'Biarritz Yellow'

Chrysanthemum 'Tom Pearce'

Chrysanthemum 'Tedcha Yellow'

Chrysanthemum 'Kermit'

Chrysanthemum 'Tedcha Orange'

Chrysanthemum 'Stallion'

Hedera

Hedera helix 'Goldchild'
VARIEGATED IVY
Season All-year evergreen.
Length shown 35in (90cm).
Care Cut, scrape, and stand in deep water for several hours.
Vase life 4–7 days.

Hedera helix 'Kolibri'
IVY
Season All-year evergreen.
Length shown 9in (23cm).
Care Cut, scrape, and stand in deep water for several hours.
Vase life 10 days.

Hedera helix f. *poetarum*
POET'S IVY
Season All year; berries winter to spring.
Length shown 12in (30cm).
Care Cut, scrape, and hammer woody stems, then stand in deep water.
Vase life 14 days.

Heliconia aurantiaca
HELICONIA
Season Early summer.
Length shown 18in (46cm).
Care Cut, scrape, and hammer woody stems, then stand in deep water.
Vase life 10 days.

Heliconia psittacorum
PARROT FLOWER
Season All year from florists.
Length shown 25in (62cm).
Care Cut, scrape, and hammer woody stems, then stand in deep water.
Vase life 10 days.

Heliconia rostrata
LOBSTER CLAW
Season All year.
Length shown 39in (1m).
Care Cut, scrape, and hammer woody stems, then stand in deep water.
Vase life 10 days.

Helleborus

Helianthus annuus
SUNFLOWER
Season Late summer to autumn.
Length shown 28in (70cm).
Care Cut and scrape, then give hot water treatment *(see pp.310–313)*.
Vase life 7 days.

Helianthus annuus 'Autumn Beauty'
SUNFLOWER
Season Late summer to autumn.
Length shown 22in (55cm).
Care Cut and scrape, then give hot water treatment *(see pp.310–313)*.
Vase life 7 days.

Helichrysum italicum subsp. *serotinum*
CURRY PLANT
Season Summer to autumn.
Length shown 20in (50cm).
Care Condition before arranging *(see pp.310–313)* or air dry hanging.
Vase life Indefinite once dried.

Heliconia stricta 'Fire Bird'
HELICONIA
Season Early summer.
Length shown 20in (60cm).
Care Cut, scrape, and hammer woody stems, then stand in deep water.
Vase life 10 days.

Heliconia stricta
HELICONIA
Season Early summer.
Length shown 20in (60cm).
Care Cut, scrape, and hammer woody stems, then stand in deep water.
Vase life 10 days.

Helleborus niger
CHRISTMAS ROSE
Season Winter to spring.
Length shown 6in (15cm).
Care Cut, scrape, and prick stem below flower. Good for floating.
Vase life 4–6 days.

Helleborus

Helleborus orientalis hybrids
LENTEN ROSE
Season Late winter.
Length shown All stem length removed.
Note The flowers last well if cut short
and floated in water.
Vase life 3–4 days; 7 days if floated.

Hermodactylus tuberosus
WIDOW IRIS
Season Spring.
Length shown 16in (40cm).
Care Cut, scrape, and stand in deep
water for several hours.
Vase life 6 days.

Hibiscus sabdariffa
RED SORREL
Season Autumn to winter.
Length shown 9in (22cm).
Care Condition *(see pp.310–313)*. Air
dry standing. Use flowers to make tea.
Vase life Indefinite.

Howea bemoreana
SENTRY PALM
Season All year.
Length shown 20in (50cm).
Note The olive-like fruits take two years
to ripen.
Vase life 21 days.

Humulus lupulus
HOPS
Season Autumn.
Length shown 32in (80cm).
Care Condition *(see pp.310–313)* or air
dry by hanging in a dry, dark place.
Vase life Indefinite, but will lose color.

Hyacinthus orientalis 'Anna Liza'
HYACINTH
Season Spring.
Length shown 11in (28cm).
Care Condition *(see pp.310–313)*.
Support with wires inside stems.
Vase life 7 days; 21 days growing.

Hyacinthus

Hippeastrum 'Liberty'
AMARYLLIS
Season Winter.
Length shown 27½in (70cm).
Care Cut and fill stems with water *(see pp.310–313)*, then stand in deep water.
Vase life 10 days.

Hippeastrum 'Masai'
AMARYLLIS
Season Autumn to winter.
Length shown 26in (65cm).
Care Cut and fill stems with water *(see pp.310–313)*, then stand in deep water.
Vase life 10 days.

Hosta 'Francee'
PLANTAIN LILY
Season Summer to autumn.
Length shown 14in (35cm).
Care Submerge leaves, then condition before arranging *(see pp.310–313)*.
Vase life 4-7 days.

Hyacinthus orientalis 'City of Haarlem'
HYACINTH
Season Spring.
Length shown 9in (23cm).
Care Condition *(see pp.310–313)*.
Support with wires inside stems.
Vase life 7 days; 21 days growing.

Hyacinthus orientalis 'Lady Derby'
HYACINTH
Season Spring.
Length shown 9in (23cm).
Care Condition *(see pp.310–313)*.
Support with wires inside stems.
Vase life 7 days; 21 days growing.

Hyacinthus orientalis 'White Pearl'
HYACINTH
Season Spring.
Length shown 9in (23cm).
Care Condition *(see pp.310–313)*.
Support with wires inside stems.
Vase life 7 days; 21 days growing.

Hydrangea

Hydrangea paniculata 'Praecox'
HYDRANGEA
Season Summer to autumn.
Length shown 18in (46cm).
Care Cut, scrape, and hammer woody stems, then stand in deep water.
Vase life 5 days.

Hydrangea 'Preziosa'
HYDRANGEA
Season Summer to autumn.
Length shown 24in (60cm).
Care Condition *(see pp.310–313)*. Air dry standing in a vase or hanging.
Vase life Indefinite once dried.

Hydrangea 'Preziosa'
HYDRANGEA (Drying on plant)
Season Summer to autumn.
Length shown 24in (60cm).
Care Condition *(see pp.310–313)*. Air dry standing in a vase or hanging.
Vase life Indefinite once dried.

Ilex verticillata
WINTERBERRY
Season Autumn to winter.
Length shown 24in (60cm).
Care Cut, scrape, and hammer woody stems, then stand in deep water.
Vase life 21 days.

Ilex verticillata
WINTERBERRY
Season Autumn to winter.
Length shown 24in (60cm).
Care Cut, scrape, and hammer woody stems, then stand in deep water.
Vase life 21 days.

Iris 'H.C. van Vliet'
IRIS
Season Spring; all year from florists.
Length shown 18in (46cm).
Care Cut, scrape, and stand in deep water for several hours.
Vase life 5 days.

Larix

Ilex aquifolium 'Madame Briot'
VARIEGATED HOLLY
Season All-year evergreen.
Length shown 24in (60cm).
Care Cut, scrape, and hammer woody stems, then stand in deep water.
Vase life 14 days.

Ilex aquifolium 'Golden van Tol'
HOLLY
Season All-year evergreen.
Length shown 28in (70cm).
Care Cut, scrape, and hammer woody stems, then stand in deep water.
Vase life 14 days.

Ilex x meservcae 'Blue Prince'
BLUE HOLLY
Season Winter.
Length shown 26in (65cm).
Note This holly has rich, shiny green foliage and dark purple-green stems.
Vase life 14 days.

Iris 'Professor Blaauw'
IRIS
Season Late spring to summer.
Length shown 16in (40cm).
Care Cut, scrape, and stand in deep water for several hours.
Vase life 5 days in water.

Kniphofia 'C.M. Prichard'
RED-HOT POKER
Season Summer.
Length shown 18in (46cm).
Care Flowers open over long period; remove the lower flowers as they die.
Vase life 7 days.

Larix decidua
EUROPEAN LARCH
Season Winter for twigs.
Length shown 20in (50cm).
Note In winter the branches have a good shape with their small cones.
Vase life Several weeks.

Lathyrus

Lathyrus odoratus
SWEET PEA
Season Summer; spring from florists.
Length shown 12in (30cm).
Note Condition *(see pp.310–313)*. They are often long-life treated by growers.
Vase life 3–7 days.

Laurus nobilis
BAY
Season All-year evergreen.
Length shown 5in (13cm).
Care Cut, scrape, and hammer woody stems, then stand in deep water.
Vase life 14 days; 1 day out of water.

Lavandula angustifolia
LAVENDER
Season Summer.
Length shown 22in (55cm).
Care Cut, scrape, and stand in deep water for several hours.
Vase life 7 days.

Leptospermum scoparium ‘Gaiety Girl’
NEW ZEALAND TEA TREE
Season Spring. Also autumn and winter.
Length shown 22in (55cm).
Note Cut, scrape, and hammer woody stems, then stand in deep water.
Vase life 7 days.

Leucadendron laxum
LEUCADENDRON
Season All year from florists.
Length shown 13½in (35cm).
Care Condition before arranging *(see pp.310–313)* or air dry hanging.
Vase life 14 days.

Leucadendron laureolum
LEUCADENDRON
Season All year from florists.
Length shown 13½in (35cm).
Care Condition before arranging *(see pp.310–313)* or air dry hanging.
Vase life 14 days.

Liatris

Lavandula stoechas
FRENCH LAVENDER
Season Summer.
Length shown 16in (40cm).
Care Cut, scrape, and stand in deep water for several hours.
Vase life 7 days.

Leonotis leonurus
LION'S EAR
Season Late autumn.
Length shown 24in (60cm).
Care Cut and scrape, then give hot water treatment *(see pp.310–313)*.
Vase life 5 days.

Leptospermum scoparium
NEW ZEALAND TEA TREE
Season Flowers spring; foliage all year.
Length shown 20in (50cm).
Care Cut, scrape, and hammer woody stems, then stand in deep water.
Vase life 7 days; 6 hours out of water.

Leucadendron platyspermum
LEUCADENDRON
Season All year from florists.
Length shown 11½in (30cm).
Care Condition before arranging *(see pp.310–313)* or air dry hanging.
Vase life 14 days.

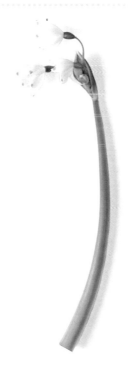

Leucojum vernum
SPRING SNOWFLAKE
Season Spring.
Length shown 9in (22cm).
Care Cut, scrape, and stand in deep water for several hours.
Vase life 6 days.

Liatris spicata
GAYFEATHER
Season Spring; all year from florists.
Length shown 20in (50cm).
Care Cut, scrape, and stand in deep water for several hours.
Vase life 14 days.

LILIUM

 WITH THEIR LARGE, trumpet-shaped flowers (several on each stem) and many with delicious, sweet, spicy perfumes, lilies must be among the best of all flowering plants. The main types available as cut flowers are the *longiflorum* hybrids, which have a sweet but non-pervasive perfume; the Oriental hybrids, which are invariably larger than other varieties, often with spotted petals, and with a wonderful sweet, spicy scent; and the Asiatic hybrids, which have no perfume.

The flowering season of lilies is from early summer with *Lilium candidum* to *Lilium speciosum* in late summer, and this is when lilies are at their best and strongest. Many varieties of lilies are available all year round from florists, however.

Lilies last extremely well, and once they are conditioned and arranged, most of the buds should open. It is important not to buy lilies that are too tightly budded: choose stems that have a base bud just showing color. Remove lower flowers as they start to wilt, and this will help the upper buds to open.

Some lilies with very large flowers can become top-heavy as the flowers open, causing the stem to break. To prevent this from happening, prop large-flowered lilies against the stems of other plant material.

Lilium 'Pompeii'

Lilium 'African Queen'

Lilium 'Woodriff's Memory'

Lilium Golden Splendour Group

Lilium 'Jet Fire'

Lilium 'Medusa'

Lilium 'Salmon Classica'

Lilium 'Grand Paradise'

NARCISSUS

 THESE CHEERFUL FLOWERS, of which the daffodil is the most well known, bloom naturally out-of-doors from late winter to late spring. They are forced for the flower trade so that the first narcissus can usually be purchased in early autumn; but it is in spring (when one of the most uplifting sights in nature is their golden yellow drifts against fresh green grass) that narcissus seem most appropriate for the home. The predominant colors are yellow and gold, but there are whites, creams, oranges, and quite a few with salmon-pink cups. Many have intense, fresh, sweet perfumes. Narcissus bulbs can be forced into flower indoors by early or mid-winter, the first usually being the highly scented variety known as 'Paper White'.

Once cut, narcissus flowers last best in a cool place and are ideal candidates for standing outside where they can be viewed from a living-room or kitchen window; this way they will last for a couple of weeks. In a dry, centrally heated room, however, they will last for less than a week.

Choose narcissus with plenty of buds: even when they are backward and showing no color they will come out once they start taking up water. Always use flower food or a few drops of bleach in the water to prevent the stems from becoming slimy.

Narcissus 'Tahiti'

Narcissus 'Johann Strauss'

Narcissus 'Golden Harvest'

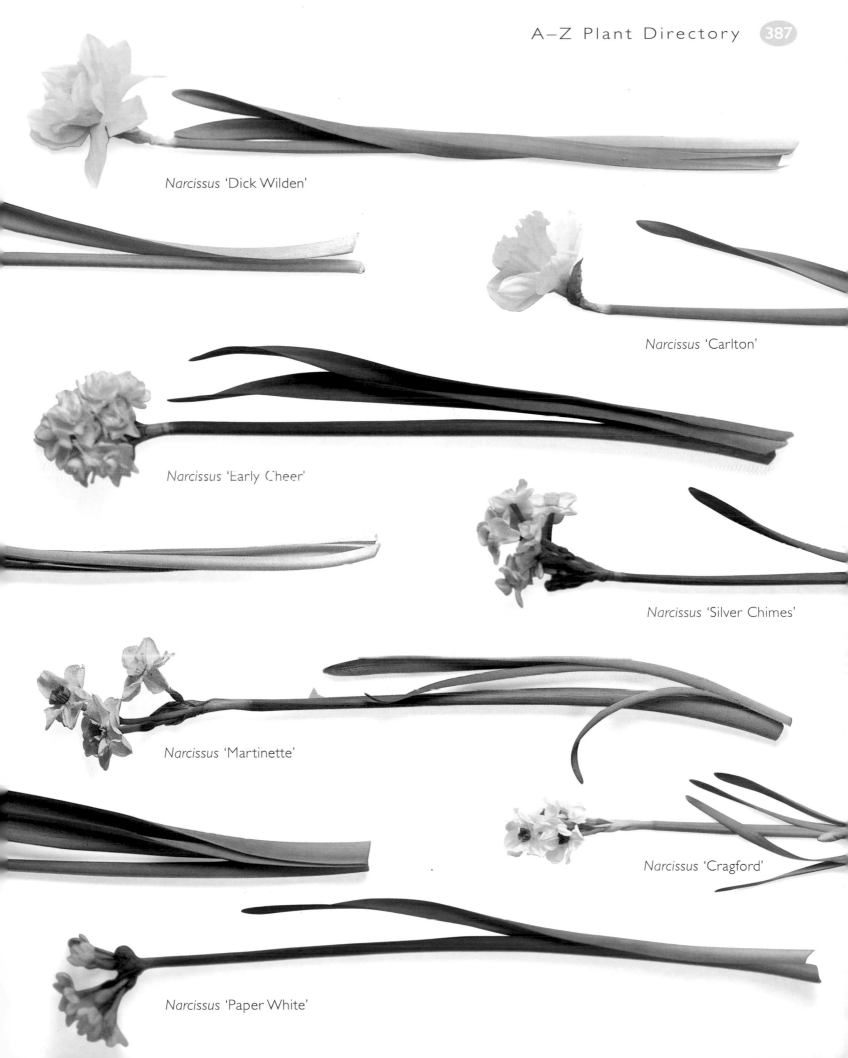

Narcissus 'Dick Wilden'

Narcissus 'Carlton'

Narcissus 'Early Cheer'

Narcissus 'Silver Chimes'

Narcissus 'Martinette'

Narcissus 'Cragford'

Narcissus 'Paper White'

ORCHIDACEAE

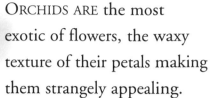

ORCHIDS ARE the most exotic of flowers, the waxy texture of their petals making them strangely appealing. They come in a huge range of colors and sizes and, because there are quite a few earthy colored varieties, they work equally well in both rustic and elegant displays.

Cymbidium is the most commonly grown orchid, both as a house plant and for cut flowers, closely followed by *Dendrobium*. The moth orchid, *Phalaenopsis*, must be the most elegant orchid: flowers in whites, pinks, yellow, and green, looking like exotic, hovering moths, are produced on long arching stems. The amazing slipper orchids, *Paphiopedilum*, have flowers that can be striped and spotted in browns, plums, and greens, making them look like large insects. Some *Cattleya* have very large flowers that look as if they are made of satin, but they are short lived compared to other orchids.

Most orchids are long lasting, particularly if left to flower on the growing plant. It can be difficult, however, to coax them into flower in subsequent years. In temperate and cooler climes, orchid plants benefit from being moved to a semi-shaded place in the garden for the summer. They must be kept well watered (they should never be soggy) – ideally sprayed with rainwater, because they dislike the additives in tap water.

Cymbidium Christmas Angel 'Cooksbridge Sunburst'

Phalaenopsis Yukimai

Cymbidium 'Showgirl'

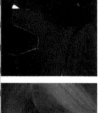

Arachnepedium 'James Story'

Paphiopedilum insigne

x Aranda majala

Arachnis flos-aeris

Dendrobium 'Mme. Pompadour'

Vanda Rothschildiana

Dendrobium 'Joan'

Ornithogalum

Ornithogalum dubium
STAR-OF-BETHLEHEM
Season Spring and early summer.
Length shown 18in (46cm).
Care Condition *(see pp.310–313)*. Very
long lasting. Remove flowers as they die.
Vase life 18 days.

Ozothamnus rosmarinifolius
TASMANIAN ROSEMARY
Season Summer.
Length shown 18in (46cm).
Care Cut, scrape, and hammer woody
stems, then stand in deep water.
Vase life 7 days.

Paeonia 'Baroness Schröder'
PEONY
Season Early summer.
Length shown 14in (36cm).
Care Cut, scrape, and stand in deep
water for several hours.
Vase life 4–7 days.

Papaver nudicaule
ICELAND POPPY
Season Summer.
Length shown 12in (30cm).
Care Seal stem ends by hot water
treatment *(see pp.310–313)*.
Vase life 6 days.

Papaver somniferum
OPIUM POPPY
Season Summer.
Length shown 9½in (25cm).
Note Dried poppies can be spray-
painted as festive decorations.
Vase life Indefinite.

Papaver somniferum 'Hen and Chickens'
OPIUM POPPY
Season Summer.
Length shown 22in (55cm).
Care Extraordinary seedheads air dry
very easily hanging or standing.
Vase life Indefinite.

Philadelphus

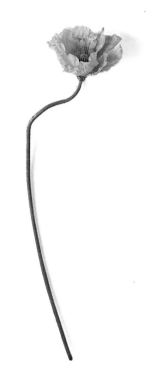

Paeonia 'Globe of Light'
PEONY
Season Summer.
Length shown 3½in (9cm).
Care Cut, scrape, and stand in deep
water for several hours.
Vase life 1–4 days.

Papaver nudicaule 'Summer Breeze'
ICELAND POPPY
Season Summer.
Length shown 16in (40cm).
Care Seal stem ends by hot water
treatment (*see pp 310–313*).
Vase life 6 days.

Papaver orientale
ORIENTAL POPPY
Season Summer.
Length shown 16in (40cm).
Care Seal stem ends by hot water
treatment (*see pp.310–313*).
Vase life 6 days.

Pelargonium 'Rollisson's Unique'
GERANIUM
Season Summer.
Length shown 10in (25cm).
Note The flower heads are good for
floating in water.
Vase life 5 days; 3–4 days floating.

Petroselinum crispum
PARSLEY
Season Summer; all year from groceries.
Length shown 6in (15cm).
Note Condition (*see pp.310–313*). Out
of water it will keep for 6 hours.
Vase life 5 days.

Philadelphus 'Belle Etoile'
MOCK ORANGE
Season Early summer.
Length shown 18in (46cm).
Care Condition (*see pp.310–313*).
Remove most leaves to prolong its life.
Vase life 5 days. *Philodendron*

Philodendron

Philodendron bipinnatifidum
PHILODENDRON
Season All year.
Length shown 18in (46cm).
Care Cut, scrape, and stand in deep water for several hours.
Vase life 10 days.

Phlox 'Kelly's Eye'
PHLOX
Season Late summer to autumn.
Length shown 26in (65cm).
Care Cut, scrape, and stand in deep water for several hours.
Vase life 7 days.

Phlox paniculata 'Fujiyama'
PHLOX
Season Late summer to autumn.
Length shown 26in (65cm).
Care Cut, scrape, and stand in deep water for several hours.
Vase life 7 days.

Pinus bungeana
LACEBARK PINE
Season Bark available all year.
Length shown 6in (15cm).
Note The stunning, peeling bark is mottled gray, cream, and green.
Vase life Bark lasts indefinitely.

Pinus nigra
AUSTRIAN PINE
Season All-year evergreen.
Length shown 22in (55cm).
Note Condition *(see pp.310–313)*. This pine lends itself well to arranging.
Vase life 10 days.

Pinus strobus
EASTERN WHITE PINE (CONE)
Season Autumn.
Length shown 3½in (9cm).
Care Use cones either on stems or wired *(see p.320)*.
Vase life Indefinite.

Polianthes

Phoenix dactylifera
DATE PALM
Season All year.
Length shown 14in (36cm).
Note Fruiting stems last a long time in or out of water.
Vase life 21 days.

Physalis alkekengi
CHINESE LANTERN (FRUITS)
Season Autumn.
Length shown 24in (60cm).
Care Pick as orange lanterns develop and remove leaves. Condition or air dry.
Vase life Several weeks; indefinite if dried.

Picea pungens
COLORADO SPRUCE (CONE)
Season Autumn.
Length shown 5in (13cm).
Note Use cones either on stems or wired *(see p.320)*.
Vase life Indefinite.

Pinus sylvestris
SCOTS PINE (CONE)
Season Autumn.
Length shown 5½in (14cm).
Care Use cones either on stems or wired *(see p.320)*.
Vase life Indefinite.

Pittosporum tenuifolium 'Silver Queen'
PITTOSPORUM
Season All-year evergreen.
Length shown 12in (30cm).
Care Cut, scrape, and hammer woody stems, then stand in deep water.
Vase life 9 days; 12 hours out of water.

Polianthes tuberosa 'The Pearl'
TUBEROSE
Season Summer; all year from florists.
Length shown 14in (36cm).
Note Condition using hot water treatment *(see pp.310–313)*.
Vase life 5 days.

Polygonatum

Polygonatum x *hybridum*
SOLOMON'S SEAL
Season Early summer.
Length shown 19½in (50cm).
Care Cut, scrape, and stand in deep water for several hours.
Vase life 4–7 days.

Polystichum setiferum
HEDGE FERN
Season All-year evergreen.
Length shown 18in (46cm).
Care Cut, scrape. and stand in deep water for several hours.
Vase life 4 days.

Primula Polyanthus Group
POLYANTHUS
Season Spring.
Length shown 6in (15cm).
Care The cut flowers last quite well, or use as a potted plant.
Vase life 7 days; 14 days inside.

Prunus mume
JAPANESE APRICOT
Season Spring.
Length shown 18in (46cm).
Care Cut, scrape, and hammer woody stems, then stand in deep water.
Vase life 7 days.

Quercus macrocarpa
BUR OAK
Season Summer to autumn.
Length shown 24in (61cm).
Care Condition or preserve using glycerin with dye added.
Vase life 7 days; indefinite if preserved.

Ranunculus asiaticus Turban Group
PERSIAN BUTTERCUP
Season Spring.
Length shown 11in (28cm).
Care Condition *(see pp.310–313)*. Use other plants to support lower stems.
Vase life 7 days.

Rhododendron

Primula Polyanthus Group
POLYANTHUS
Season Spring.
Length shown 6in (15cm).
Care The cut flowers last quite well, or use as a potted plant.
Vase life 7 days; 14 days inside.

Protea cynaroides
KING PROTEA
Season Summer.
Length shown 6½in (17cm).
Care Cut, scrape, and hammer woody stems, then stand in deep water.
Vase life 14 days.

Prunus avium
CHERRY
Season Spring.
Length shown 20in (50cm).
Care Cut, scrape, and hammer woody stems, then stand in deep water.
Vase life 7 days.

Ranunculus asiaticus Turban Group
PERSIAN BUTTERCUP
Season Spring; from autumn in florists.
Length shown 13in (32cm).
Note Flowers in yellow, pink, orange, red, and white. Some stripes and spots.
Vase life 7 days.

Reseda odorata
MIGNONETTE
Season Summer to autumn.
Length shown 18in (46cm).
Care Condition *(see pp.310–313)*. Sweet hay-scented flowers will air dry.
Vase life 6 days.

Rhododendron 'Sweetheart Supreme'
AZALEA
Season Late spring.
Length shown 18in (46cm).
Care Keep pots well watered but not soggy. Heating shortens life of flowers.
Vase life 3 weeks.

Rhododendron

Rhododendron yakushimanum 'Isadora'
RHODODENDRON
Season Late spring.
Length shown 8in (20cm).
Care Pot-grown plants need lots of water,
especially in central heating.
Vase life Up to 3 weeks.

Ribes rubrum
REDCURRANT
Season Summer flowers and fruits.
Length shown 16in (40cm).
Care Cut, scrape, and hammer woody
stems, then stand in deep water.
Vase life 10 days.

Ricinus communis
CASTOR BEAN (SEEDHEADS)
Season Autumn.
Length shown 16in (40cm).
Care Condition *(see pp.310–313)*. All
parts are toxic and may irritate skin.
Vase life 7 days.

Rumex obtusifolius
DOCK
Season Summer.
Length shown 16½in (42cm).
Care Use fresh or air dry. Spray with
hairspray to prevent seeds dropping.
Vase life 14 days.

Rumex sanguineus
BLOODY DOCK
Season Late summer to autumn.
Length shown 18in (46cm).
Care Cut, scrape, and stand in deep
water for several hours.
Vase life 7 days.

Rumohra adiantiformis
LEATHER FERN
Season All year.
Length shown 14in (35cm).
Care Cut, scrape, and stand in deep
water for several hours.
Vase life 6–7 days.

Rosmarinus officinalis
ROSEMARY
Season Flowers spring; foliage all year.
Length shown 8in (20cm).
Care Cut, scrape, and hammer woody
stems, then stand in deep water.
Vase life 7 days; 4 hours out of water.

Rosmarinus officinalis 'Miss Jessopp's
Upright' ROSEMARY
Season Spring flowers; evergreen leaves.
Length shown 24in (60cm).
Care Cut, scrape, and hammer woody
stems, then stand in deep water.
Vase life 7 days.

Rubus fruticosus
BLACKBERRY, BRAMBLE
Season Autumn.
Length shown 14in (35cm).
Care Condition *(see pp.310–313)*. The
berries may stain as they drop.
Vase life 7 days.

Ruscus hypophyllum
BROOM
Season All year from florists.
Length shown 21½in (55cm).
Care Cut, scrape, and stand in deep
water for several hours.
Vase life 14 days.

Ruscus hypoglossum
BROOM
Season All year; winter berries.
Length shown 24in (60cm).
Care Cut, scrape, and stand in deep
water for several hours.
Vase life 14 days; 4 days out of water.

Ruta graveolens 'Variegata'
VARIEGATED RUE
Season Summer.
Length shown 10in (25cm).
Care Condition *(see pp.310–313)*. All
parts of the plant can irritate skin.
Vase life 6 days.

ROSA

THE ROSE has been cultivated and valued for perhaps 5,000 years, its origin appearing to have been with the China rose, *Rosa chinensis*. Around 500 BC, the rose was introduced into Egypt and from there it traveled to the Middle East, where it became known as the damask rose and was highly prized for its perfume.

There are now more than 4,000 species and hybrids of roses available, and each month seems to see new florists' roses appearing. The color range of cut roses is extraordinary: apart from the usual reds and pinks, there are exquisite peaches, mauves, lilacs, brilliant orange, bicolored and picotee, splashed and dappled, even green and parchment colors. Fortunately, perfumed roses have become valued again, and many of the roses that we can now buy smell deliciously sweet, fruity, and spicy.

Although I love the old-fashioned roses, their cut life is not as long as that of the hybrid teas. If roses are well conditioned, however, they should last from bud for a week (*see pp.310–313*). If cut roses start to droop – and this can be a problem with the longer stemmed blooms – give them a hot water treatment (*see p.313*). This will often revive them if they are not too far gone. Remember also that most roses will last longer with a short stem.

Rosa 'Grand Prix'

Rosa 'Emerald'

Rosa 'Diadem'

Rosa 'Yellow Texas'

Rosa 'Vicky Brown'

Rosa 'Leonidas'

Rosa 'Lydia'

Rosa 'La Minuette'

Rosa 'Candy Bianca'

Rosa 'Vendella'

TULIPA

THESE ELEGANT, spring-flowering bulbs have been treasured for centuries for their beauty, exquisite shapes, and remarkable colors.

Originating in the Middle East, tulips passed, in the sixteenth century, from Turkey to Europe, where they quickly became the most fashionable of all flowers. Growers vied to produce the most exotic of flower variations, and tulip bulbs became astoundingly expensive.

We can now choose from hundreds of tulip colors and flower shapes – from the purest white, through creams, the palest of pinks, mauves, lilacs, and apricots to the richest of purples, scarlets, oranges, greens, and yellows, in single and double, cup, bowl, and goblet, lily, frilled, and parrot forms. The latter are extraordinary, with petals like parrot feathers, sometimes gaudily splashed with different colors, sometimes demure.

The tulip season has been so extended that it is now possible to buy them throughout the year. Although I think that it is generally best to use flowers in their natural season, when they look and last well, tulips are invaluable in winter when there is limited choice. The only drawback of tulips is that their acidity shortens the lives of any blooms that share their vase. If it is only for a day or so, there is no problem, but for longer periods they are best kept to themselves.

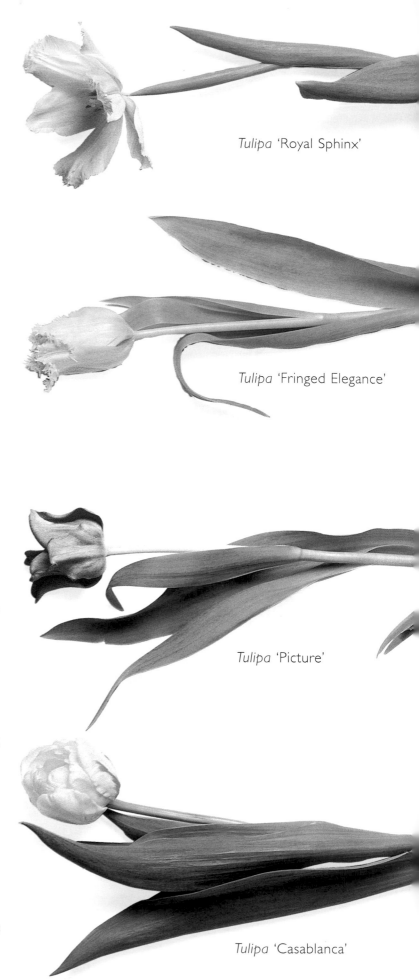

Tulipa 'Royal Sphinx'

Tulipa 'Fringed Elegance'

Tulipa 'Picture'

Tulipa 'Casablanca'

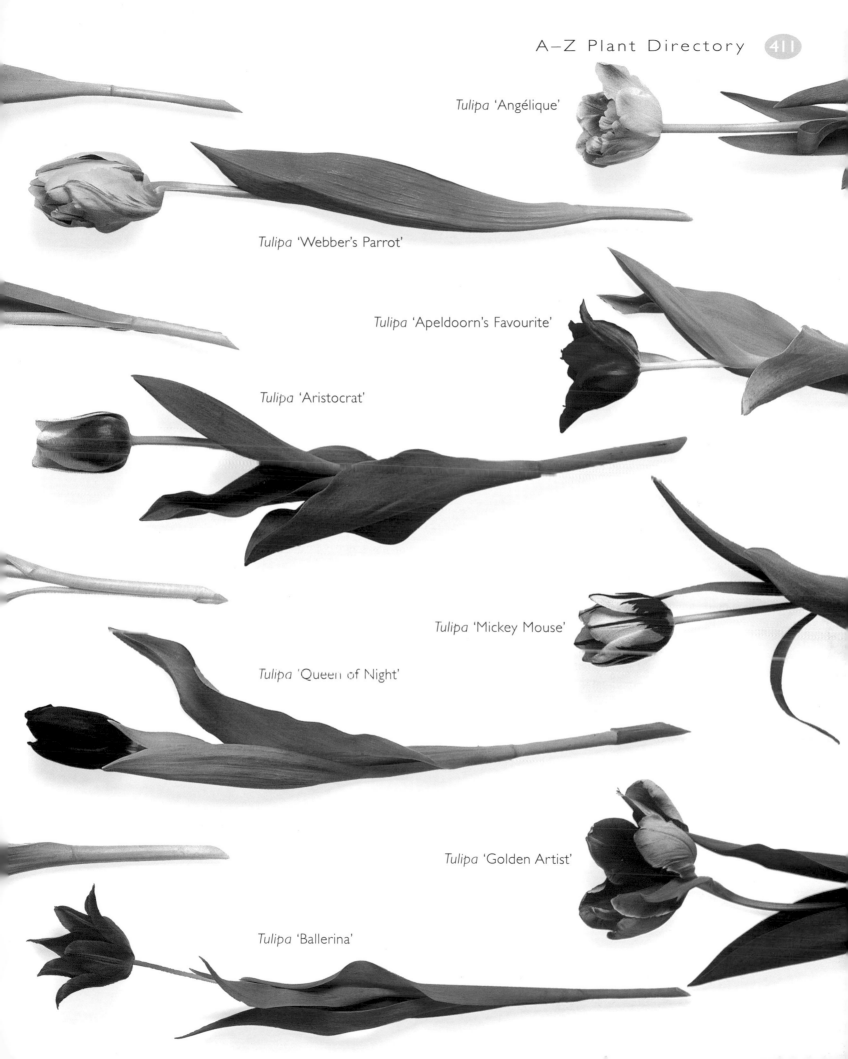

Tulipa 'Angélique'

Tulipa 'Webber's Parrot'

Tulipa 'Apeldoorn's Favourite'

Tulipa 'Aristocrat'

Tulipa 'Mickey Mouse'

Tulipa 'Queen of Night'

Tulipa 'Golden Artist'

Tulipa 'Ballerina'

RED

RED IS THE hottest color in the spectrum. It is also the most intense of all colors, especially when it is set off by its contrasting opposite color green (as it frequently is with foliage). It is a loud color that not only shouts out its dominance but also spawns a whole series of pinks, which are composed of varying mixtures of red and white. Red is jazzy, deliberate, and very demanding. It puts us in our place and does not suffer other colors lightly. The contrast of red and white is arguably the hardest of all color combinations to use successfully, but it can look stunning when interesting textures are involved. Crimson and purple – the two colors that sit very close to red in the color spectrum – often look excitingly lurid when mixed with it.

Rosa 'Leonidas'

Chrysanthemum 'George Griffiths'

Author's Choice

Long-lasting red flowers

Anthurium andraeanum
 (Flamingo flower)

Heliconia stricta (Heliconia)
Hippeastrum (Amaryllis)

Strongest red flowers

Anemone coronaria
 'Mona Lisa Red' (Anemone)
Antirrhinum majus
Coronette Series (Snapdragon)
Celosia argentea (Cockscomb)
Crocosmia 'Lucifer'
 (Montbretia)

Gerbera jamesonii
 'Ruby Red' (Gerbera)
Hippeastrum 'Liberty'
 (Amaryllis)
Rosa 'Estelle de Meilland'
 (Rose)
Tulipa 'Cassini' (Tulip)

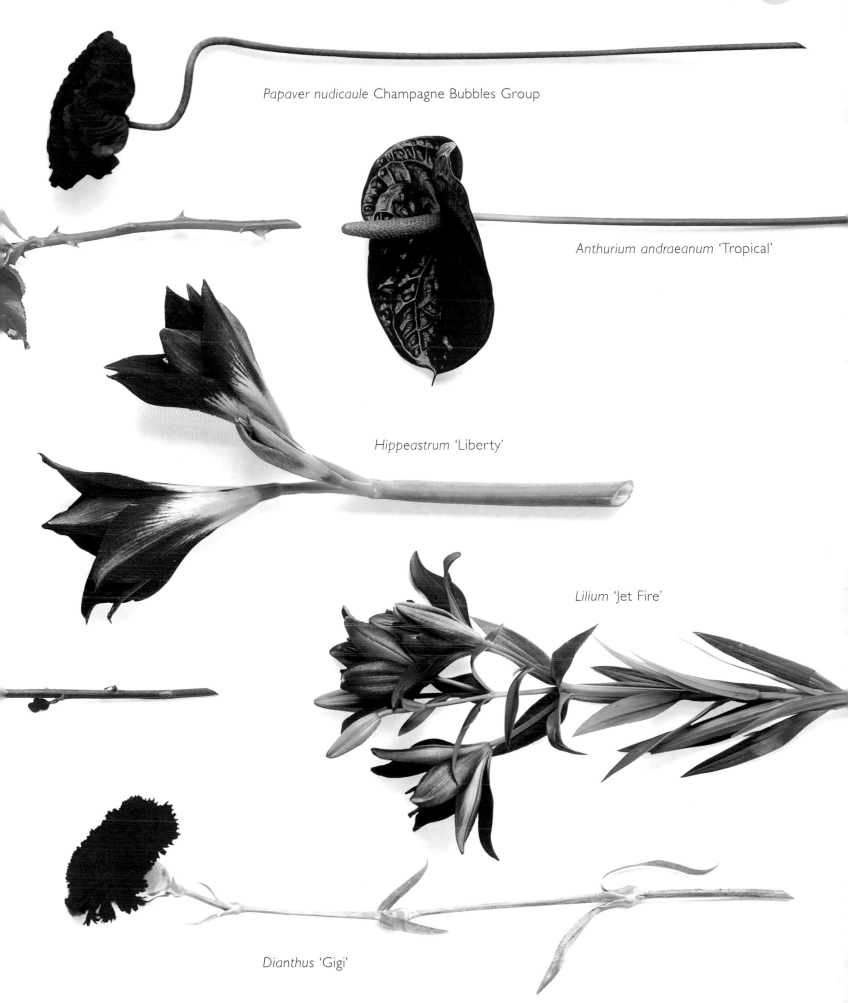

Papaver nudicaule Champagne Bubbles Group

Anthurium andraeanum 'Tropical'

Hippeastrum 'Liberty'

Lilium 'Jet Fire'

Dianthus 'Gigi'

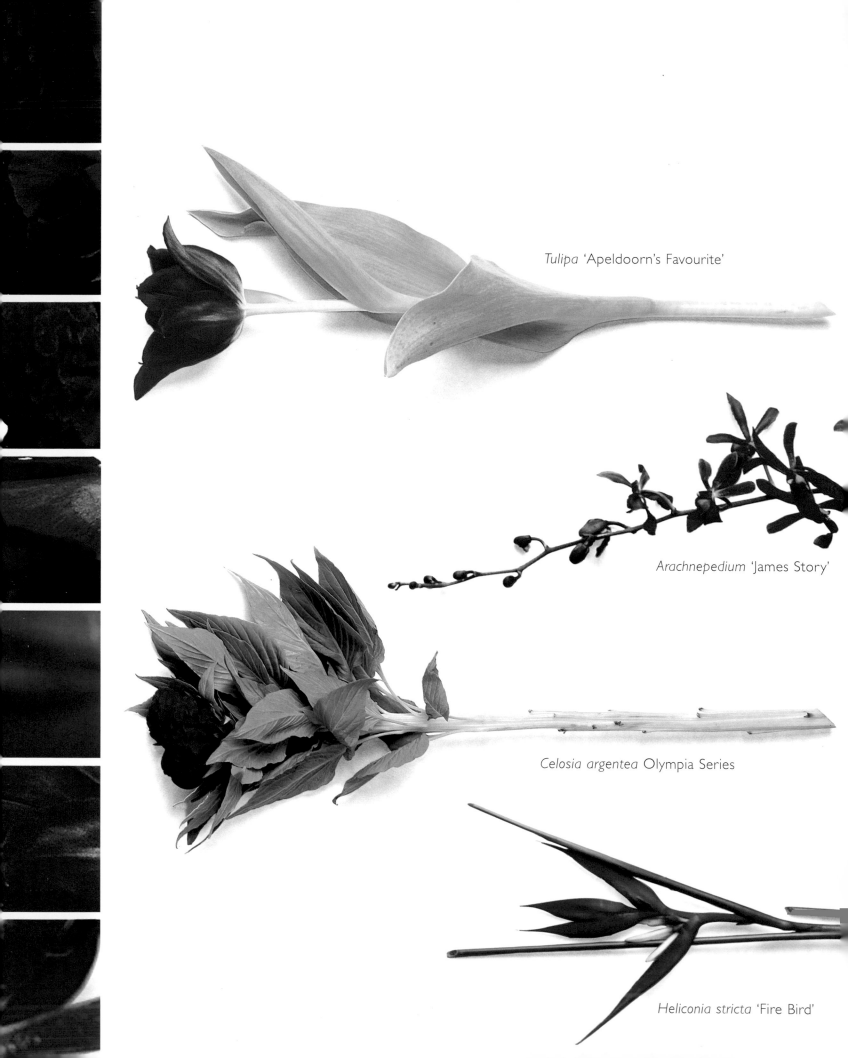

Tulipa 'Apeldoorn's Favourite'

Arachnepedium 'James Story'

Celosia argentea Olympia Series

Heliconia stricta 'Fire Bird'

Rosa 'Prima Donna'

Clarkia amoena

Dahlia 'John Prior'

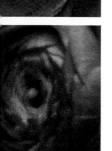
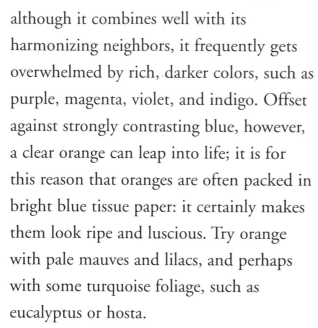

ORANGE

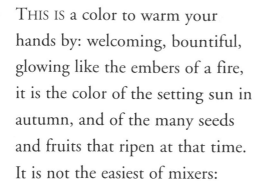

THIS IS a color to warm your hands by: welcoming, bountiful, glowing like the embers of a fire, it is the color of the setting sun in autumn, and of the many seeds and fruits that ripen at that time. It is not the easiest of mixers: although it combines well with its harmonizing neighbors, it frequently gets overwhelmed by rich, darker colors, such as purple, magenta, violet, and indigo. Offset against strongly contrasting blue, however, a clear orange can leap into life; it is for this reason that oranges are often packed in bright blue tissue paper: it certainly makes them look ripe and luscious. Try orange with pale mauves and lilacs, and perhaps with some turquoise foliage, such as eucalyptus or hosta.

Tulipa 'Ballerina'

Ranunculus asiaticus Turban Group

Author's Choice

Long-lasting orange flowers and berries

Alstroemeria (Peruvian lily)
Celastrus (Bittersweet)
Heliconia (Heliconia)
Ilex (Holly)
Lilium (Lily)
Protea (Protea)
Pyracantha (Firethorn)

Strongest orange flowers

Chrysanthemum 'Sally Ball'
 (Chrysanthemum)
Dianthus 'Malaga' (Carnation)
Gerbera jamesonii 'Sunset'
 (Gerbera)
Kniphofia 'Prince Igor'
 (Red-hot poker)
Rosa 'Confetti' (Rose)
Rosa 'Jazz' (Rose)
Tulipa 'Ballerina' (Tulip)

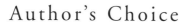

Crocosmia 'Jackanapes'

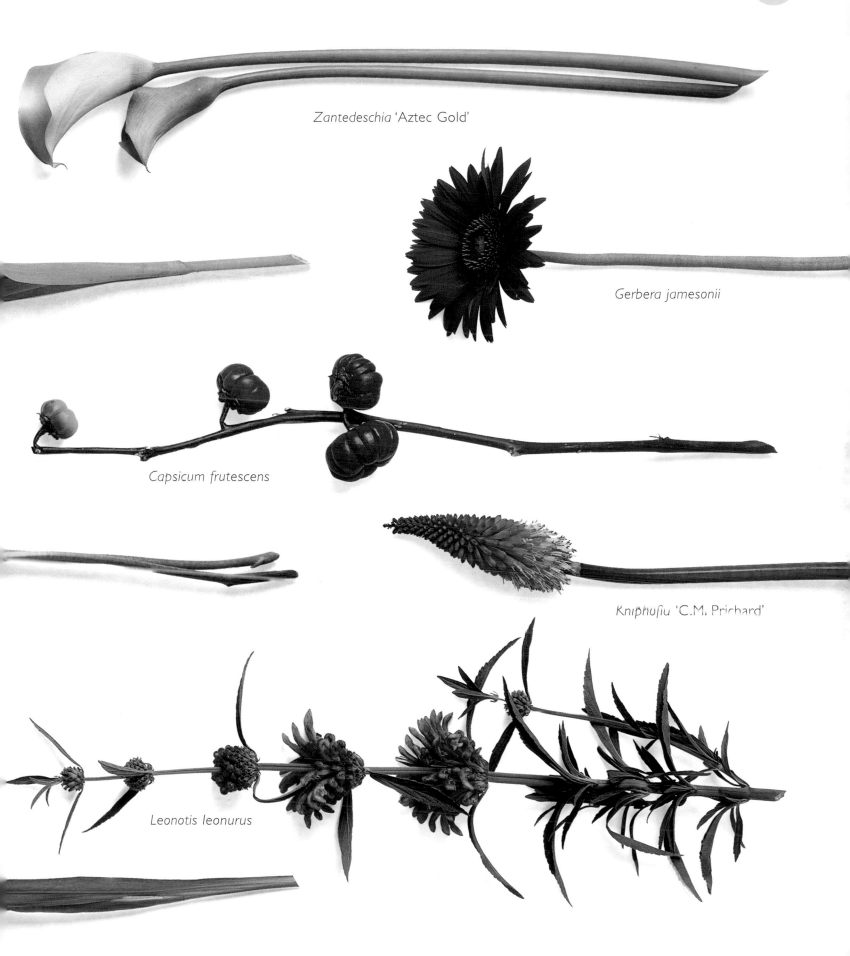

Zantedeschia 'Aztec Gold'

Gerbera jamesonii

Capsicum frutescens

Kniphofia 'C.M. Prichard'

Leonotis leonurus

Sandersonia aurantiaca

Eremurus x *isabellinus*

Chrysanthemum 'Biarritz Yellow'

x Aranda majala

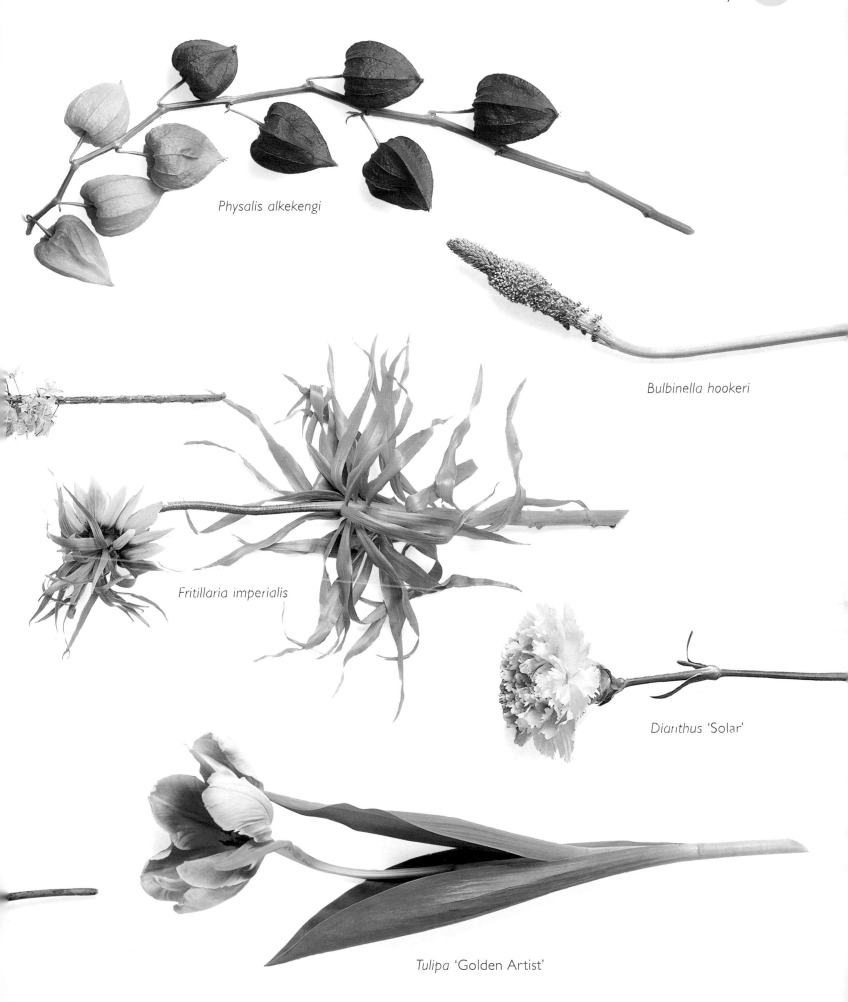

Physalis alkekengi

Bulbinella hookeri

Fritillaria imperialis

Dianthus 'Solar'

Tulipa 'Golden Artist'

YELLOW

THE BRIGHTEST COLOR in the color spectrum is yellow: in flower arrangements, it positively shines and leaps forward. Always looking cheerful and sunny, yellow has a wonderful ability to raise the spirits. Like its close neighbor lime green, it is also good at lifting other colors. Yellow is very well represented in the world of flowers: it is the color most associated with spring, when forsythia and daffodils dominate our parks and gardens. In summer and autumn, too, there is always a plethora of yellow flowers, and even winter has a few fragile beauties. For the brightest yellow effect, team it with its contrasting opposite color, violet; for its most harmonizing effect, on the other hand, team it with orange.

Lilium 'African Queen'

Rosa 'Pistache'

Author's Choice

Long-lasting yellow flowers

Achillea filipendulina (Yarrow)
Alstroemeria (Peruvian lily)
Eustoma grandiflorum (Texas bluebell)
Lilium (Lily)
Orchidaceae (Orchid)
Solidago (Goldenrod)
Zantedeschia (Calla lily)

Best scented yellow flowers

Acacia (Mimosa, Wattle)
Freesia (Freesia)
Hamamelis (Witch hazel)
Hyacinthus orientalis (Hyacinth)
Lilium (Lily)
Narcissus (Daffodil)
Primula (Primrose)
Rosa (Rose)

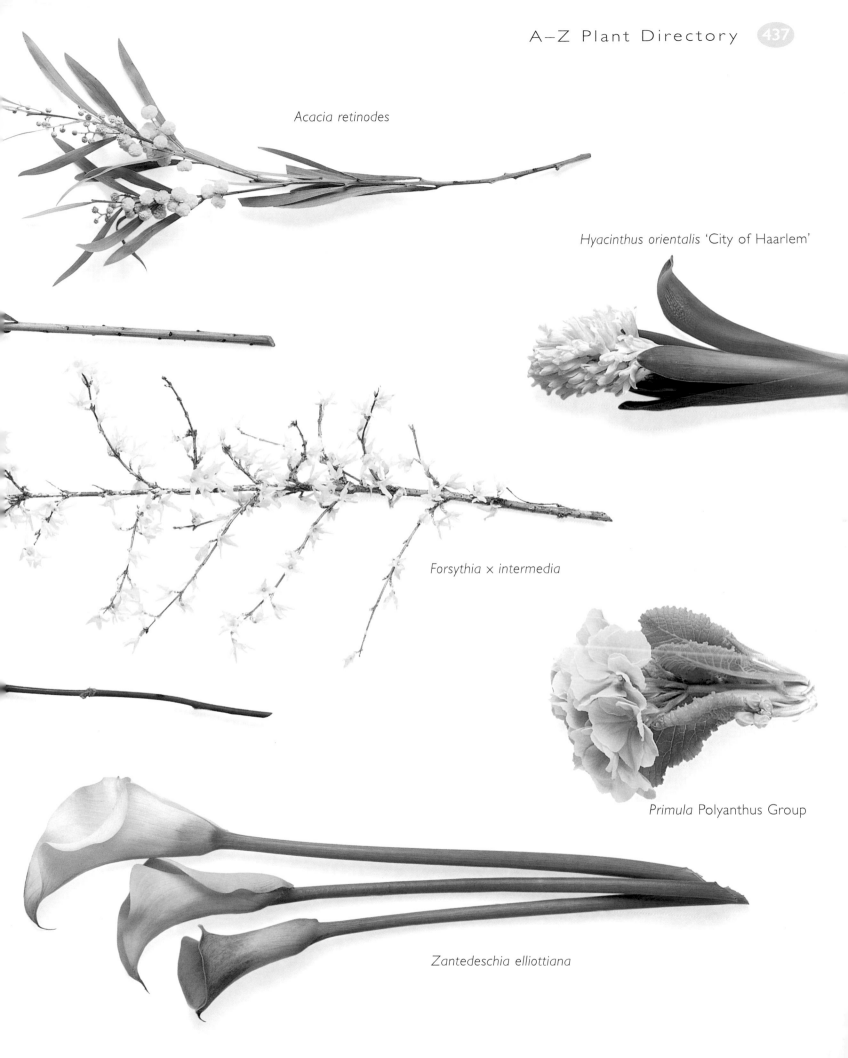

Acacia retinodes

Hyacinthus orientalis 'City of Haarlem'

Forsythia × *intermedia*

Primula Polyanthus Group

Zantedeschia elliottiana

Narcissus 'Dick Wilden'

Tulipa 'Fringed Elegance'

Narcissus 'Martinette'

Carthamus tinctorius 'Summer Sun'

Achillea filipendulina

Papaver nudicaule Champagne Bubbles Group

Narcissus 'Golden Harvest'

Dianthus 'Cobra'

Rosa 'Gold Strike'

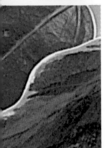
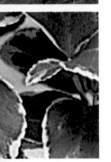

GREEN

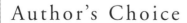
IN THE COUNTRYSIDE, in our parks and gardens, and in flower creations, green is a color that is always with us. Even in deepest winter, there are evergreens to evoke memories of summer. It is rare for there to be no green leaves at all in an arrangement, so it is fortunate that green works easily with all other colors. As a foil to other-colored flowers, green does an excellent job of showing them off to their best advantage. Restful, serene, and easy on the eye, green is also beautiful when it is used on its own: there are many leaves in different shades of green, as well as a few flowers, and all of these have their own unique shapes and textures.

Colocasia esculenta

Hedera canariensis 'Gloire de Marengo'

Author's Choice

Long-lasting green flowers and foliage

Anthurium (Flamingo flower)
Areca lutescens (Areca palm)
Galax urceolata (Wandflower)
Hedera helix (Ivy)
Philodendron (Philodendron)

Most dramatic green leaves

Acacia (Mimosa, Wattle)
Freesia (Freesia)
Hamamelis (Witch hazel)
Hyacinthus orientalis
  (Hyacinth)
Lilium (Lily)
Narcissus (Daffodil)
Primula (Primrose)
Rosa (Rose)
Strelitzia (Bird of paradise)

Carex oshimensis 'Evergold'

Hedera helix f. poetarum

Polystichum setiferum

Euonymus fortunei 'Silver Queen'

Cryptomeria japonica

Hedera helix 'Congesta'

Abies procera 'Glauca'

Eucalyptus gunnii

Anthurium crystallinum

Cyperus alternifolius

Galax urceolata

Aspalathus sp.

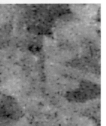

LIME-GREEN

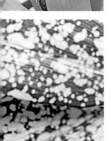

LYING BETWEEN GREEN and yellow on the color wheel, lime-green (or chartreuse) has a very special property – it has the ability to lift every other color in the spectrum. Be it with reds, pinks, oranges, yellows, or blues, the addition of luminous, lime-green flowers or foliage immediately brings other colors in the arrangement to life, giving them a fresh clarity and sparkle. Fortunately there are plenty of lime-green leaves and flowers to choose from. Like yellow, lime-green is also a particularly good color in positions that do not get much light, so it is excellent for use in brightening church arrangements or with flowers in a dimly lit hallway.

Moluccella laevis

Chrysanthemum 'Green Spider'

Author's Choice

Best lime-green leaves and bracts

Acer (Maple)
Asparagus (Asparagus)
Chamaecyparis (False cypress)

Euphorbia palustris (Spurge)
Hosta (Plantain lily)
Moluccella (Bells of Ireland)

Best lime-green flowers

Alchemilla mollis (Lady's mantle)
Anethum graveolens (Dill)
Anthurium andreanum (Flamingo flower)

Chrysanthemum (Chrysanthemum)
Gladiolus (Gladiolus)
Orchidaceae (Orchid)
Rosa (Rose)

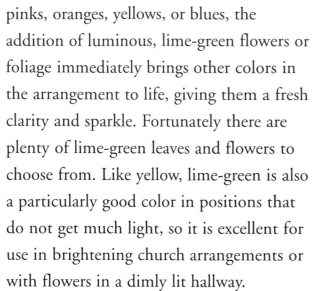

Rosa 'Emerald'

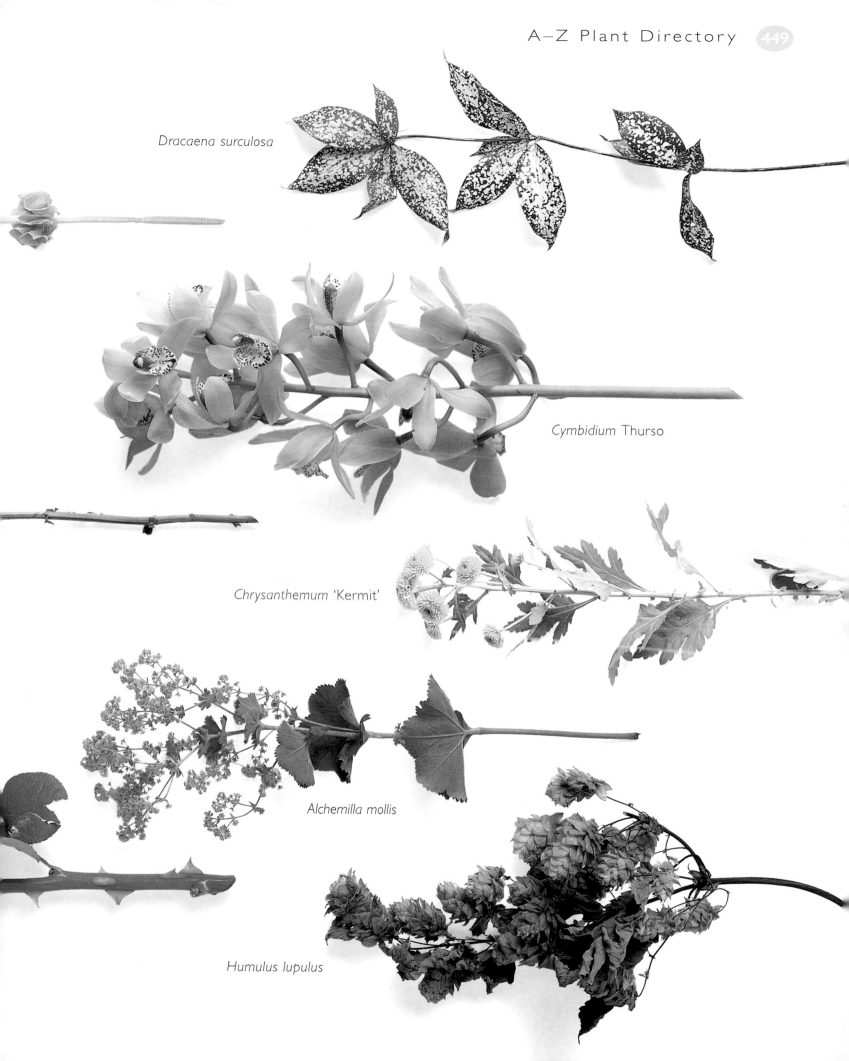

Dracaena surculosa

Cymbidium Thurso

Chrysanthemum 'Kermit'

Alchemilla mollis

Humulus lupulus

BLUE

 THIS IS A COMPLICATED color when it comes to flowers, for there are, in fact, very few true blue specimens. Many flowers listed as blue in plant catalogs have some red in their coloring, making them closer to mauve and violet than to true blue. The eye also plays tricks with blue, and often a flower that we see as blue is not quite what it seems.

Blue is the color of distance: remote, cool to the point of coldness, but at the same time serene and timeless. It is the color of the skies and seas of our dreams – although these are usually far from true blue.

Blue mixes easily with greens, whites, creams, and yellows, but becomes quite violent when it is paired with orange and hot reds. Paler shades combine beautifully with all other colors but work particularly well with the entire range of pinks.

Gentiana asclepiadea

Delphinium 'Lord Butler'

Author's Choice

Best true blue flowers

Anchusa (Alkanet)
Delphinium (Delphinium)
Gentiana (Gentian)
Iris (Iris)

Meconopsis (Poppy)
Muscari (Grape hyacinth)
Scilla (Siberian squill)
Erysimum (Wallflower)

Best deep blue flowers

Agapanthus campanulatus
  (African blue lily)
Hyacinthus orientalis
  'Blue Jacket' (Hyacinth)
Gentiana 'Kingfisher' (Gentian)

Iris 'Professor Blaauw' (Iris)
Lithodora diffusa 'Heavenly
  Blue' (Lithodora)
Lobelia erinus 'Sapphire'
  (Lobelia)

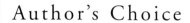

Myosotis sylvatica 'Music'

Agapanthus campanulatus

Iris 'Professor Blaauw'

Muscari armeniacum

Aconitum carmichaelii 'Barker's Variety'

PURPLE AND VIOLET

MOVING FROM RED toward blue, we find purple and violet followed by indigo. Purple is a richly glowing regal color like crimson and magenta, though without their striking brilliance. Lying next to purple, violet is the most withdrawn of all the colors and springs to life only when combined with its opposing partner, yellow. Violet is a dark and moody color with an old-fashioned air about it; it can look muddy and congested when mixed with warm oranges and scarlet. The color violet takes its name from the common or garden sweet violet (*Viola odorata*), but there are very few truly violet-colored flowers.

The darker shades of purple and violet are somber, but their lighter variants – mauve, lilac, fuchsia, lavender, and rose madder – harmonize exquisitely with each other and with the nearby crimson and magenta.

Tulipa 'Queen of Night'

Hydrangea 'Preziosa'

Author's Choice

Boldest purple and violet flowers

Anemone coronaria (Anemone)
Campanula (Bellflower)
Eustoma grandiflorum Heidi Series (Texas bluebell)
Gladiolus (Gladiolus)
Hydrangea (Hydrangea)

Iris (Iris)
Limonium sinuatum (Statice)
Primula Polyanthus Group (Polyanthus)
Tulipa 'Blue Heron' (Tulip)
Viola (Violet)

Best scented purple and violet flowers

Freesia (Freesia)
Matthiola incana (Stock)
Phlox (Phlox)

Rosa (Rose)
Syringa vulgaris (Lilac)
Viola (Pansy, violet)

Anemone coronaria De Caen Group

Callicarpa bodinieri var. *giraldii*

Vanda Rothschildiana

Limonium sinuatum Pacific Series

Eustoma grandiflorum Heidi Series

MAUVE AND LILAC

IN BOTH SUMMER and autumn, mauve, lilac, and lavender- and wisteria-colored flowers are freely available in gardens and flower shops. From the early irises, through hardy geraniums and campanulas, lilac and wisteria, one or two roses, china asters and eustomas, to autumnal Michelmas daisies and chrysanthemums, there are countless varieties in these hues.

Mauve and lilac are gentle colors that harmonize exquisitely with each other and also with the richer purples, violet, and magenta – the colors from which they derive. They also mix deliciously with pinks, blues, silver-grays, green, and turquoise. These paler variants are also interesting when juxtaposed against clear orange, lemon, and cream, but they tend to be deadened by bright red and gold.

Freesia 'Blue Heaven'

Hydrangea 'Preziosa'

Author's Choice

Best mauve and violet flowers

Ageratum houstonianum
  (Floss flower)
Hyacinthus orientalis
  'Ostara' (Hyacinth)
Hydrangea (Hydrangea)

Iris (Iris)
Orchidaceae (Orchid)
Phlox (Phlox)
Primula (Primrose)
Viola (Pansy)

Best-scented mauve and violet flowers

Freesia (Freesia)
Hyacinthus (Hyacinth)
Matthiola (Stock)
Phlox (Phlox)

Primula (Polyanthus)
Rosa (Rose)
Syringa (Lilac)
Viola (Violet; Pansy)

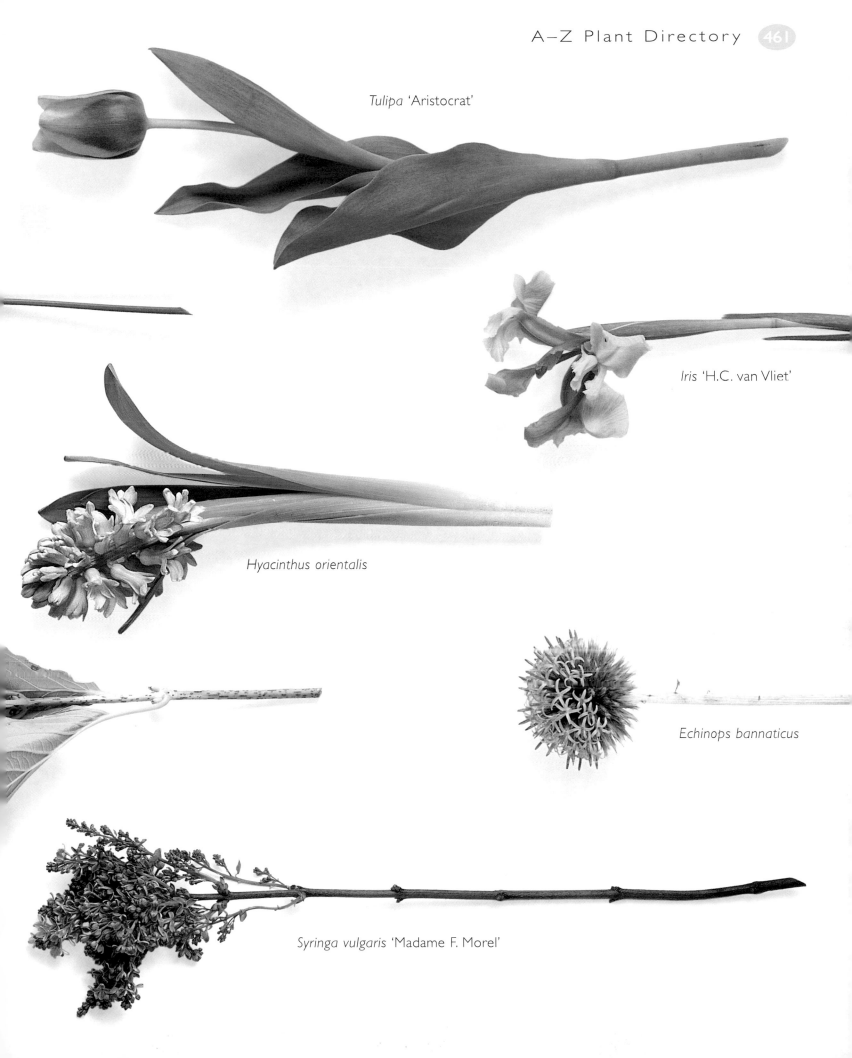

Tulipa 'Aristocrat'

Iris 'H.C. van Vliet'

Hyacinthus orientalis

Echinops bannaticus

Syringa vulgaris 'Madame F. Morel'

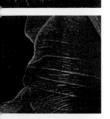
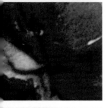

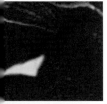

MAGENTA

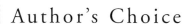

A GREAT DIVERSITY of flowers lies in the color range between red and purple. Crimson, magenta, carmine, and blood red – these are rich and regal colors with a luminous warmth. They are colors that we associate with pageantry and, as one might expect, they do not mix as easily with the bold hoi polloi of orange, scarlet, and yellow as with the more stately, sedate, and withdrawn violets and blues. They look particularly stunning when mixed with silver or turquoise foliage, or simply on their own in a harmonizing group.

These colors, along with the various pinks, mauves, lilacs, and plums so closely related to them, are a mainstay of the summer flower palette – starting with peonies, progressing through roses, and culminating in chrysanthemums.

Chrysanthemum 'Delaware'

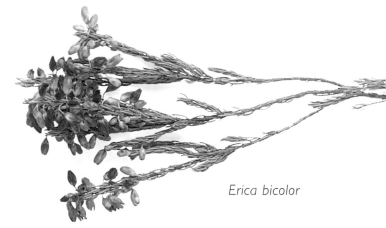

Erica bicolor

Paeonia 'Globe of Light'

Author's Choice

Long-lasting magenta flowers

Allium (Ornamental onion)
Alstroemeria (Peruvian lily)
Aster novi-belgii (Michaelmas daisy)
Dianthus (Carnation; Pink)
Eustoma (Texas bluebell)

Gladiolus (Gladiolus)
Liatris spicata (Gayfeather)
Lilium (Lily)
Limonium sinuatum (Statice)
Orchidaceae (Orchid)
Trachelium (syn. *Diosphaera*)

Best scented magenta flowers

Dianthus (Carnation; Pink)
Lathyrus odoratus (Sweet pea)

Matthiola incana (Stock)
Rosa (Rose)
Syringa (Lilac)

Anemone coronaria De Caen Group

Celosia argentea Olympia Series

Dendrobium 'Madame Pompadour'

Fritillaria meleagris

Vanda sp.

Dianthus 'Cranmere Pool'

Clarkia amoena Grace Series

PINK

ONE OF THE MOST COMMON colors in the garden, pink is a paler, white-added scion of full-blooded red and can be as bright as it can be gentle. It is a color that is full of good associations (the expression "in the pink" indicates that someone is in peak condition) and, true to that form, pink mixes readily with colors from all parts of the spectrum. From "shocking" pink to the softest pastel shade, there is a great range of pinks, some with a hint of orange and others with more than a suggestion of purple. Shocking, fuschia, cerise, salmon, rose, flesh, and blush – as well as baby – are all named shades of pink from the brightest to the palest. All mix easily and look particularly good with purple, mauve, and silver-green. I particularly like pink in combination with primrose, lemon-yellow, and with cream.

Clarkia amoena Grace Series

Dahlia 'Wootton Cupid'

Cymbidium 'Showgirl'

Author's Choice

Long-lasting pink flowers

Anthurium (Flamingo flower)
Chrysanthemum (Chrysanthemum)
Eustoma (Texas bluebell)

Lilium (Lily)
Limonium sinuatum (Statice)
Nerine bowdenii (Nerine)
Orchidaceae (Orchid)

Best scented pink flowers

Buddleja (syn. *Buddleia*)
Dianthus (Carnation; Pink)
Hyacinthus (Hyacinth)
Lilium (Lily)
Lathyrus odoratus (Sweet pea)

Paeonia (Peony)
Phlox (Phlox)
Prunus (Ornamental cherry)
Rosa (Rose)
Syringa vulgaris (Lilac)

Eustoma grandiflorum Heidi Series

Limonium sinuatum

Rosa 'Bo'

Chamelaucium uncinatum

Anthurium andraeanum 'Lunette'

Symphoricarpos × *doorenbosii*

Eustoma grandiflorum 'Mariachi Pink'

Rosa 'Radox Bouquet'

Dahlia 'Rhonda'

Lilium 'Vivaldi'

Tulipa 'Angélique'

Rosa 'Candy Bianca'

Ranunculus asiaticus Turban Group

Rosa 'Curiosa'

Hyacinthus orientalis 'Lady Derby'

Prunus triloba

Clarkia amoena Grace Series

CREAM AND PEACH

THESE LUSCIOUS, gentle colors, with just a hint of warmth, are among the most mouth-watering hues to be found. I like to place their soft mixes of pink, orange, and yellow with pale lilacs, mauves, and blues – combinations that are both fascinating and under used. Peach and cream also combine easily with the two warm primary colors, red and yellow, particularly in autumn arrangements. In the peach range, alstroemeria, gerberas, roses, and tulips are well represented, while among the creams, there are wonderful perfumed roses, freesias, lilies, and stocks. Try combining cream flowers with any of the other colors in the spectrum – they are less contrasting and demanding than white.

Rosa 'Champagne Cocktail'

Viburnum tinus

Author's Choice

Long-lasting peach and cream flowers

Alstroemeria (Peruvian lily)
Anthurium (Flamingo flower)
Eustoma (Texas bluebell)
Gladiolus (Gladiolus)
Lilium (Lily)
Orchidaceae (Orchid)
Protea (Protea)
Zantedeschia (Calla lily)

Best scented peach and cream flowers

Freesia (Freesia)
Lathyrus odoratus (Sweet pea)
Lilium (Lily)
Lonicera (Honeysuckle)
Matthiola incana (Stock)
Narcissus (Daffodil)
Polianthes tuberosa (Tuberose)
Rosa (Rose)

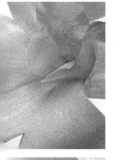

Zantedeschia 'Dusty Pink'

Narcissus 'Silver Chimes'

Dendrobium 'Joan'

Anthurium andraeanum 'Fantasia'

Matthiola incana

WHITE

THROUGHOUT HISTORY, white has been a color associated with purity; both the white lily and the white rose have been used symbolically in this way. White has great clarity and ethereal transparency. Pure white is, in fact, pure light and all the whites we see contain hints of other colors. White flowers combine easily with other colors. The strongest contrasts – white with bright red or strong violet – are like the opposing color contrasts in the color wheel, producing violent effects; harmonious effects are achieved, however, by combining white with pastel shades.

Because white is not the showiest of flower colors, many white flowers have delicious perfumes to help them attract insects to pollinate them. Their perfume is, of course, a great additional bonus in our creations.

Zantedeschia aethiopica 'Crowborough'

Phalaenopsis Yukimai

Author's Choice

Long-lasting white flowers

Anthurium (Flamingo flower)
Ornithogalum thyrsoides (Chincherinchee)
Lilium (Lily)
Orchidaceae (Orchid)
Zantedeschia (Calla lily)

Best scented white flowers

Gardenia (Gardenia)
Jasminum officinale (Jasmine)
Lilium (Lily)
Matthiola incana (Stock)
Narcissus (Narcissus)
Nicotiana (Tobacco plant)
Philadelphus (Mock orange)
Rosa (Rose)

Astilbe 'Irrlicht'

Achillea 'Hartington White'

Anemone coronaria 'The Bride'

Salix caprea

Narcissus 'Paper White'

Syringa vulgaris 'Jan van Tol'

Polianthes tuberosa 'The Pearl'

Tulipa 'Casablanca'

Lilium 'Navonna'

Dendrobium bigibbum

Dianthus 'Delphi' ®

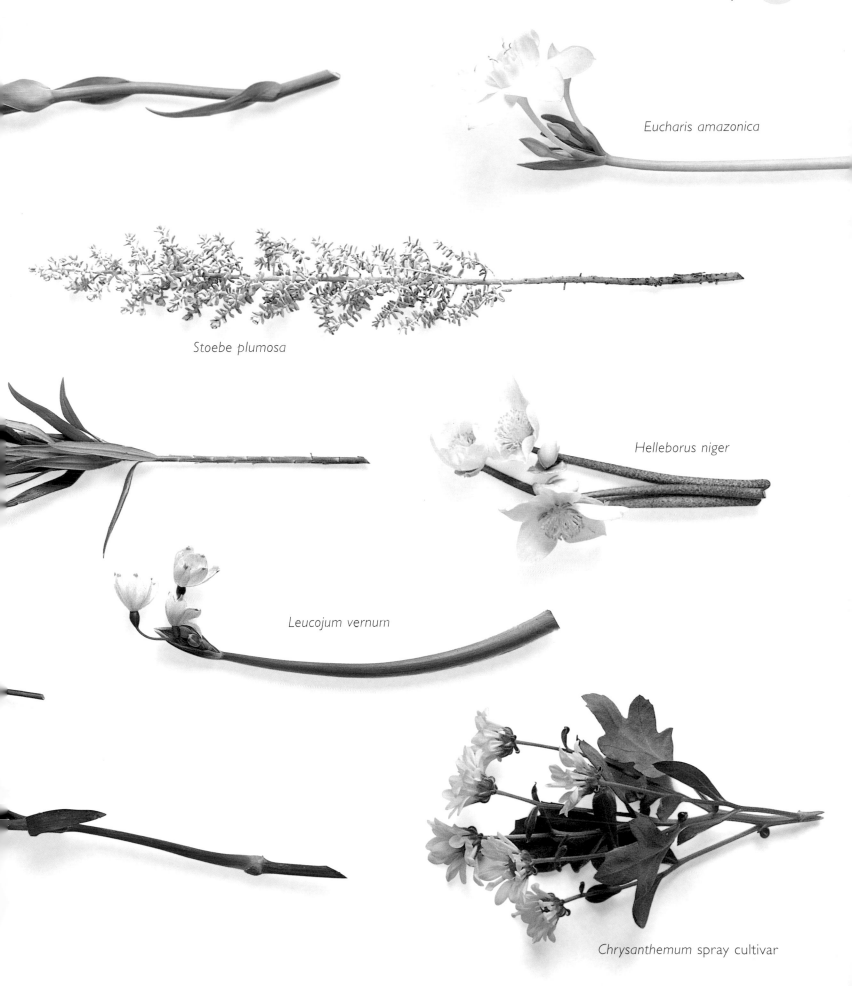

Eucharis amazonica

Stoebe plumosa

Helleborus niger

Leucojum vernum

Chrysanthemum spray cultivar

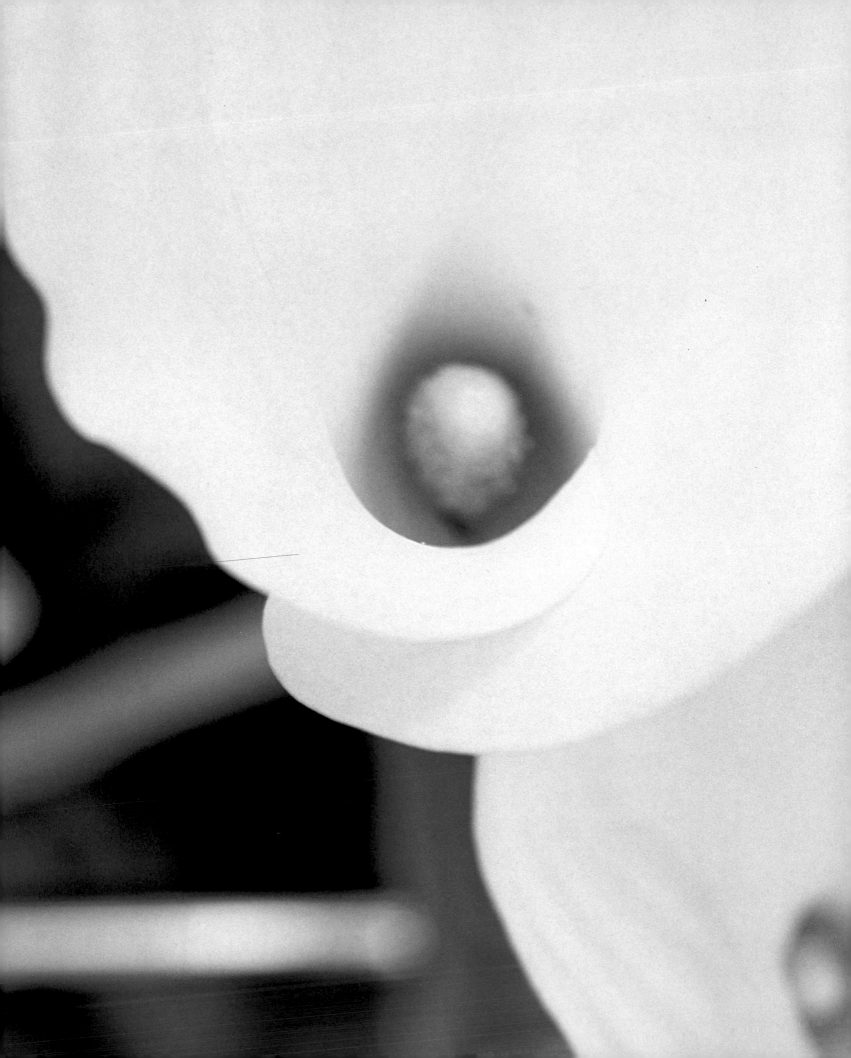

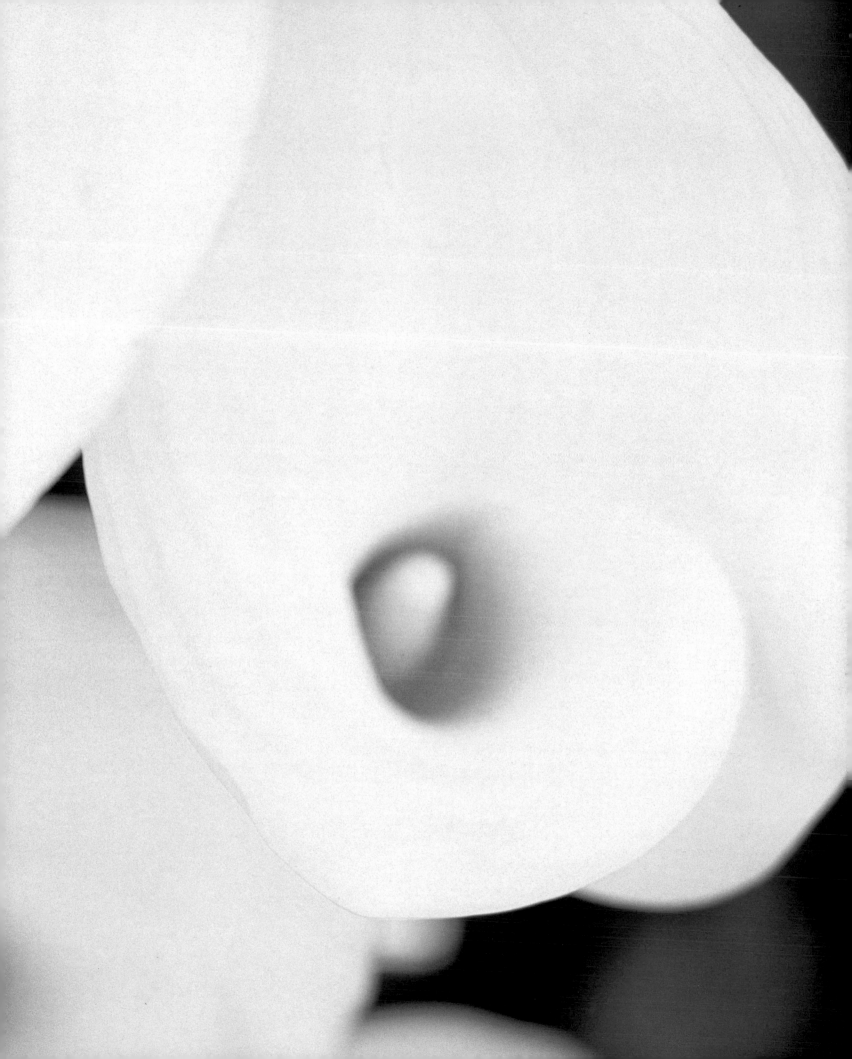

MAJOR IMPACT PLANTS

THERE ARE OCCASIONS when we want our flower displays to have impact and star quality. Creations for large spaces (such as the inside of a church or synagogue or a large reception area) or for a special event in the home must make an immediate statement. Not all the flowers in such arrangements need to be visually powerful; it is usually better if only one or two of the flowers and leaves are bold, because then they will stand out even more.

Color and texture also play their part in impact, and sometimes just a small amount of one color placed against a large amount of its contrasting opposite in the color wheel can give a dramatic effect (*see p.34*).

Here, though, we are talking about scale and, used judiciously, these major players in the plant world can give our creations just the impact that they need.

Delphinium 'Lord Butler'

Heliconia nutans

Chamaerops fortunii

Author's Choice

Large-scale and decorative plants

Aconitum carmichaelii (Monkshood)
Anthurium (Flamingo flower)
Aspidistra elatior (Cast-iron plant)
Bambusa multiplex (Bamboo)
Cynara scolymus (Artichoke)
Cyperus alternifolius (Papyrus)
Delphinium (Delphinium)
Eremurus × *isabellinus* (Foxtail lily)
Ficus carica (Fig)

Helianthus annuus (Sunflower)
Heliconia (Heliconia)
Hippeastrum (Amaryllis)
Kniphofia (Red-hot poker)
Lilium (Lily)
Magnolia (Magnolia)
Paeonia (Peony)
Philodendron (Philodendron)
Protea (Protea)
Rheum (Rhubarb)
Strelitzia (Bird of paradise)
Zantedeschia (Calla lily)

Zantedeschia elliottiana

Hippeastrum 'Masai'

Dypsis lutescens

Helianthus annuus

Paeonia officinalis 'Rubra Plena'

Anthurium andraeanum 'Lunette'

Kniphofia 'C.M. Prichard'

Cyperus alternifolius

Alocasia macrorrhiza 'Variegata'

Ficus carica

Lilium 'Ascari'

Anthurium 'Trinidad'

Hippeastrum 'Liberty'

Protea cynaroides

Hydrangea 'Preziosa'

Brassica Northern Lights Series

Colocasia esculenta

Cynara scolymus

DELICATE PLANTS

WHILE THE FLOWERS and leaves of bold plant material can be invaluable for dramatic displays, the beauty of more fragile specimens cannot be ignored. Delicate flowers and foliage create an ethereal look, making creations that, though maybe not as powerful from a distance as those using large plants, are nonetheless beautiful and often enchanting from a closer viewpoint. The fact that some of these plants will last for only a brief time adds to their appeal, for the ephemeral has a great attraction.

To show off delicate plants to their best advantage, place arrangements composed mainly of such material in positions where they will be easily seen, such as on a dining or coffee table; or combine them to accentuate the contrasting forms.

Crocosmia 'Jackanapes'

Astrantia major

Gypsophila paniculata

Author's Choice

Delicate plants

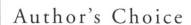

Acacia (Mimosa; Wattle)
Anethum graveolens (Dill)
Aquilegia (Columbine)
Asparagus plumosus
  (Asparagus fern)
Aster novi-belgii (Michaelmas
  daisies)
Astrantia major (Masterwort)
Chamelaucium (Waxflower)
Cytisus (Broom)
Helenium (Sneezeweed)
Lathyrus odorata (Sweet pea)

Leptospermum scoparium
  (Tea tree)
Lysimachia clethroides
  (Loosestrife)
Malus (Apple blossom)
Narcissus 'Paper White'
  (Narcissus)
Nerine (Nerine)
Oncidium (Orchid)
Pelargonium (Geranium)
Prunus (Cherry blossom)
Thalictrum (Meadow rue)

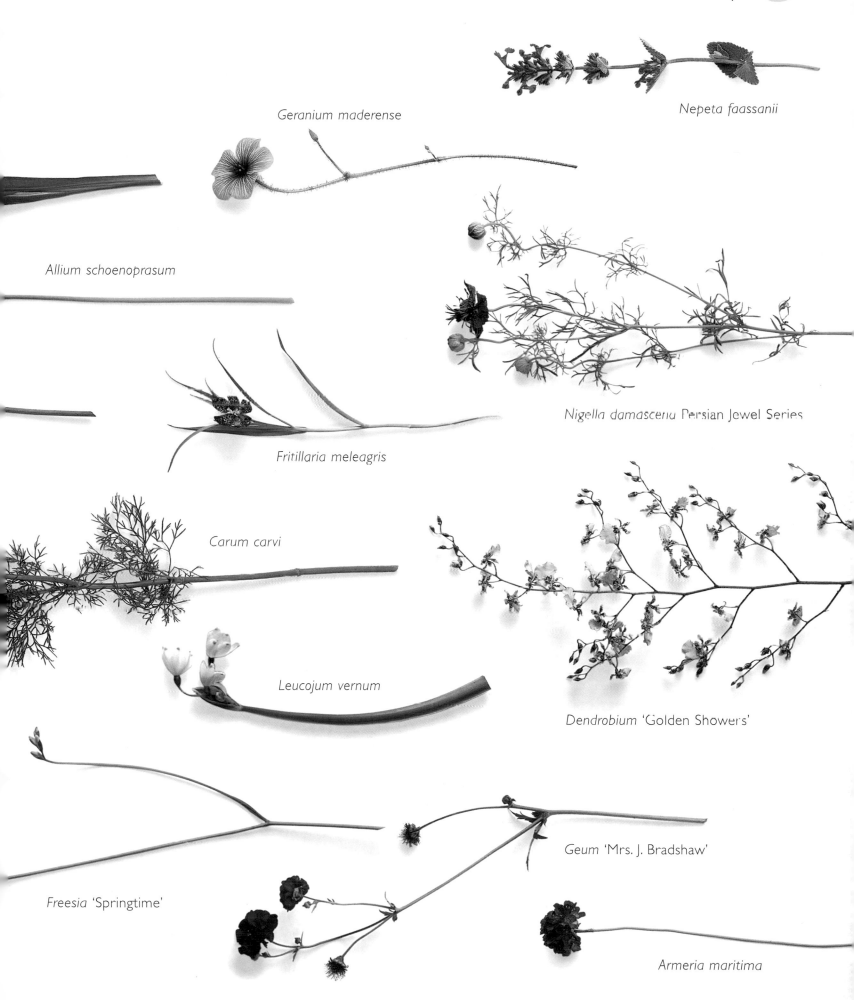

Nepeta faassanii

Geranium maderense

Allium schoenoprasum

Nigella damascena Persian Jewel Series

Fritillaria meleagris

Carum carvi

Leucojum vernum

Dendrobium 'Golden Showers'

Freesia 'Springtime'

Geum 'Mrs. J. Bradshaw'

Armeria maritima

SCENTED PLANTS

PERFUME PLAYS an important role in any display of flowers and foliage. I like to use scented plants and aromatic foliage as often as possible, but it is important to consider the position of the display when selecting them. The flowers on a dining table, for example, should not be too strongly perfumed, otherwise they will clash with the smells of the food.

The scent of flowers can be extremely welcoming: some perfumed lilies, freesias, roses, sweet peas, or stocks in the hallway will immediately make guests feel comfortable and happy. Even sprigs of herbs, such as bay and rosemary, will fill the house with delicious aromas. If you are having guests to stay, a small jug or vase of sweetly perfumed flowers on the bedside table will identify you as the best of hosts.

Philadelphus × *lemoinei*

Lilium 'Journey's End'

Rosa 'Leonidas'

Author's Choice

Favorite scented plants

Acacia dealbata (Mimosa)	*Lilium* (Lily)
Aloysia (Lemon verbena)	*Lonicera* (Honeysuckle)
Artemisia (Lad's love)	*Melissa officinalis* (Lemon
Convallaria (Lily of the valley)	balm)
Cytisus (Broom)	*Mentha* (Mint)
Daphne (Daphne)	*Philadelphus* (Mock orange)
Erysimum (Wallflower)	*Rosa* (Rose)
Eucalyptus (Gum)	*Rosmarinus officinalis*
Jasminum officinale (Jasmine)	(Rosemary)
Lathyrus odorata (Sweet pea)	*Ruta* (Rue)
Laurus nobilis (Bay)	*Santolina* (Santolina)
Lavandula (Lavender)	*Syringa* (Lilac)

Polianthes tuberosa

Freesia 'Pink Marble'

Muscari armeniacum

Syringa vulgaris 'Jan van Tol'

Stephanotis floribunda

Dianthus 'Ciao Bianca'

Lavandula spica

Prunus triloba

Cestrum diurnum

Acacia retinodes

Eucalyptus gunnii

Narcissus 'Early Cheer'

Paeonia 'Baroness Schröder'

Viola odorata

Matthiola incana

Convallaria majalis

Lathyrus odoratus

Hyacinthus orientalis 'Anna Liza'

LONG-LIVED PLANTS

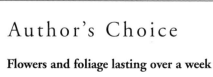 THERE ARE MANY cut flowers, as
well as much foliage, that will last
for two weeks or more provided
they are not placed in too warm a
location; the hot, dry atmosphere
created by central heating, however, will
very quickly kill off most flowers and leaves.
The range of long-lived plant material is
quite varied, though naturally it is the
evergreen rather than deciduous foliage that
stays with us longest once it is cut.

The life of any cut flower or stem of leaves
depends totally on conditioning: even long-
lived flowers will die quickly if their stems
are inadequately prepared (*see pp.310–313*).

I believe, however, that one of the beauties
of flowers is their very transience. The week
for which most cut flowers last gives us such
great pleasure that we should not be overly
concerned about choosing only flowers with
long-lasting attributes.

Eustoma grandiflorum Heidi Series

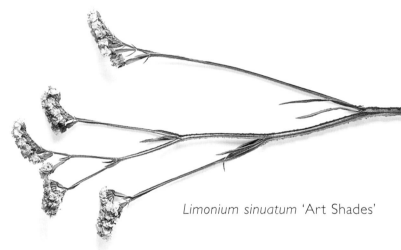

Limonium sinuatum 'Art Shades'

Author's Choice

Flowers and foliage lasting over a week

Achillea (Yarrow)
Anthurium (Flamingo flower)
Aspidistra elatior (Cast-iron
  plant)
Bracteantha (Strawflower)
Carthamus (Safflower)
Chamaecyparis (False cypress)
Echinops bannaticus (Globe
  thistle)
Eryngium alpinum (Sea holly)
Eucalyptus (Gum tree)

Euonymus (Spindle tree)
Galax urceolata (Wandflower)
Gaultheria (syn. *Pernettya*)
Liatris spicata (Blazing star)
Lilium (Lily)
Limonium sinuatum (Statice)
Philodendron (Philodendron)
Protea (Protea)
Ruscus hypophyllum (Broom)
Solidago (Goldenrod)
Strelitzia (Bird of paradise)

Camellia japonica 'Elegans'

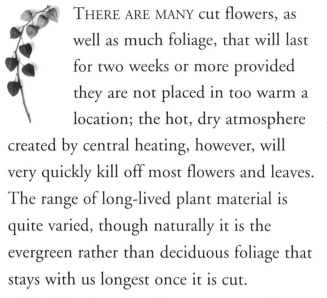

Liatris spicata

Allium aflatunense

Echinops bannaticus

Physalis alkekengi

Chrysanthemum 'George Griffiths'

Eryngium alpinum

Hedera helix f. *poetarum*

USEFUL ADDRESSES

Societies and Organizations

GARDEN CLUB OF AMERICA
www.gcamerica.org

IKEBANA ARTS
580 N. 6th Street
San Jose, CA 95112
(408) 279-8342
www.ikebana-arts.com

NATIONAL COUNCIL OF FEDERATED
  GARDEN CLUBS
www.gardenclubs-of-
(Fill in individual state after "-of-")

Florists/Wholesale suppliers

FLORAL HOME
(800) 622-7372
http://floralhome.com

FRESH FLOWER SOURCE
(800) 246-5665
www.freshflowersource.com

PAHOA ORCHIDS–TROPICAL FLOWER
P.O. Box 346
Pahoa, HI 96778
www.tropicalflower.com

Online flower supplies

www8.proflowers.com

www.plantshop.com

www.justflowers.com

www.800florals.com

Supplies

BEES KNEES GARDEN PRODUCTS
424 Narcissus
Corona Del Mar, CA 92625
(800) 834-8008
http://beesbotanical.com

CALYX & COROLLA
185 Berry Street
San Francisco, CA 94107
(415) 626-5511, (888) 88-CALYX
www.calyxandcorolla.com

FOREVERGREENS
2823 S. Patterson St.
Sioux City, IA 51106
www.forevergreens.com

ASIAN ARTS & MEDITATION SUPPLIES
1813 Pearl St.
Boulder, CO 80302
(800) 961-2555
www.chopa.com/ikebana.htm

Flower-arranging courses

FLORAL DESIGN INSTITUTE
Career-building programs for professional
and amateur floral designers.
(800) 819-8089
www.floraldesigninstitute.com

GARDEN WEB
On-line forums, information, events
calendars, links to other related sites.
www.gardenweb.com

Flower-arranging magazines

FLOWER ARRANGING
Martha Stewart Living
Random House

Various editions of the following magazines:

COUNTRY LIVING
GARDEN DESIGN
CANADIAN FLORIST GREENHOUSE & NURSERY
FLEUR DESIGN
FLOWER & GARDEN MAGAZINE
GOOD HOUSEKEEPING
SUNSET PUBLICATIONS

Previous publications by the author

MALCOLM HILLIER'S CHRISTMAS
Dorling Kindersley © 1992

MALCOLM HILLIER'S WREATHS AND GARLANDS
Dorling Kindersley © 1994

MALCOLM HILLIER'S COLOR GARDEN
Dorling Kindersley © 1995

MALCOLM HILLIER ENTERTAINING
Dorling Kindersley © 1997

INDEX

A

A

Abies grandis 202–3, 338
    A. 'Glauca' 218–19, 338, 434
    A. nordmanniana 212–13
    A. procera 176–7, 198–201, 338
abrotan *see Berzelia abrotanoides*
Acacia 284, 436, 442, 490
    A. baileyana 74–5, 339
    A. dealbata 494
    A. retinodes 230–3, 339, 436, 437, 496
Acer
    for color 448
    preservation 316
Achillea 152, 500
    A. filipendulina 338, 436, 438
    A. 'Hartington White' 120–1, 339, 479
Aconitum carmichaelii 484
    A. c. 'Barker's Variety' 154–5, 338, 453
Acorus calamus 'Variegatus' 174–5, 338
African containers 84–5
Agapanthus campanulatus 126–7, 339, 452, 453
    A. 'Lord Butler' 86–7
Ageratum houstonianum 460
air drying 314–15
Alcea rosea 'Chater's Double' 258–9, 339
Alchemilla mollis 100–1, 116, 240–1, 258–9, 339, 448, 449
Alexandrian rose *see Rosa × damascena* var. *bifera*
Allium sativum 88–9

A. aflatunense 114–15, 340, 501
A. giganteum 340
A. glutinosa 341
A. schoenoprasum 340, 491
A. stipitatum 96–7, 464
Alnus glutinosa 144–5, 200–1
Alocasia macrorrhiza 'Variegata' 214–15, 341, 486
Aloysia 494
Alpine sea holly *see Eryngium*
Alstroemeria 426, 432, 436, 464, 474
    A. 'Capri' 254–5, 341
    A. 'Victoria' 268–9, 340
Amaranthus caudatus 156–7, 340
amaryllis *see Hippeastrum*
America, flowers in 24–5
Ananas bracteatus 'Striatus' 124–5, 340
    A. nanus 144–5, 341
Anchusa 452
Anemone 60
    A. coronaria 456
    A. c. 'Mona Lisa Purple' 76–7
    A. c. 'Mona Lisa Red' 420
    A. c. 'The Bride' 220–1, 341, 479
    A. c. De Caen Group 62–3, 72–3, 80–1, 132–3, 292–3, 341, 457, 465
    A. × hybrida 186–7, 342
anemone, Japanese
    see Anemone × hybrida
Anethum graveolens 74–5, 100–1, 342, 448, 490
Anigozanthos 144–5
    A. flavidus 156–7, 342
Anthriscus sylvestris 100–1, 128–9, 236–7, 298–9, 343
Anthurium 442, 468, 474, 478, 484, 500

A. andraeanum 420, 448
    A. a. 'Fantasia' 204–5, 343, 474
    A. a. 'Lunette' 280–1, 469, 485
    A. a. 'Tropical' 280–1, 342, 420, 421
    A. crystallinum 280–1, 342, 444
    A. 'Midori' 242–3
    A. 'Trinidad' 150–1, 342, 486
Antirrhinum majus Coronette Series 130–1, 343, 420
apricot 16
    Japanese *see Prunus mume*
Aquilegia 82, 490
    A. McKana Hybrids 100–1, 343
    A. vulgaris 21
Arachnadendron 144–5
Arachnepedium 'James Story' 393, 422
Arachnis flos-aeris 270–1, 393
× *Aranda majala* 393, 428
Areca
    A. catechu 344
    A. lutescens 343
Armeria maritima 344, 491
Artemisia 494
artichoke, globe
    see Cynara scolymus
arum lily *see Zantedeschia*
Asclepias curassavica 118–19, 344
    A. tuberosa 246–7, 262–3, 345
Aspalathus sp. 200–1, 345, 445
Asparagus 448
    A. myriocladus 268–9, 272, 345
    A. officinalis 276–7, 344
    A. plumosus 490
Aspidistra elatior 484, 500
aster, China *see Callistephus*
Aster novi-belgii 464, 490
    A. n-b. 'Chequers' 84

A. n-b. 'Mount Everest' 298–9, 344
    A. n-b. 'Sungal' 344
Astilbe
    A. 'Irrlicht' 290–1, 345, 478
    drying 314
Astrantia major 345, 490
attar of roses 14
autumn displays 142–7, 150–1, 154–63, 180–97, 266–9, 296–7
avens *see Geum*
azalea *see Rhododendron*

B

B

baby's breath *see Gypsophila*
bamboo containers 18, 158–9
    see also Bambusa
Bambusa 16, 164
    B. multiplex 345, 484
banksia *see Grevillea robusta*
base-making 322–7
baskets 17, 44, 306
    displays 100–1, 122–3, 134–5, 138–9, 154–5, 176–7, 180–1, 184–5, 188–9, 204–5, 220–1, 232–3, 236–7, 282–3, 290–1, 298–9
bay laurel *see Laurus nobilis*
beauty berry *see Callicarpa bodinieri* var. *giraldii*
Begonia tuberhybrida 346
bellflower *see Campanula*
Bellis perennis cultivar 288–9, 346
bells of Ireland *see Molucella*
bergamot/bee balm *see Monarda*

ACKNOWLEDGMENTS

Author's Acknowledgments

I would like to thank the following for their help in creating *Flowers*: photographer Stephen Hayward, with assistant Paul Lund, for his stunning images, infinite patience, and for never being daunted by a studio floor that was constantly awash with flowers; not to mention the Dunsfold village store for a constant supply of doughnuts.

The team from Dorling Kindersley who were wonderful to work with: editors Lesley Malkin (carrying baby Finlay) and Irene Lyford, and art editor Wendy Bartlet.

Dennis Edwards, Lee Ward, and David Donovan at John Austin; David Hancock, Ian Potter, and Tony Flavin at Baker and Duguid; and David Bacon at A & F Bacon – all at New Covent Garden Market, London, who helped me search out most of the plant material for the book. Also Terracottas of New Covent Garden for many pots; Stephen Camburn of Gaudiamus, New Kings Road, London, for lending some of his stunning terracotta containers; Babylon Design, Fulham Road, London; HRW Antiques, 26 Sulivan Road, London, for lending the table photographed for pages 218–219; Whiteway & Waldron Ltd, 305 Munster Road, London, for the loan of the pew photographed for pages 230–231.

A special thank you to Dr C. Andrew Henley, who traveled to various locations in Australia to photograph plants for us; and to the following people who helped him:

Albert's Garden, Pialligo, ACT; Marcus Harvey, Hillview Rare Plants, Hobart, Tas; Dean Havelberg, Hillview, Exeter, NSW; Marcia Voce, Birchfield Herbs, Bungendore, NSW; Dirk Wallace, Wodonga, Vic.

Lastly, and most importantly, I would like to thank Rodney Engen for all his help and tremendous inspirational input.

Publisher's Acknowledgments

Dorling Kindersley would like to thank Sue Barraclough, Joanna Chisholm, Jane Cooke, Candida Frith-MacDonald, Jenny Jones, Jane Laing, Kathryn Lane, Frank Ritter, and Susannah Steel for invaluable editorial assistance; Fiona Wild and Henrietta Llewelyn Davies for punctilious proofreading; and Michelle Clark for compiling the index. Alison Lotinga, Alison Shackleton, and Ann Thompson for design assistance; Wesley Richards for design assistance and artwork on the flower symbols. Amanda Russell for painstaking picture research. Mark Bracey and Robert Campbell for DTP support.

Commissioned Photography

All photographs by Stephen Hayward except: Andreas Einsiedel 304–305, 316–317, 318–319, 320–321, 328–329; Dr C. Andrew Henley; Dave King 304–305, 312–313, 316–317, 318–319, 320–321, 330–331; Diana Miller 316–317, 320–321; Matthew Ward 306–307, 314–315, 334–335.

Agency Picture Credits

The publisher would like to thank the following sources for their kind permission to reproduce their photographs in this book.

(a=above; c=center; b=below; l=left; r=right; t=top)

The Art Archive: 16; Archaeological Museum, Naples, Italy, 12tr, 12bl; Galleria Borghese, Rome, Italy, 22tr; Egyptian Museum, Cairo, Egypt, 10c; Louvre, Paris, France, 21bl; V&A Museum, London, UK, 17.

Bridgeman Art Library, London/New York: Bonhams, London, UK, 23; Galleria Dell'Academia, Venice, Italy, 20; Galleria Borghese, Rome, Italy, 21tl; National Gallery, London, UK, 27tl; Private Collection, 22br, 25br; V&A Museum, London, UK, 19bl.

Corbis UK Ltd.: Burstein Collection, 18.

© Michael Holford: 11b.

NAFAS (National Association of Flower Arrangement Societies): Arranged by Marjorie Watling and Mary Napper, photography Peter Chivers, 26bl.

Christine Osborne: 89, 14l, 15tr.

Scala: Museo Pio-Clementino Vaticano, Vatican City, Italy, 13t; National Portrait Gallery/Smithsonian/Art Resource, 24-5b; Washington National Museum of American Art/Art Resource, US, 24cl.

V&A Picture Library: 15bl, 19tl.

Wessel & O'Connor: 27tr.